MW00878762

The Office of Shaman

A Hermeneutic Rationale for the Inclusion of a Soul
Concept in the Genesis of Human Thought

John Worthington

Fifth Edition Copyright © by John Worthington, 2007-2014
http://mentalartsnetwork.com

All rights reserved. No part of this book may be used or reproduced in any manner whatsoever without written permission except for brief passages in connection to a review.

Cover design: Bri Sienkiewcz

Layout & Design: Robert Sink

ISBN: 978-1502766427

Table Of Contents

Dedication and Acknowledgments

To Tooke

I would like to thank all the people I've met, talked to, and learned from. Special thanks go to John C. Lilly, Howard Tooke, Eugene Albright, Doc Romero, and Glen Robinson who were my benefactors.

To my wife Lucy, whose insight and Agreement have made for a better book, but more importantly, for a much more interesting life.

This book may not have happened had it not been for my editor Paul Bowersox. He has been the guardian of the Agreement that made this book real.

To those individuals who agreed to read and comment on the early versions of this work, even those who never commented at all. Your input, or lack of it, spoke volumes and made for an improved manuscript.

And lastly,

To those of you willing to give up your personal history and move forward into a brave new world of your own making. This book was written for you with the hope that it will help you make sense of where you have been, where you are now, and how to get where you want to go. You are the new Shamans to hold the Office and rebuild the wisdom base. Welcome.

Foreword

If you are reading this book there is a good chance you are someone who is interested in exploring and understanding the nature of reality. You have been "called" to explore the depths of the Mind in a way many people never achieve. It may be that you sense this calling because you had a traumatic event early in your life resulting in disadvantageous behaviors. It could be you want to resolve things from the past. Perhaps you have simply always been driven to understand how your mind works, or you want to increase your performance or enhance your relationships. Regardless, something in you has been "sparked" and that spark led you here.

My intention with this foreword is to give you a foundation for reading *The Office of Shaman* by John Worthington. The best foundation I can provide is to set a context for the book in relation to where we have been, where we are, and where we are going as a society and as a World.

People have been collectively insisting that we are separate from one another, and it has caused a lot of problems ranging from war to domestic and human rights abuses. I recently read a novel where the main character travels back in time to live in 1958-1963 in different parts of the United States. The author adroitly described the manner of speech and the local color of that time period. At the time, the U.S. (and the world) was transitioning after a war ending with the explosion of nuclear bombs in Japan. What became known as the "military industrial complex" was just taking shape, television was still relatively new, computers were on the verge of increasing throughout the world, and people kept in touch largely through telephone and handwritten letters. Things were more simple back then because we still did not have the internet and smart phones, but it was a "heavier" time weighed down by the shared belief that people of color must be separate from Caucasian people. To many people that belief was as real as the sky is blue and the grass is green. The only way to maintain such a belief was to objectify other people and insist they were only their bodies. As long as people were "objects," people could rationalize mistreating African Americans and even killing them because of the color of their skin.

Gandhi represents an example of someone who did not Agree with the belief that people are objects. To Gandhi (and to people who aligned with him) people were not just their bodies. They considered people to have a spiritual essence, which was connected among all people. Therefore, if someone mistreated another person, they were affecting all other people in existence. A good example was the scene in the movie *Gandhi* when he was living in South Africa. There was a point when he chained himself to a post in protest of the apartheid practices. A police officer beat Gandhi, who was defenseless. The officer hit Gandhi over and over and over and Gandhi just sat there and took it. The scene impacted me deeply because the man who was beating Gandhi could only do so if he treated Gandhi as an object and, therefore, considered Gandhi separate from him. However, the only way Gandhi was able to stay there and take the beating was because Gandhi treated everyone as "part of" him. He knew taking the beating was going to have an impact because it would wake people up to recognize they were connected to him. It worked. It was because Gandhi treated everyone as "part of" him that he was motivated to stand up against racism in South Africa and (later) in India. To Gandhi (and to people like Martin Luther King, Mother Theresa, and other social and spiritual progressive icons of the last one hundred years), to treat one person poorly was to treat oneself poorly because all people are interconnected at a spiritual level. As time has progressed, the influence of Gandhi and people like him has resulted in massive changes in laws that align with the belief that all people are connected. For example, Gandhi helped emancipate India from British rule and Martin Luther King played a key role in African Americans not only have the right to vote, but in having an African American in the Office of the President. Those are big changes. However, many challenges abound as we deal with war in different parts of the world, and other social ills, such as domestic and sexual abuse.

All people (and therefore all ideas) have many pieces, and one of the pieces contributing to people treating one another as objects is the schism between the scientific approach to understanding reality and the spiritual/religious approach. The scientific approach asserts everything has only a physical origin, including intelligence. Only things that can be measured matter. The spiritual/religious approach asserts everything comes from a non-physical source, and that science has no importance in finding the origin of intelligence. When people lean purely in either of those directions it causes problems. Modern day examples are the food manufacturing/agriculture practices and ISIS (Islamic State of Iraq and Syria). There are food production companies that are polluting the environment and taking away people's rights to grow certain crops in the name of science and "the law." Such practices are sometimes so focused on scientific data and financial gain that the impact on people outside the "company" are considered unimportant. In other words, such companies use "science and measurements" to justify objectifying and mistreating people the way the officer who beat Gandhi used his belief that Gandhi was just an object. On a related note, ISIS has been committing serious human rights violations, such as beheading Westerners and other violators, in the name of religion. They attribute (or more accurately blame) God as the reason why they are killing people and they eschew basic human rights in God's name.

The dichotomy of "science versus religion" seems to be slowly losing ground as more and more people realize solutions lie in the middle or (at least) in something outside of the polarization. As a gay man with an interest in different spiritual practices, I have participated in Native American ceremonies throughout the years. In some Native American traditions, gay people are considered a third gender known as "two spirits" or "walk betweens." In those cultures, as well as in some cultures throughout the world, gay people are known as filling a different slot in the society - in different ways, such as storyteller, singer, poet, or holy person. The reason I share this is because societies that eliminate the dichotomy of "straight man" and "straight woman" and make room for something other than those roles stand to benefit. Even a recent meeting among bishops in the Catholic church indicated an awareness and a desire to discuss the topic that gay people have something important to offer the Church and the community at large. When society embraces solutions other than "this way" or "that way," there are many other solutions that present themselves. Recognizing the benefits of gay people is a great example of integrating science and religion/spirituality. One can recognize the scientific aspect, such as that gay people are productive members of society, such as Tim Cook, Apple's CEO, and the spiritual aspect, such as that gay people are Souls (like all people) who have an impact that is profound but also hard to measure, such as in the poetry of Walt Whitman.

The place where the non-physical (the Soul) meets the physical (the Body) is in the Mind and the increasing integration of humans and technology underscores the importance of finding a way to describe and navigate that meeting place. The leaders of the world are being given access to increasingly powerful technologies. These leaders might be able to see into any place in the world with powerful computers, and conquer towns and cities with the words "Go ahead." However, are they able to see into and rule their mind? Alfred Korzybski noted that until humans, and especially the leaders of the world, resolve the conflicts in their mind, the world will continue to be insane. We have come far as a human civilization. However, advancements are speeding up. We can create beautiful things, such as bountiful food, music, art, and constructive technologies. However, we also have the power to kill one another easily. The increasingly sophisticated world requires us to understand our mind.

If you are called to understand how the energy from the Soul integrates with the physical mind, you're in for a treat by reading this book (and by taking the classes associated with this book). If you want to see people as Souls instead of as objects, and to find solutions outside of "this" or "that," you have come to the right place. The world needs people to fill a slot that is outside of dichotomies. It needs people who see they are connected to all other people on the planet, and who act from that knowledge. Filling that slot (what John Worthington calls "the office" of "shaman") is like being the one who blows the glass into whatever forms one's community requires instead of the one who simply drinks from a glass. The world needs "glass blowers." It needs people who will shape the world from an understanding of how the Soul expresses through the mind and body.

This book is meant to be the first step in learning a set of tools in the Mental

Arts. Upon finishing this book, I recommend you sign up for your first Mental Arts class (called *The Introduction to the Art of Rewriting*). To learn and sign up:

http://mentalartsnetwork.com

This book is helpful but the classes are necessary for you to have the experience of understanding how the Soul expresses through your mind.

Through my experience, I observe we all are changing moment to moment. May the act of reading this book and taking classes in the Mental Arts enable you to make changes that facilitate the expression of who you really are and what you are meant to do in this world. May you stand in the slot you are meant to stand in, and thereby help maintain Harmony in your communities and, therefore, the World.

— *David Conneely*
Certified Floatation Facilitator
Certified Program Facilitator
http://ifloatct.com

How to Approach This Book

You don't need to be a Shaman to benefit from this book. In fact, you don't even need to know or care what a Shaman is to step into the Shamanic Point of View described herein. The reason this is true is because this book is less about the dream and myth of Shamanism and is more accurately about the *do* and the functions employed in embracing a Shamanic life. This book is most specifically about awareness, the awareness of self, soul, mind and actions. It provides a framework you can use to understand why you do what you do and how you can make choices with applied insight, rather than blind reactivity. In a very real sense, it throws the doors and windows of the locked and shuttered mind wide open so you can live life unified in body, mind, and spirit, having eliminated any division or conflict of self.

This book identifies and explains the levels of consciousness, the nature of perception, the dynamic functions of the soul, and the mechanics of change. It is written to resonate simultaneously with multiple layers of your being and consciousness. It should be no surprise that the rhythm and words used to speak to logical cognition are not necessarily the same rhythm and words most effectively used to speak to the soul. Because of this, *The Office of Shaman* is not a book that can or should be read with expectations for full and complete understanding using your day-to-day conscious mind. The words that are used, the flow of the work, even the structure of the sentences, which can at times be challenging and non-traditional, are designed to speak to the deeper realms of your being; indeed to your very soul. Over the course of the book, a subtle connection is made between this deeper soul level and your conscious mind. As this is achieved, you will become aware of your issues, your condition-ing, and your central beliefs. These can be enormous and devastating areas of inquiry that you may perceive as frightening or intimidating. For this reason, we offer here an approach to reading this book that might be helpful and which will assist you in avoiding this trap of fear.

The Office of Shaman is a book best taken in small sips rather than large gulps. Because it defines and illuminates all facets of the thinking machinery and therefore reorders those structures, reading only a couple chapters at a sitting allows the material greater impact at each stage of that reordering process. That said, it is also recommended that you consistently read each block of chapters in a timely manner, not allowing days to elapse before taking the next "sip." This maintains the intensity of the process and establishes an Intent to shift awareness that your thinking machinery will recognize.

No matter what, if you start the book, finish it. Whether you understand it consciously or not, whether you enjoy the story, the characters or the concept, make the effort to complete reading the entire text. Once you have finished the book, the laying of the informational foundation is complete and you can find further instruction, get personal help with any aspect of the program and take your training to the next level by emailing the author himself, talking with the person from whom you got this book or by getting in touch with whomever has identified themselves for contact in the end pages of this work.

By adopting this approach to the book, the work that *The Office of Shaman* is meant to do will be accomplished efficiently and completely to your ultimate benefit and increased awareness, clarity, and personal freedom.

Introduction to Part 1

The Shamanic Office has existed for thousands of years. It may have been born out of necessity but it grew from those early roots to become an integral part of society. Of course, in the beginning there was a scarcity of scientists, doctors, and other learned folk, so the Shaman was pretty much the only game in town. Shamans were educated people. Their tradition was oral and the body of knowledge maintained from generation to generations was extensive. The knowledge included information concerning healing, herbs, spirits, behavior, and of course, tribal lore. Some of their accumulated knowledge pertained to astounding things that only Shamans did. Things continued in this vein for thousands of years with each successive generation of Shaman adding to the knowledge pool. As city-states and kingdoms began to replace tribal societies, the knowledge of the Shamans became less necessary. The Shaman actually began to be a threat to emerging social structures. Learning was more widespread and the closely guarded secrets of the Shaman came under suspicion.

As Christianity gained popularity, the Shamanic office experienced an even sharper decline. Part of the decline had to do with a struggle for power between the Church and the Shamans. The Church recognized that Shamanic learning posed a threat to Church doctrine. Since the Church was an organized force and the Shamans were, as they always had been, a somewhat closed society which generally did not share their information even with other Shamans, the Church had the upper hand. What the Church represented to society was an idea whose time had come. The Church provided a new type of societal arrangement. People could have pageantry, a central meeting place where ideas were explored, peaceful leadership within limits, and a new idea called forgiveness. Forgiveness was, perhaps, the most important idea of all for the emergence of the Church. Forgiveness meant that an individual could go to Church, talk to a priest, and leave in a few minutes without having to make a blood sacrifice, lose an eye, or even look over his shoulder, no matter what he had done. He didn't have to worry about some Shaman finding out that he had been a bad boy and broken some taboo in his tribe. Forgiveness freed up thinking space in the brain because the Church represented a less fear-filled society. It was the idea of forgiveness that resulted in more free space in the brain that actually brought Shamanism down in its traditional form. More space in the thinking machinery freed up the brain to deal with ever more complex abstractions.

The original Shamans were not, as is commonly believed, priests of the dark underworld, but rather observers of nature and extremely practical and pragmatic individuals, or perhaps even groups of individuals. They were people who were born to their office and the small communities of those times recognized them from their early childhood. Sometimes the young Shamans-to-be had physical abnormalities, sometimes they were wise beyond their years, and sometimes they could simply dream dreams which helped in some manner the community in which they lived.

While the Shaman was not a priest, he was the repository of the community beliefs. The beliefs he guarded were not about pagan gods and goddesses nearly as much as they were beliefs about what the community viewed as real. In some societies, gods, goddesses, or even spirits were presented to the general populace as though real and in many cases as actually real. The Shaman had to have the appropriate mystical hold over the people because in tribal times he helped the leader lead by using his knowledge to keep the populace in line. While Shamans themselves formed a mystical part of the tribal society, they also had specific responsibilities to the tribe. Through rituals, for instance, they could allay the fears of their people about strange occurrences such as unexpected death, poor hunts and weather phenomena, while maintaining tribal unity. What they did and how they did it was not common knowledge. It was secret knowledge reserved for the Shaman alone.

There were good reasons for keeping the Shamanic knowledge secret in those early days. Education as we know it was not widespread, to say the least. The Shaman was more often than not the most educated individual in a given society due to the information that was passed down through succeeding generations of Shamans. In tribal cultures the Shaman was, without doubt, the most educated and mentally agile member of the tribe. The information he held simply could not be entrusted to anyone who had not gone through the rigors of Shamanic initiation. There were too many pieces of that knowledge puzzle.

As Christianity gained strength, the clergy began to assume some of the duties which the Shaman had traditionally performed. The Shamanic hierarchy was threatened and a power struggle ensued. Shamans, being human, had allowed their power to go to their heads and had begun to practice more and more bizarre behavior that actually threatened the emerging societal reforms. An example of this strangeness is the practice of human sacrifice in the Aztec society in Mexico, and this was not the only part of the world where this practice was widespread. Archeological evidence of human sacrifice can be found in nearly every part of the world. At the time of the Churches' emergence as the spiritual leader of the world, the common man didn't have to think very hard about his choices.

Clearly, the advent of the Church marked the fall of the Shaman. However, there remains a question. After thousands of years and countless generations of people being born to the Office of Shaman, where did today's potential Shamans go? It is difficult to accept that Shamans during millennia were possessed of the devil. It is fairly clear that the Church put a socially unacceptable spin on Shamanic activities but it is not clear how, after generations of Shamanic activity, the Shaman himself suddenly became a vile creature to be cast out of this earthly paradise. The reality is that he wasn't. The Shaman did not disappear. He simply began to apply his unique personage to other endeavors.

By the time the industrial revolution was in full swing, many of those born to the Office of Shaman were finding other outlets for their talents. The vast Shamanic knowledge had dwindled away. The Shamanic teachers became fewer and fewer. The methods which are born into the fledgling Shaman were, from time to time, brought to fruition by very talented and often Machiavellian individuals, but the rules of Shamanic behavior were no longer taught. Perhaps those talented individuals never knew that they were but one in a long line of Shamans born to the Office.

Another byproduct of forgiveness was that it made it easier for people to forge Agreements. As Agreements were made and energy was gathered by the holders of the Agreements, a new type of Shaman came to be. He was the modern day Shaman. Captains of Industry. Inventors. Bankers. Scientists. They, like their predecessors, fell into two categories. One category dreamed dreams and invented things or discovered micro-worlds, or even gazed at stars and developed mathematical formulas to explain their findings to others. This type of Shaman is called a Dreamer. The other type of modern day Shaman dealt with people. They got them to agree to do things. Wondrous things. They convinced people to build interstate highways and skyscrapers and bridges and dams. This type of Shaman is called a Stalker. They worked together with the Dreamers. The Dreamers conceived the wondrous things then the Stalkers gathered the Agreements to accomplish those wondrous things.

People such as Edison show all the earmarks of a Shamanic Dreamer. Carnegie may well have been a Shamanic Stalker. These are but a couple of many, many examples which could be sited of individuals who may well have been born to the Office of Shaman and in reality practiced as though they actually were Shamans. It is relatively certain that they did not receive Shamanic instruction in the course of their lives even though they performed Shamanic feats. In the present day and time there are many, many people who may also have been born to the Office of Shaman but lack the instruction that would make them functional as Shamans simply because our society has deemed Shamanism to be bad, antiquated, or maybe silly. It is certainly true that some of the practices commonly associated with Shamanism no longer have the same relevance they once had but this suggests that Shamanism has not kept itself relevant with changes in society.

It is time, once again for those born to the Office of Shaman to acknowledge who they are and to rebuild the Shamanic knowledge base. As the knowledge base is rebuilt it will, no doubt, incorporate more modern explanations, practices, and ideas than was ever thought possible by earlier Shamans. Some ideas will remain intact and some ideas will be modified. The practice of Shamanism always has and should continue to garner remuneration for services rendered. It must, at least at first, be self-governing. But for this type of global change to occur a more nearly complete idea of Shamanic practice must be set forth. This work is the first of a series designed to this end. It is not a complete set, but it is a primer for those who see Shamanism as an alternative life style and who would like to have a reference guide for common, basic Shamanic practices.

It should be noted here that the word Shaman covers many aspects of the "mystical arts." Here the word is used for anyone who uses the thoughts inherent in the Shamanic discipline. At one time it was necessary for Shamans to guard their information. In today's world the educational level of the populace is different than it was during the time of Shamanic secrecy. In our current society, nearly anyone can avail themselves of those secrets. All that is required is a modicum of study and a good deal of application.

There are several basic ideas which need to be covered as a primer in order for an individual to conceptualize a Point of View conducive to understanding Shamanic activities. One of the first ideas necessary to this type of understanding is the concept of describing the world in terms other than equal opposites. In other words, it is difficult to understand any Shamanic principle if one describes the world as black being the opposite of white, as male being the opposite of female, as up being the opposite of down, as good being the opposite of bad and so on. In common language between ordinary people, this type of linguistic shorthand is acceptable, but it is not accurate enough for the Shaman's purpose. The Shaman would have to say that black is an absence of color and white includes all the colors and both are visual perceptions. Or, the Shaman might say that males and females are two aspects of humanity. Or, the Shaman might say that up is relative to down. Or, the Shaman might say that good and bad describe advantageous and less than advantageous behaviors. A Shaman would have to make the distinction that nearly any linguistic dichotomy is actually a relative measure of extremes.

One of the reasons for such linguistic nit-picking is that Shamans must pay attention to actual events in all their myriad levels. To the Shaman, the world, as a sentient being, addresses seemingly ordinary events in non-ordinary ways, which make some of those events extraordinary. To the Shaman, people do extraordinary things that they themselves may think of as coincidences. A Shaman must pay attention to miniscule events which pass by ordinary people as though merely a hiccup in the continuum of daily life. Attention to detail is one of the hallmarks of the Shamanic experience. It is in the details of living life that much of the Shaman's knowledge takes on importance.

Anyone who is seriously considering the way of the Shaman must give himself over to the discipline of speaking about, exploring, and considering the minute aspects of life which escape many individuals. Part one of this book will examine some of the common tools that Shamans use to examine their own lives and bring discipline to bear on their activities.

Points to Consider:

1. Shamanism became irrelevant because Shamans did not acknowledge changes in society or because they resisted those changes.

2. Shamanism lost a great deal of its accumulated knowledge because Shamans were silenced due to their resistance to change.
3. The Shaman has always filled a necessary niche in society.
4. That niche is not currently being filled.
5. It should be filled.
6. Anyone can understand Shamanic concepts.
7. Shamanic concepts apply to all people.
8. If we don't learn from history we are damned to repeat it.
9. The application of the full spectrum of Shamanic principles adds value to any way of life including the Shamanic way of life.

Introductory Story

Here he comes again; all full of himself and so sure that he is in control of his universe. But such energy! He doesn't have a clue why he is at my place and he keeps coming back. This is the fourth time in a week. There is something about this guy that has captured my attention.

He looks like he is a Stalker. He certainly has the mental agility, but every time I ask him how he knows what he is talking about, he defends his Point of View well. If he only knew what he was defending, or even why, he would be a bit more palatable. But he doesn't know, and for this reason he is at once maddening and intriguing.

He says his name is Robert. I call him Bob and, of course, he corrects me. But since I want to see if I can run him off, I persist in calling him Bob, but he keeps coming back. I shouldn't be surprised, but I am. I should really wait until he asks for information, but since he doesn't know what to ask for I need to pay attention to his actions to tell me what he is asking. Sometimes people just don't have the words.

If most folks could only listen to themselves talk, they would know that they are running scared. Bob is no exception. The poor guy talks non-stop. There's no doubt that he's threatened at a fight or flee level. The only question is what button or buttons will evoke the response. He's got to take a breath sooner or later.

"So Bob, you think you can stop talking about yourself long enough to let me ask you a couple of questions?"

"Am I talking about myself again? You know, you aren't the first one to ever say that to me. My current girlfriend tells me that a lot."

"I'll bet she does."

"Yeah, she tells me I talk about myself. I don't think I talk about myself that much, but she does."

A problem common to many people is that they put themselves in situations to learn about all manner of things, but then prevent that learning from ever taking place. It seems as though learning new things is some kind of threat.

"Bob, I have these questions."

"Oh yeah, well, ask away."

"Thanks. Well, why do you think you keep coming by here?"

"You're a nice guy and you listen to me and I like your place and I don't think you're as grouchy as everyone says. Everyone says you're a real..."

Let's cut that off at the pass.

"Well I am a grouchy old fart and I've worked hard for people to think I'm like that so don't you go telling them any different. So tell me, why do *you* think you keep coming by here?"

"Like I said, people say you're all grouchy..."

"Bob."

"…but you seem like a nice guy to me…"

"Bob."

"…and this is a great place and…"

"BOB."

"Yes?"

"Why do *you* think you keep coming by here? I didn't ask you what someone else said, I asked you about what *you* think. Would you answer that, please?"

"Sure. I don't really know why."

That is, without doubt, true. Bob can't possibly know why he comes by. He doesn't have the tools to know and I'm betting that is precisely why he's coming by – to get the tools.

"Let's just say I've had some experiences in my life which allow me to talk about things and see things a little differently than a lot of folks. In fact, you might say that I have a set of unique experiences. At least they would be unique as far as *you* can tell."

"Well, I didn't fall off the turnip truck just last week, you know."

"Oh?"

"I've been around. I know some things. I…"

You know some things, all right. Let's see how much you know. My guess is that the next subject will either run him off or glue him to the spot.

"Bob."

"Yeah?"

"Have you ever thought about the spirit of man or about the soul?"

"Yeah, lots of times."

"What do you think about that?"

"What do you mean?"

"I mean, what do you think about that?"

This question is designed to pull him up short. Another way to say this would be that I am trying to "stop his world." If I can stop his internal dialogue for a few minutes I will be able to introduce the idea of being born to the Office of Shaman and see what his reaction to that is.

"Do you mean about religious stuff and things like that?"

"No, I mean what do you think about the spirit of man or about the soul?"

"Well, I don't know. I guess we have a soul, at least that's what they say."

"Well, let me ask you something about that. If you think we have a soul, is it bigger than a breadbox? Do you think it has a function?"

"What do you mean?"

"I mean do you think that the soul is bigger than a breadbox?"

"I don't understand."

"I know. Bob, I don't want to overload you with information or anything, but if you were to think about the soul, would you say that you have a soul or would you say that you are a soul?"

"I don't understand."

"It's pretty simple, really, because if I wanted to know what you think I could only ask you. Out of all the people in the world, you are the only one I would trust about what it is that you think. From that perspective then, would you say that you have a soul or that you are a soul?"

"Well, I don't think I know what you are talking about. Are you asking me if I am a religious person?"

"No, I'm asking you if you think you *have* a soul or if you *are* a soul."

"Well, I think that's kind of personal. I don't think you have the right to ask me about that kind of personal stuff."

"Bob, it's just you and me here and you said that you come by here because I'm a nice guy and this is a nice place, right? Didn't you say that?"

"Yeah, but..."

"Bob, you know what? I'm going to tell you what I think about this subject, okay?"

"Yeah, but that doesn't mean that I'm going to agree with you."

"I'm not asking you to agree or to disagree. I am asking you what you think, but you don't seem to be able to respond to that so I'm going to tell you what I think so you won't feel so threatened, okay?"

"Yeah, but that doesn't mean I'm going to agree."

"Fair enough. Well, I think we *are* souls. I think you are a soul, I think I am a soul, I think everyone either of us knows is a soul. Not only that, I think that the soul is really in charge of nearly everything any of us does. There are exceptions, to be sure, but when it comes to major turning points in our lives, it is the soul who is in charge. Not only that, but I think that the reason you are here is because your soul put you here and I think that the reason your soul has put you here is that you may be one of those people who were born to the Office of Shaman. What that means for me, at least, is that you are being drawn to come by and talk to me about something that you can only sense. Something that may be of great importance to you, but that you can't quite put your finger on. If that should prove to be the case then you are being directed by your very soul to discover that to which you were born. Would that be all right with you?"

"Yeah, but that doesn't mean I'm going to agree with anything you say."

You didn't say you wouldn't either. Will you continue to deny this if you're consciously aware of it?

"Fair enough, but if you continue to come by here we'll cross that bridge when we get to it. But for right now let's say that I think you were born to learn certain things and that you have been chasing down those things your whole life. For instance, I'll bet that you have a series of memories about doing things that were life threatening, surviving, and not knowing exactly how you managed to live through the thing. That's true isn't it?"

"Well, I do have one memory like that, kind of."

I'll bet you have more than one, but I'll settle for this one because it's the most important to you.

"Tell me about it."

"Well, I was driving on a mountain road one night and it was snowing. For some reason I lost control of the car. I started to spin, and I don't mean the tires were spinning, either. I mean the car went around three times. On one side of the road there was a rock cliff and on the other side of the road there was a 100-foot drop off. Somehow I managed to steer the car right down the middle of the road and not hit the cliff or the drop off. When the car came to a stop, I was headed down the hill in the direction I was going and so I put the car in first and drove off. The weird thing is that I don't know how I did any of that. My memory is kind of blurred, really."

I could very well be wrong about this guy. As he told his story, I could see the entire event unfold even though I doubt Bob will ever qualify for the World Raconteur Round-Up. I do believe we have a real live Dreamer here. Who knew?

"Is it like you remember watching the whole event unfold and not knowing how your body was doing the things it was doing?"

"Exactly like that."

"I would say, then, that you, as the soul, took over from you, as your consciousness, and guided your body to react so you as body, consciousness and soul didn't die that night. Otherwise you wouldn't be here talking to me."

From the color of his face, I'd say that he's about to invoke the flee part of fight or flee.

"What is this, the twilight zone?"

"No this is just a conversation we are having about what you think."

"I'll see you later. I gotta go."

"See you later, Bob."

He overloads pretty quick. I'll have to work on that. He did tell me his story though. I doubt he's told that story to many people in his life. What he told me was that his soul has been trying to express through him for a long, long time. I think he may have been born to the Office of Shaman.

Points to Consider:

1. Bob has made himself available to the Spirit.
2. Even though he could not verbalize his desires, when he was presented with what the teacher thought, he did not deny the possibility of being born to the Office of Shaman.
3. Bob has at least one memory that would indicate that he has been chosen, if that is the word, for something important.
4. The teacher successfully guided Bob to consider, at least, the idea that the soul or spirit of man has a function.
5. Bob reached a certain threshold of understanding and couldn't continue without giving himself more time.
6. The teacher pushed Bob as far as was possible, then gave Bob the time he will need to process the new information he received.

The teacher managed to "draw a line in the sand" for Bob which if crossed will indicate his willingness to continue, even without verbal consent.

Chapter 1: Programming

"Once a program has been written
it becomes the rule of our life until recognized and changed."

John C. Lilly: *Programming and Metaprogramming in the Human Biocomputer*

The first tool a Shaman must understand how to use is Programming the brain. This is as true today as it was when the first Shamans began to learn about what would become their calling. Much has been written about this process and Programming is the first place that the kind of discipline necessary to the Shamanic experience becomes apparent. Although early Shamans couldn't have ever understood the concept, the brain works, acts and can and should be considered to be a computer. Even though they could not have understood the concept as we can, they still practiced Programming by teaching young Shamans how to behave.

Programming is nothing more than telling yourself or allowing someone else to tell you how to do something or what to do about something. A program can be as simple as repeating to yourself, "Relax, relax, relax." It can also be more complicated as with telling yourself how to behave in certain situations and it can consist of several parts. It can even be as complicated as writing a business program for a new or existing business where the program tells numbers of people what to do and how to do it. Exact wording in a program will result in the brain thinking and acting in an exact or precise manner. Inexact wording in Programming will result in the brain acting on all the ways it can conceive the words to mean. Shamanic training begins with Programming so that the Shaman can learn how exact and how precise he must be in every aspect of his life. The early Shamans taught this by insisting on a code of conduct which they called the warrior's way. This code was probably named different things in different cultures but essentially was a method of teaching young people the way they should act within the tribe or culture.

In order to achieve Programming in oneself, one needs to understand that the brain works a lot like a computer. It is a very large computer, to be sure, but it behaves like a computer. We can refer to the brain as the biocomputer and be most accurate. On the computer I am using to write this, for instance, there is a program which checks for computer viruses. It runs without me doing anything to make sure that it is doing its job. It checks to see if it is current whenever I log on to the Internet, it checks all my e-mail when they arrive and when they leave. In other words, it is part of the rule of the life of my computer. It will continue to do the things it does until I decide that it is no longer necessary and remove the program. Programs in the biocomputer work in exactly the same way.

One of the problems inherent to changing ones mindset or Point of View to that of Shaman is how to change Programming which may have existed since childhood. The human operating system just doesn't come with instructions and it is true that once a program or a set of behavioral instructions have been written they are in effect in our life until recognized and changed. To complicate matters, Programming is not a simple set of instructions such as, "If attacked by a large animal, run!" Perhaps they once were, but in our modern world, who knows what a large animal looks like? About the only threatening animal we see nowadays is at the movies.

There are many instructional manuals about how to reprogram the thinking machinery to lead a better life. Most start with counting backwards from five to one or some other numerical sequence, then there is a prewritten Programming sequence which states that you are a better person than before you listened to the program. Essentially, this is self-hypnosis in one of its various forms. There is nothing wrong with self-hypnosis. It is a great Programming tool. The problem is that most of the prewritten Programming is too ambiguous to be much help for changing intensely personal Programming. What is needed is a method of writing programs for each individual need.

Of course, it is easiest to have someone else do it for you, but that method isn't very effective and can be downright confusing. It is much more effective to sit down and write a program for yourself being as specific as possible. One of the easiest forms of this type of Programming to understand is the Goals/Means Program developed by John C. Lilly. Lilly is the author of several books on how the brain works. He was involved for many years in dolphin research and wrote extensively on the correlation of the two brains. He also developed the physical isolation tank.

The reason the Goals/Means program form works is that it can be used for nearly any need which arises in the realm of human endeavor and it is easy to remember. It uses body parts as keys to how to interpret use. For instance, Goals are connected to the hands and feet because they are the body parts which reach a Goal first. Means are connected to the wrists and ankles because wrists and ankles support the hands and feet reaching the goal. Elbows and knees are connected to Charisma because they provide the attitude of approach, and so on as follows.

This Programming form consists of 11 parts. Each part is correlated with a body part to make it more understandable. The 11 parts of the program are: Goals, which is related to hands and feet; Means, which is related to wrists and ankles; Charisma, which is related to elbows and knees; Orientation, which is related to the genital area; Elimination, which is related to the lower abdomen; Assimilation, which is related to the upper abdomen; Impulses, which is related to the chest area; Needs, which is related to the mouth; Possibilities, which is related to the nose; Form which is related to the eyes; and Substance, which is related to the ears.

A Goal is defined as something you want to achieve or somewhere you want to go. It should be stated in a single sentence. The goal should be stated in a positive manner. The brain will follow the instructions given it. For example, it is one thing to say that you want to go to 1492 Columbus Drive in Columbus, Ohio and quite another thing to say that you would someday like to visit the Midwest. These two examples illustrate the attention to detail that is the hallmark of the practicing Shaman.

A program to purchase a house would, perhaps, be an ideal method of demonstrating the exact wording necessary in self-Programming. The goal could be stated in a variety of ways. "To buy a house," would be a very simplistic goal. "To buy a house that is within my financial ability to pay," would be a better and more nearly exact goal. "Buy a two bedroom, three bath house with attached garage for no more than $250,000.00 in Wooded Hills," would be a nearly perfect goal. The more exact the wording in the goal, the fewer options the brain has for interpreting the instructions and the easier it is to complete the next portion of the program.

Means is defined as how the goal is to be achieved. As the hands are the part of the body which actually pick up the desired goal, the wrists must be aligned with the hands so the goal can actually be picked up. "Get the down payment together," would be a simplistic means segment for buying a house. "Save some money out of my paycheck and put it in the bank until I have the money to make the down payment," would be better. "Save 22% of all income and place that in a high yield account until I accumulate $25,000.00 while reducing my credit load," would be even more accurate. Remember that the means part of this program describes how the goal will be achieved.

Charisma can be defined as an attitude of approach. The elbow needs to be at an appropriate angle if the hands are to pick something up off a table like a bag of flour, for instance. The same is true for Programming. Charisma, or the attitude of approach, must be correct to empower the Goals and Means. "I'll talk to the bank about what I need to do to get a loan," would be a simple charisma segment for buying a house. "I'll go down to the bank and fill out a credit application and submit it," would be better. "I'll make an appointment with Ralph, the branch manager at my bank, to talk to him about how much money I need to have in my account and what level of credit I should have in order to qualify for a loan of $250,000.00" would be even better. The idea behind charisma or attitude of approach is to define your attitude so that you can ride that attitude to your goal.

Orientation is defined as the direction you face in order to accomplish the goal. If your genitals are facing away from that table with the bag of flour on it, you will have even more trouble picking it up than if your elbows are at an inappropriate angle. This may be a silly example, but it does define the problem that orientation is designed to overcome. If you aren't facing the right direction, it is nearly impossible to solve a problem coming in that direction. "I want to buy a house because I don't want to pay rent," is a simple statement of orientation. "I want to build equity for my future by buying a house," is a better direction. "I will employ my money in a house purchase to further my financial standing so that I can begin to guarantee my own retirement insurance and future financial well-being," is even better. Each of these examples point in a single direction, but each successive statement better defines the direction you want to go through time.

Elimination is defined as the stuff you wish to eliminate from your life in order to accomplish your goal. It seems that there is no gain without a corresponding loss. "I'll pack my lunch so I can save for the down payment on my house," is a good, if simple, elimination. "I'll work an extra shift instead of watching television at night to make the down payment," is an ambitious elimination. "I'll eliminate my fear of owning a home and making the payments and eliminate my pride about how important I am in my present job so that I can do something that makes more money," would be even better. The elimination part of this Programming form requires that one address things that actually make a difference.

Assimilation is defined as the things you need to put into your life in order to accomplish your goal. At first glance one might think that in the house purchase program we have been following, you would want to assimilate money into your life in order to purchase the house. That would be true, but misleading. "I'll develop pride of ownership," is a step in the right direction. "I will work overtime and join the Rotary Club so I can meet people who can possibly help me further my opportunities," is several steps in the right direction. "I am going to take some night courses so that I qualify for that management opening and use that position as a stepping stone to move up to the front office and I will take responsibility for my own future well-being by being responsible for my current state in life," would be one defining course of assimilation. As with elimination, assimilation requires actual differences to be realized.

Impulses are exactly what they seem to be. Some negative impulses are good survival tools and need to be left in place. As in all other parts of the Programming, it is well to word the program so there is no margin for error. You don't want to tell the brain to do something unless you are absolutely sure that is exactly what you want the brain to do. Always think about all the possibilities that your verbiage could mean. Your brain will even if you don't. "My impulse is to buy the house I want," could be defined by the brain in funny ways that could result in buying the house before you are ready, for instance. "My impulses direct me to take advantage of opportunities in the work place and to avoid office politics that could result in losing my job," would be a much better statement to program impulses. "My impulse is to accept responsibility for my actions and learn from my mistakes." "My impulses direct me, always to the best course of action to build for my future," is even more to the point and leaves very little room for brain interpretation.

Needs is defined as what you actually have to have in order to accomplish your goal. This part of the program can be tricky. We tend to think of the word *need* in ways that confuse the brain. Needs are things that are necessary. Air is necessary. Water is necessary. An attitude that makes money for you and for others is necessary in business. Buying a home is business. "I'll work hard and do what the boss asks me so I can make the money I need to buy my house," is a great start, but it still leaves something to be desired. "I need to understand what my company does to earn money so that I can do more to make the company succeed and to do that, I need more education," is better. "I need to understand what my talents are so that I can use those talents to make money for myself and others so that I can earn the money and stability I need to buy my house," is still better.

Possibilities is defined as the ways the program could be made real. In particular it is the way *your* program is going to be made real. As in the old adage of "be careful what you wish for, you might just get it," this can be a two edged sword. You want to be sure here that you direct the brain to stay within these limits. "There is a possibility that I could lose my job, but I could always sell this house for a profit and be ahead," leaves the brain the option to look for a way to fulfill this possibility. "I have the possibility of making a few repairs to this house and selling it for a profit and I have the possibility of living here for the rest of my life," is a much better set for possibilities. "If I do get that promotion through taking night classes, I could pay off the mortgage in 15 years instead of 30 and would end up paying much less for the house," is still better and much more self-serving.

Form is defined as the structure of the reality you wish to create. In other words, you are forming something that is becoming real for you. How do you want it structured? It is at this point in the Programming process that the hoped for reality starts to become real. You are committing to this program you are writing. Your decision is becoming final. "When I buy the house and get the promotion, I'll have a party in the back yard and invite all the neighbors," would be a simple form. "Living in this house in this neighborhood will allow me to cut 30 minutes off my commute and the kids will have a better school system." "I'll only be a few minutes from shopping, yet it is peaceful here and with the work I want to take on, being able to relax here will be like taking a small vacation everyday," would be a much better definition of form.

The substance of the program is noted when you know that the program has jumped from the idea to the reality of everyday existence. You actually write the definition of that moment here. "When I come home every day I'll have my shop in the garage so I can build model widgets and set up the den so that I can go online and study trends in the widget market so that I can use this place as a relaxing extension of work." "I'll be able to invite people from work to brainstorm new ideas for product and services and still maintain a relaxed atmosphere for everybody." "I can put a big couch in the living room and a large table in the den so that we can examine drawings and I'll make it low enough so we can all sit around and eat afterwards." These are the types of statements that make a program real.

This Programming form is very powerful. It is simple if you remember to define each element as precisely as possible. It is not necessary to change brain wave levels as it is with other types of Programming. Writing does that anyway. In order to write a program in this format you will have to leave conscious thought to a certain degree anyway, but that is an automatic response. You will not be able to simply chatter to yourself and accomplish this feat. Once you have written a program for yourself, you have taken the first step toward becoming a Shaman.

Some things to do to better understand Programming

Programming is a fairly simple exercise. There are several ways anyone can use it to begin to write programs and examine their usefulness. The simplest type of program is to find a word or statement which sums up a desired activity. For example, someone who deals with the public in a stressful situation may find it helpful to repeat often, "Be kind." Someone who works in government, a bank, or an insurance office may want to repeat, "Take the time to explain the rules." New parents may want to repeat, "Patience is good." These are examples of "mantra" type Programming. This type of Programming is a simple and effective behavior modification tool.

The *Goals/Means* type of Programming covers a much broader scope. This type of program would be employed for changing, not modifying, behavior. For this program to be most effective it must be written. This can be a challenging task, but for an individual who is exploring the Office of Shaman it is a necessary step. Even for those who are simply trying to see if Programming can be effective in their lives the only method to employ this Programming tool is by writing it out.

The advantage of any type of Programming is that it gives the individual control over what he wants to do and where he wants to go in his life. There is no longer any reason for anyone to be chained to childhood Programming. There is no reason to allow Programming foisted upon an individual from parents or society to remain in control of anyone's life. This is one of the secrets that Shamans have always known about, but had no way of explaining. Until the advent of the computer, there simply wasn't a language that could cover the events taking place in the brain. In the last fifty years, or even less, such a language has emerged and it can be used to explain this aspect of brain/mind function. Programming is no longer wrapped in mystery. It is a concept which is available to anyone at any time. It is simply a matter of learning how to apply information to the thought process.

Programming can even be applied to business because everyone has a job. There is a business program called MBO (Management By Objective) which can be utilized by anyone who has a job to make that job more understandable and productive. The program form was developed by Peter Drucker many years ago and has since been modified by Big Businesses to be ever more effective. In its most simple form it consists of only four parts. There is the Objective, which is a one-sentence statement about what the job or the business is to accomplish. This sentence may not contain any numbers, dates, or amounts. It is simply a statement which defines the... well, Objective.

Next are the Goals. Goals are defined as the numbers, dates, and amounts that must be achieved to reach the Objective. There may be many Goals, but all of them must define numbers, dates and amounts. Most often the Goals are all defined in the wording of the Objective or should be.

The next part is the Strategy. Again this is only one sentence. This sentence defines how every Goal will be achieved. Although this may sound like an impossible task, it can be as simple as, "Smile at all the customers."

The last part of this program is the Recurring Events. Be careful here to think about this one carefully. Recurring Events are not re-occurring events. They are the things that happen every day, or every hour or even once a week which cause the Goals to be achieved. They are, obviously, done in the manner described by the Strategy.

This Programming form can be applied to any job or business. A simple example for a convenience store clerk is as follows:

Objective: Make my shift the most profitable shift in the store.

Goals: 1) Remember all the regulars' names and what they normally buy. 2) Greet each regular, calling him by name. 3) Learn the names by keeping notes in a notebook. 4) Leave space after each name to make notes about his family. 5) After calling the customer by name, ask if there is anything else I can get for him today. 6) Make notes for other things he may buy.

Strategy: Always present myself as though I am overjoyed to see the customer.

Recurring Events: 1) Have the customers "behind the counter" purchases ready when they come to pay. 2) Check the notebook at the end of every shift to make sure that his special needs are met during ordering. 3) Make a show of writing down his order and getting his phone number and then actually call to tell him the order is in.

This is a flippant example, perhaps, but it shows how this program works. This program must be written to be effective. All Programming forms must be put to use in order to see how they work and where they work. With practice, Programming skills can be developed and honed. There is no substitute for experience.

Points to Consider:

1. The first tool a Shaman must learn is Programming. Programming teaches exactness.
2. There are many Programming forms which range from one-word mantras to multi-level business programs.
3. The Shaman will want to learn how to utilize as many types of Programming as is possible.
4. Programming teaches a Shaman the limits of his influence. Those limits may be wider in some ways than one would think and in other ways they may be less than one would think because sometimes we limit ourselves through our Programming and sometimes we act as though we are more than we actually are because of our Programming.
5. By teaching other people how to write programs the Shaman will learn more than all his students combined.
6. By answering for himself how Programming works the Shaman will learn a great deal about how his own thinking machinery works.

Story Chapter I

It's been a week or so since Bob stopped in for a visit. His last visit was a bit hard on his current view of the world. When you get right down to it, his current view of the world has been mortally wounded. It will take a long time to actually succumb, but the fatal blow has been delivered.

He could still recover, I suppose, but he would always know that he survived the event on the mountain road because of the soul's intervention. He can't just walk away from that. The Spirit chose him that night. I might even say that the Spirit tapped him on the shoulder. His consciousness doesn't know what to do with that memory. The last visit was probably the first time in his life that he had even a halfway reasonable explanation for it.

The problem he has now is that the idea of the soul being in control of his body will begin to grow. It is like giving water to last year's seed after having lain on the ground all winter. The problem is that there isn't a genetic map of what he's supposed to do with that information. It isn't likely that he can find a support group even on the World Wide Web. If I don't help him, he won't have anyone.

He must have some mettle or the Spirit wouldn't have tapped him on the shoulder and he wouldn't have sought me out. The next time he comes by, I'll start his "formal training." I can't even tell him that, but I have to start anyway. He won't have enough information to deal with what I'm going to tell him for quite a while. I wouldn't wish this on anyone.

"Damn, Bob, are you still here? I thought you took off for parts unknown."

"No, I'm still here."

"You're not mad at me, are you?"

"No, why should I be mad?"

"Well you left in a huff the other day."

"No, I didn't. I was thinking about what you were saying was all."

"What did you think about that?"

"I don't know. I can't remember what we were discussing right now."

"Weren't we discussing the soul and being chosen for the Office of Shaman?"

"Yeah, I guess we were, but I don't believe in that shit."

"What do you believe in?"

"I don't believe in much of anything, I guess."

"Really? Do you believe in this table?"

"What do you mean? I don't have to believe in this table. I can touch it and that tells me it is real. What does belief have to do with that?"

"So you believe it's real, eh?"

"It *is* real. I don't have to believe in that."

"But you'll have to admit that at one time this table was simply an idea in someone's head. Then that guy went down to Denny's with his buddy and they drew this thing out on a napkin. The two of them made an agreement to make the table real. Don't you think?"

Challenging him on his belief in "real" could backfire, but I need to challenge his Programming at this point. I need to get him to think about something other than himself, something that he doesn't understand.

"I don't know if they went to Denny's and I don't know if they drew it out on a napkin."

"All good ideas are drawn out on a napkin down at Denny's, Bob. Don't you know anything?"

"If you say so."

"Okay, maybe they went to Starbucks. But you have to admit that they made an agreement about a thing, then the thing became real. We both know that because we can touch their agreement."

"I don't know what you are talking about."

"All right, this subject is probably something that we need to discuss at another point in time anyway. What else is going on in your life?"

"I talked with my dad today."

I figured that idea about real tables would get him moving.

"How is your dad?"

"He's okay, I guess. He still scares me."

"He scares you? What? Is he ugly?"

"No. He just scares me is all."

Now that can't be true. I need to get to the bottom of this, I think. Of course it could be a can of worms, but even if it is I can't let a grown man suffer with a childhood fear of his dad.

"Bob, what in the name of Sam Hill are you talking about? You talked to the man on the phone, for the love of Christ. What is scary about that?"

"I don't know. He just scares me."

"How long have you been scared of your daddy? Doesn't he love you?"

"I guess so."

"What *are* you talking about, Bob? The man has been your dad for as long as you can remember and you're scared of him? Did he beat you, or what?"

"Naw, he just talks to me using that tone of voice. You know."

"No, I don't know. You are not making any sense at the moment and I don't understand what you're saying."

This ploy is actually nothing more than making him explain his abstractions. After four or five questions about any personal abstraction, people always get defensive. Once he gets frustrated I can ask him about what is really bugging him and he'll tell me, I hope. If I don't go through this step, he's liable to dance around it all night.

"So are you on his side?"

"Bob, I don't even know your dad, remember?"

"Well, you're talking about things like I'm wrong, just like he does."

"Yo, kid. If the shoe fits, wear it."

"Well, I'm not wrong."

I wonder if he's ever heard the story about the country doctor who told his patient who complained of pain when he lifted his arm above his head, "Well, don't lift your arm above your head, then." I would think not.

"Right. If you don't think you are wrong, then why does he scare you?"

"He wants me to do things like he says. I have a mind of my own and I don't need him telling me what to do all the time."

"You mean you can't listen to what someone who is old enough to be your father thinks without being threatened? How are you going to learn anything like that? You want to cut your nose off to spite your face too?"

I don't need to waste time with this. If I act like I think his dad acts with him, maybe he'll act with me the same way he acts with his dad. I already know he's not going to run, so I might as well whack this good and hard so he can get past it as quickly as possible. He may get his feelings hurt, but he'll get over that.

"You don't have to be nasty. You can tell me things without putting me down. I don't need this shit; I get enough of that from my old man. What do I need this from you for?"

I'm going to show you the way out of this box you're in, so just hang on. The intensity is over, for the moment anyway.

"I'll tell you what. Why don't you just sit down and write yourself a program to treat your dad like a human being?"

"What do you mean?"

"I mean, sit yourself down and write yourself a program which will direct you to find the ways to show your father some degree of respect. He deserves it and you know he does or you wouldn't be talking about what he is supposedly doing to run your life. You do as you please. So why blame him for what you do?"

"I'm not blaming him."

"Right. You're just 'scared' of him. Have I got that right?"

"Well, he does scare me."

"If he actually scared you then you would be doing what he tells you to do. You never do what the man says. What you do is anything and everything he tells you not to do. Then you claim that the reason you are doing all that stuff is that he can't tell you what to do. You claim to be your own person, but you just happen to be reacting to something that isn't even real."

He actually has convinced himself that it's his father's fault that he's scared. He isn't even aware that his fear requires huge amounts of energy to maintain. Let's free up some of that energy for reprogramming the old biocomputer.

"Look, if I was as bothered as much by something as you seem to be about the supposed control that your dad visits on you, I'd write myself a program to address the situation."

"So according to you, all I have to do is write a program and I'll magically stop being afraid of my dad. Right?"

If you only knew. But we're about to remedy that situation.

"If you haven't tried it, don't knock it."

"So how do you write a program?"

I need to make sure he's ready to actually write a program before I start off into this.

"You mean you don't know?"

"I'm willing to give it a try."

"So you're willing to 'give it a try.' I don't have to 'give it a try.' I've been writing programs for nearly as many years as you've been alive. I don't even have to believe in it. I know, and know how I know, that if you recognize a program and change it, you will have a new rule in your life that your brain will follow until you change that. You're still running on the original set of programs that you wrote as a child. The problem is you've never even examined your own Programming for the first time."

"How do you know what I have examined and what I haven't?"

"You still scared of your daddy?"

"Well…"

"I'll take that as though you have recognized that you are still running a childhood program of being afraid of your dad telling you what you have to do. If that's true, then what would you like to change?"

"What do you mean? I don't know if I want to change anything."

Oh, you bad, bad man! I'll bet you have your hog parked right outside in my driveway, don't you? There really isn't much choice here, bad man. I'm not going to give up on you until you agree to write the program, so we might as well cut to the chase.

"You mean you want to continue to be afraid of your dad?"

"No! I don't want to be afraid of my dad."

"Well, that's good but what does that mean, 'I don't want to be afraid of my dad?' You aren't afraid of him. You may be afraid that he'll find out what you do, but you aren't afraid of him."

"Why do you say that?"

So you're willing to admit that one. I do believe we're making progress here.

"Because it's true. You do as you please. You may be afraid your dad will try to explain why you should be doing something else, but you don't give a fig about what he says."

"All I know is that he scares me."

God doesn't like backsliders, Bob. Keep the slate clean here.

"Look, if you aren't going to be honest with me then I'm not going to help you."

"I am being honest."

"Sure you are. You are just jumping right on the idea that you aren't really afraid of your dad, right?"

"Well, I am afraid of him."

He's been ducking out of this one for a long time. I think I'll beat him to the punch.

"Bye."

"What do you mean?"

"I mean good bye, adios, hasta la vista, see you later, get out of here."

No one's ever pulled it up that tight that quickly. The boy's gotta decide right now. This is something new.

"What did I do?"

"Nothing you haven't been doing for your whole life."

"What do you mean?"

"Look, let me say this another way. You ain't the least bit afraid of your dad. You do whatever you want whenever you want. I will agree that you feel fear when you talk to him, but he isn't generating it. You are. You generate it by doing exactly the things you know he won't approve of and you don't want him to know what you are doing because you are ashamed of what you do."

"I'm not ashamed of what I do."

How long has this guy been running this? He's certainly been pushed up against it before. I wonder if it came from his mom.

"Then why do you feel fear when you talk to your dad? Remember, I won't buy into the idea about him scaring you."

I should just wait about 20 minutes to see if he will ever come up out of it. I won't, but only because he's new at this. Innocence didn't work for him, so now he's going to try to stick his head in the sand and pretend he didn't hear me.

"You don't have an answer, do you? Well, let me offer a solution that just maybe will solve the problem. Okay?"

"Okay."

"What is your goal when you talk to your dad?"

"I don't have a goal."

"Of course you do. What do you want him to know when you talk with him?"

"I want him to know what I do."

"Exactly! You want to tell him what you do but you experience fear when you start to tell him because you know already he won't approve, right?"

"Kinda."

"Why don't you change your goal to find out what he is doing, or even better, what he is thinking?"

"What good would that do?"

Don't give up too quickly. Don't want you to lose face. Okay, I'll play along.

"It would set you up to respect him for a change."

"I don't know if I can do that."

"Bye."

"What? Every time I have a doubt, you say bye? What kind of help is that?"

"If you aren't serious about helping yourself then I'm wasting my time."

"You're not wasting your time."

Now that didn't hurt, did it?

"Then you *can* respect your dad?"

"Yeah."

"Want some cheese with that whine?"

"No."

"Then cut it out. I don't have the time you have to waste. If you want to actually learn how to program yourself to make things better, then act like it. Writing a program is like deciding to go somewhere. If you wanted to go to New York, for instance, that would be your goal. Then you need to decide on the means of going to New York, like are you going to drive, or take public transportation, or walk, or something, get it?"

"Yeah."

"The next thing is to decide what charisma you will employ."

"What?"

"Charisma can mean attitude of approach. Are you going to go first class? Are you going to go within your budget? That might mean for you that you hitchhike, but let's pretend you are a man of means and can decide on any attitude of approach you want. What would that be for you?"

"I'd fly in, then take a taxi to Queens."

"Why take a taxi to Queens?"

"I have a cousin who lives there."

"Of course you do. Then what would be your Orientation if you wanted to go to New York?"

"I'd have to be oriented toward going to New York. It wouldn't do me any good to be oriented toward going to New Orleans, would it?"

"No. I don't think it would. Okay, the next part of the program is what you would eliminate in order to go to New York."

"I'd eliminate my job and having to listen to you."

"The whole world loves a smart ass; you know that, don't you? Why would you eliminate your job? How will you pay for the flight?"

"Okay, I get it. How do I write a program so my dad doesn't scare me?"

"You write a program to respect your dad."

"You won't give up on that, huh?"

"Not if you want to be successful with not being scared when you talk to him or anyone else you perceive to be in authority."

"So how do I do that?"

"There are 11 parts to this program. The first part is goals and they are related to your hands and feet. Are you going to remember this? Maybe you should get a piece of paper and write this down. I don't want to have to do this again tomorrow when you forget what we were talking about."

Besides, if you write it down then you will integrate it into your body.

"Okay."

"The next part is means, which is related to wrists and ankles. Write it down. After that comes charisma, which is related to knees and elbows. Then orientation, which is related to the genital area. If you aren't pointing in the right direction then you won't see what you need to get done, in other words. After that comes elimination, which is related to your lower intestine. You have to let some things go in order to gain something else, most often. Then comes assimilation, which is related to your upper intestine. After that is impulse, which is related to the chest. Not all impulses are bad, you know. Are you writing all this down? Then comes needs, which is related to the mouth. Be careful on this one to write the things you actually need and not the things you think you want. Then comes possibilities, which is related to the nose. Next is form which is related to the eyes. And last is substance, which is related to the ears."

"Are you going to help me write this? This sounds complicated."

"I could, I suppose, but if you want to change then you should write it yourself. When I want to change something in my life, I write my own program. I don't want anyone else messing with my Programming. Do you?"

"No, but I have never done this before."

"And that means...?"

"You have experience and I don't."

"Do you know how you get experience?"

"How?"

"You have experiences. Once you get it done, bring it back and I'll look it over. It won't make any difference because you will have told yourself what you should be doing anyway. But if it will make you feel better, I'll look it over.

Poor Bob, he doesn't know it, but the program has already been written. It won't hurt a thing for him to confirm it for himself, that's for sure. He can stand to have it integrated into body and mind and it won't hurt a thing. If he brings his program for me to look over tomorrow, the next day, or whenever, I will.

Points to Consider:

1. Bob affirmed that he had been thinking about being born to the Office of Shaman.
2. Bob affirmed that he was seeking information about the soul or spirit.
3. The teacher was able to plant the seed that belief makes things real.
4. Bob couldn't accept that idea as real, however.
5. The teacher was able to use the idea of making things real by using belief to set Bob up to talk about his relationship with his dad.
6. Bob began by saying that his dad scared him and finished by almost admitting that he was the fear generator.
7. The teacher got Bob to take responsibility for that fear and agree to write a program to replace the self-generated fear with respect.
8. The teacher called on Bob's fear of rejection to illustrate the error of not taking responsibility.
9. The actual program Bob used was:
   a. Act in a manner which his father would disapprove of, which would:
   b. Reinforce the feeling of rejection that Bob attributed to his father, so he could:
   c. Blame his father for the fear he felt, then:
   d. Indulge in the feeling that no one loved him.
10. The teacher disassembled all the parts of the program to show Bob how to be responsible for himself.

Chapter 2: Changing Points of View

"If a job is worth doing it's worth doing right."

— My Dad (and probably yours)

As the Shaman develops and masters the art of self-programming, he will begin to view the world a bit differently. He will begin to notice that many people could reduce the number of problems which they think they have by simply writing a program to change a behavior or to improve a relationship. If he is adept, he will soon notice that the world has taken on a different hue; he will be more relaxed, he will be more patient, and he will be ready to take the next step in his learning process. He will be on the verge of taking that first step toward acting as Shaman.

In order for the Shaman to act, he must be able to see the world between the shadows. This event could be likened to having the ability to take a stroll through rush hour traffic on any major freeway. It is as though the Shaman is operating at a different speed than the people who surround him. It probably looks to others as though he is traveling at a speed that is faster than normal, but in reality, he is traveling slower.

One way to talk about viewing the world in this manner is to say that we want to shut off the internal dialog. There are many, many models available to describe the event, such as meditation, yoga, and even running. One is not necessarily better than another. Some are more accurate than others, but the idea is to slow down, so if you have a model that works for you, such as meditation, keep it in place. If you are going to explain to others how you shut off your own internal dialogue, then accuracy counts. A model which seems to have fewer faults than others is to use brain wave frequency control as a method of slowing down. This is a method available to everyone because we all have brains and all brains use brain wave frequencies to function. If we can identify what frequencies have which functions, then we can deduce which ones we want to use to accomplish certain tasks.

Most people use the fastest brain wave frequency to think consciously. This frequency is named Beta and seems to be the frequency most used for conscious thought. It ranges between 14 and 21 cycles per second. It seems to be the home of the internal dialogue, too. Shamans are aware that the internal dialogue is a programming tool. We constantly reinforce our existing programming by telling ourselves over and over through the internal dialogue the component parts of our world. For instance, if someone "wrongs" us it is typical human behavior to tell ourselves all the reasons that wrong should be redressed. In other words, we hold our "wronged" stance in place through the internal dialogue. Shamans simply don't have time for such silliness. They strive to rid themselves of that kind of programming. To this end Shamans have found that slowing down and relaxing the body is a good first step. In our modern world, we know that slowing down the body can produce Alpha brain waves.

For instance, most hypnotists use a slower or softer tone of voice and change the cadence or rhythm of their voice to accentuate a 10.5 cycle per second beat. This is generally considered to be an Alpha brain wave rhythm. Brain wave frequencies have definite parameters which are measured in cycles per second. Because different brain wave patterns have different functions, we can accent the different patterns to self-program or practice self-hypnosis. Brain wave groupings may work in concert and they may work as though separated. There are some popular concepts which seem to have validity concerning brain wave function, although the reality of what brain waves do and how they do it may not be fully understood even by those who are on the cutting edge of brain function discovery. Therefore, the model offered here may be fraught with inaccuracies and is probably overly simplistic, but it can be considered as a model which can act as a catalyst for thinking about the problems associated with quieting the internal dialogue.

There are four generally recognized frequencies. There is a fifth, but little is known about it and it apparently shows up in only certain individuals. We will not use this frequency in our model. The fastest brain waves are Beta waves, which are between 14 and 21 cycles per second. It is likely that Beta waves are connected to waking consciousness. Yet, as with all assumptions about what brain waves do, it is wise to remember that experimenters are still discovering how the brain functions and how the different parts interact. In the brain function model being presented here, we will say that Beta waves have to do with logical thinking and conscious thought as that relates to the internal dialogue.

Alpha waves are between 7 and 14 cps. In our model, we will say that Alpha has to do with some types of programming and we generally call this type of programming "feelings." Feelings included in this set can include feelings of friendliness, feelings of apprehension, feelings of warmth, and other sets in the language which refer to mental rather than tactile feeling. Programs are defined as, "a set of instructions which govern actions or sets of actions." Since Alpha covers the middle of the common brain wave range, many people think that 10.5 cps is the strongest of all possible programming sites. That is the reason that hypnotists use the 10.5 cps beat. 10.5 cps is one of the easiest beats to achieve and generally feels peaceful and restful. One reason may be that as we fall asleep we pass through the Alpha brain waves and this is usually a peaceful sensation.

Theta waves are between 3 and 7 cps. In our model, we will say that Theta has to do with programs which control sets of programs. We generally call this type of programming "emotions." Emotions are programs which set the body into motion and can include such things as anger, physical love, excitement about learning any new experiences, and defense, even as it pertains to arguing one's Point of View. Deliberately producing Theta waves in order to dominate emotional responses is difficult. One reason is that there is a danger of triggering emotional activity. Hypnotists tend to stay up in Alpha while doing their thing because Alpha isn't such a minefield. However, the Shaman will need to explore this part of his thinking machinery. Some emotional responses are quite pleasant and some are not. But because emotions, by their very nature, control actions then deliberate action cannot be achieved without emotional domination. As the saying goes, "The only way out of the trap is through the trap." In other words, if we avoid our strong emotions we are effectively trapped or controlled by them. If we wish to have domination over them we must experience them in all their terrible glory and learn how to dominate them through understanding their triggers.

Delta waves are between .5 and 3 cps. They actually start at zero but who can measure that? Delta waves are generally associated with deep sleep. But in our model, they hold the value of controlling belief. They do not seem to control religious belief which seems to be a logical set, but rather, belief in what is real. We learn at a very early age that certain things are real and other things are pretend. It is important for survival to know the difference. Beliefs concerning real things are the basis for emotional actions, emotional actions are the basis for feelings, and feelings are the basis for conscious thought in this model. The brain is much more complex than the model but we can treat the model "as if not false" to arrive at some conclusions about how we think and what might be better methods of thought for Shamanic activities.

Illustration:

Beta rhythms at 14 to 21 cps relate to conscious thought, logic, and therefore to the internal dialogue. Beta rhythms are supported and probably caused by:

Alpha rhythms at 7 to 14 cps, which relate to "feelings", which can be considered to be programs or sets of instructions. Alpha rhythms are supported and probably caused by:

Theta rhythms at 3.5 to 7 cps, which relate to "emotions", which can be considered to be "programs which control sets of programs". Another name for this type of program could be "meta-program." Theta rhythms are supported and probably caused by:

Delta rhythms at .5 to 3.5 cps, which relate to "belief in real things", which can be considered as "programs which control other programs, which control sets of programs." Another name for this type of programming could be "self-meta-program". Delta rhythms are supported and perhaps caused by a non-physical computer operator which could be called the "Supra-Self-Meta-Programmer" or Other.

In fewer words:

Logic - Beta
Programs (feelings) - Alpha
Meta-Programs (emotions) - Theta
Self-Meta-Programs (belief in real things) - Delta
Supra-Self-Meta Programs - Other

When considering any unknown set such as a new or different Point of View, we need to have mental agility. One method of allowing mental agility is to consider any unknown set with the following parameters. While we usually treat things as, "True" or as, "False" we are allowed to also treat sets, "as if True" and "as if False" or even "as if not True" or "as if not False." In this manner, we can examine a hypothesis or new Point of View without getting trapped in non-action that a simple True and False framework may evoke. For our model to perform its catalytic function, we need to have all the agility possible.

When we think about brain waves we consider the brain to be a computer. The question is who is the computer operator? Through the millennia, there have been many discussions about if the soul is separate from the brain or body, or if we are the soul and the body is a tool for that entity. In our model we are going to treat "as if true" the idea that the soul, spirit or Other, if you prefer, is the computer operator. We are also going to treat "as if true" the idea that the interface between the soul and the computer is found in Delta brain wave frequencies, or as another way of saying this, that our belief about what is real and what is not controls the access of the soul to the computer.

If we consider the dictates of the soul to be accessible through the Delta brain wave frequencies then the Shaman would be interested in viewing the world using those frequencies as an observation platform. He would want to view his world through his beliefs in what is real, through those programs which control sets of programs or emotions, through his programs or feelings and on up into consciousness as an end result. Not the other way around. This would define a very different Point of View for most people.

Clarification:

Most people allow themselves to be pushed around by their programming so that they resemble a balloon which has been pinched and suddenly let go. Wherever the programming pushes they hang on and go. Shamans and other responsible people take control of their programming and try to direct themselves through their programming. The best and easiest way to accomplish this is deep in the thinking machinery, not out at the surface of the thought process. Therefore, Shamans endeavor to observe the world from Delta as opposed to Beta. This is simply a logical conclusion based on how the brain functions.

In this model, we consider the body to be an instrument of communication which the soul uses. The function of Shaman is to communicate with the spirit world, and what better method is there than to access the soul or spirit directly? The question is how to change our common Point of View which seems to be seated in Beta to a Point of View which would seem to be seated in Delta. Not only would the Shaman need to view the world at a much slower pace, but he would also need to act in accordance with that Point of View.

It is obvious that if the Shaman is to act as if the body is an instrument of communication for the soul, then he would have to adjust his beliefs to accommodate that reality. In other words, he would have to believe that it is really possible for the soul to use the body as an instrument of communication. He would not have to be born believing, but he would have to deliberately believe. This is a concept which escapes many people.

Clarification:

To the Shaman, it is the soul, or Other as it is called, which allows him to do the things he does. Therefore observing the world from Delta is tantamount to being who he is. The traditional method for accomplishing the movement of awareness from Beta to Delta was to first adopt two concurrent Points of View. This action would force the brain to slow down to Alpha. Then two more Points of View would be held concurrently. This would force the brain to slow down to Theta. To hold eight Points of View concurrently would force the brain to slow down to Delta. Observing the world from Delta, then, would allow the apprentice Shaman to begin the process of allowing the Other to take over the control of the body or at least the thinking machinery. It is the soul or Other which "knows at a distance," heals, dreams, stalks, and all the other things that a Shaman does.

It isn't that the Shaman would throw out his existing beliefs, but rather, would streamline them so that he could easily adjust his view of the world to accommodate the ever-changing kaleidoscope of new experiences. He would need to be as efficient as possible when changing Points of View so as to not get lost during those changes. Deliberate belief is the only means of accomplishing such a daunting task.

If the goal is to interface with the soul, then the means is to believe it is possible. The charisma is to act as though the soul *is* communicating through the body. We would be oriented towards cultivating an understanding of what that communication actually is. We would eliminate those beliefs which contradict the soul's communication. We would assimilate new programs and sets of programs and actually think in terms of the soul using the body as an instrument of communication. Our impulse would be to expect different thought processes and actions which would be in harmony with the soul's communication even if that communication surprised us. We would need to change our view of the world to accommodate the idea that all the souls are communicating all the time and always have been. The possibilities of soul-to-soul communication being understood would depend on our Point of View and our belief structure. The form of soul communication is action, not words. The substance of soul communication is to make the body an instrument of communication.

Some things to do to understand "adopting other Points of View"

No one can see what they are looking with. The problem is that the Shaman wants to have more than one Point of View available to examine events. The easiest method of obtaining another Point of View is to borrow one from someone else. It is not necessary to agree with the other Point of View it is only necessary to understand how that other Point of View functions.

By way of example let's take two common political Points of View. On one hand, there is a liberal Point of View which holds that everyone has a right to basic human requirements such as medical aid and a dependable income. On the other hand, there is a conservative Point of View which holds that everyone has a right to earn the money to make a dependable income and could, therefore, afford medical aid. This is, obviously, a very abbreviated example of the differences between liberals and conservatives. The thing is that both ideas have good and bad elements. Neither of these two Points of View can address all the problems which could arise during a life.

The exercise here would be to take an opposing Point of View to your own and see the good and bad parts of that opposing Point of View. The idea is not to argue the other Point of View but to simply see how it works; to try it on to see if it could possibly fit. To see how it works requires that the examination not be argumentative. For instance, it is possible to accept that all people have a right to medical aid. At the same time it is possible to accept that those who provide medical aid need to be paid for their services. Both sides of this issue can be true at the same time. It is not necessary to become passionate about either side of the issue.

Another example might be a common difference between men and women. Men often feel that they may not express emotions such as crying. Women often express emotions such as crying and sometimes they express those emotions to get their way. Men sometimes express other emotions to get their way, such as forcefully stating what they want. Neither expression is "right" nor is either expression "wrong." Both expressions exist. If a man could walk in high heels (someone else's shoes) for a day, would he have a reason to understand why women sometimes use emotions such as crying to get their way? If a woman could walk in wing tips for a day, would she have a reason to understand why men sometimes use emotions such as yelling to get their way?

Can a Christian understand a "pagan" Point of View as being valid within the knowledge framework of the "pagan?" Can a Muslim understand a Christian Point of View? Can a "white" person understand a "black" Point of View?

Can conscious thought accept the existence of the "soul" Point of View?

These are all things that can be practiced in order to understand the value of changing Points of View. They must be practiced without judgment or any other type of rancor. The understanding of other Points of View is a defining factor of Shamanism.

Points to Consider:

1. Changing Points of View is a tool which Shamans use to learn how they see their world.
2. To change a Point of View, it is necessary to consider all the component parts of the Point of View including the different aspects it takes on in different brain wave frequencies.
3. Using descriptive devices other than simple True or False aid in the mental agility needed to conceive of other Points of View.
4. A common source of other Points of View can be found in other people.
5. Simply changing the way we think about ourselves constitutes a new Point of View.
6. The internal dialogue holds our present Point of View of the world in place.
7. Turning off the internal dialogue aids in viewing the world from slower brain wave frequencies.
8. Using the slowest brain wave frequencies allows us to view our programming running us and gives us the option of controlling the programming.
9. Adopting multiple Points of View and holding them concurrently necessarily lowers brain wave frequency.
10. Viewing the world from the Delta brain wave frequencies or from what we believe real to be allows us access to the soul or spirit.

Story Chapter II

Bob brought his program by. The wording was sloppy, but then it was his first try. It is important to write programs as accurately as possible. I don't know if I got that through to him as well as I would like, but then he's allowed to make mistakes and learn from the error of his ways.

The good news is that he has already begun to change his attitude with his father. That took the expected nine days. I had considered having him write a program to achieve something more material, but he beat me to the punch. He didn't do badly with the program, but he hadn't considered that the last time he thought about this particular item was several years ago and he got a model that was of the same year as when he last thought about it. I'm sure he will thoroughly enjoy his 1974 Jeep even if it does need a few repairs. Even Bob had a chuckle about that.

The next item for Bob's consideration is changing Points of View. I would like to get him to do the full Monty and actually experience a true movement of the Assemblage Point, but I'm afraid that would put the poor guy on severe overload. It's going to be stressful enough for him to handle simply changing his Point of View. He will progress to moving the Assemblage Point on his own which will be better for him. Eventually I'll show him the power of that movement, but for now, he's coming along just like Goldilocks. Not too fast nor too slow, but juuust right.

"Hey Bob, what's up?"

"Nothing much."

"How's your dad?"

"Oh, he's okay. He's going to play golf with some friends of his today and then later they're all going to go eat catfish at some Cajun restaurant."

"Cool. He told you all that or you had to ask him?"

"I just asked what he was doing today and I got the whole schedule. Jeez."

"So there's something wrong with that?"

"No. It's just he didn't want to know what I was doing."

"You mean he wasn't all worried that you have a life of your own?"

"No."

"Who knew?"

"So how does this programming stuff work, anyway?"

"The thing is that we all write programs for ourselves all the time. Mostly, we aren't aware that we are doing it because almost all programming is done in what you would call the subconscious, except for the reprogramming we all do using our internal dialogue. In our modern society we don't notice when the subconscious takes over because we are generally too busy doing stuff."

"So if we all write programs, why did you have me use the Goals/Means form to write one?"

"Because we usually don't know when or where we are writing our programs.

By deliberately using a form, we take back control. The real question is where does the program fit?"

"It fits in my head."

"Uh huh. But where does it fit in your head?"

"What do you mean?"

"You divide your thinking into conscious and subconscious and that's your limit. There are other divisions available and each one is important. For you, thought consists of the little voice in your head that keeps repeating things over and over. You probably call that talking to yourself."

"Yeah, but I don't move my lips."

"My faith in humanity has been restored. Thank you for that, Bob."

"You're welcome."

"Let's cut to the chase here, okay?"

"Sure. What are we chasing?"

"So are you a Democrat or a Republican?"

"I don't know what that has to do with anything but I'm an Independent."

"I'm sure of that, but I just had to ask. Have you ever considered thinking like a Republican?"

That screeching sound you're hearing is your world stopping, Bob. Let's get a little practice in the fine art of thinking from other Points of View, shall we?

"My dad's a Republican and I don't think like him."

"That may or may not be true, but I'll take your word on it for now. The question is if you are capable of seeing things from more than one Point of View."

"He has some good points."

"Everyone has some good points, but can you see the world the way someone else sees it? Can you simply go to how they see the world and then go to how someone else sees the world and so on?"

"Why would I want to do that?"

All right, we'll just add another abstraction to the mix. I already know that you have trouble holding more than one at a time. Your limiting Point of View is about to be exposed for what it is. Hang on Sloopy, Sloopy hang on.

"Bob, look out the window. Now while you are looking out there take a look at the color of your eyes."

"My eyes are blue."

"Why, yes they are. And you can see what color they are, right?"

"No. I need a mirror for me to see my eyes."

"Very good. I think it would be safe to say that no one can see the color of their own eyes, wouldn't you?"

"I guess."

"We could even expand that idea a bit more and say that no one can see what they are looking with, don't you think?"

This is a new idea, eh? Stretch and bend. Get those ideas up and moving. No pain, no gain.

"Yeah, but what would they be looking with other than their eyes?"

"How about the programming you've been writing since you were born?"

"What do you mean?"

"You know, Bob, you aren't anything if you aren't predictable. But I can't really expect you to be anything else because you can only use that one set of programs. Too bad."

"What's wrong with my set of programs?"

"They're boring and predictable. The shame of it all is that you can't see how boring and predictable they are because you have to use them to look at the world. You don't have any other options. Oh well. But then you can't see the reason why you would want to see the world in the way someone else sees it."

"What good does it do me to see the world the way someone else sees it? They have the right to see it any way they want to, and I have the right to see it the way I want to."

"Bob, sometimes you are such a merchant. Haven't you ever done something just for the hell of it? Is it absolutely necessary to get something in trade every time you do anything?"

"I'm not a merchant. I don't trade stuff."

"Right. Bob, you just told me that you have the right to see the world any way you want, isn't that true?"

"Of course."

Don't want to get him mad about this, I just want him to think from another Point of View.

"Then I guess you have the right to see the world in any way you want, including how someone else sees it, don't you think?"

"Okay, okay."

"The reason you would want to see the world the way someone else sees it is so you can see the color of your own eyes."

Time to pull out the Point of View I want to use and let him use my Point of View to see his.

"What?"

"If you only use that old set of programs you tote around with you all the time then you will never see anything from a different perspective. If you don't see things from different perspectives, then you won't ever have a chance to look at your own programming. What a shame that would be."

"How does that work?"

"You see the world through your consciousness. Now mind you, there's nothing wrong with seeing the world in that manner. But what if you were to see the world through your sub-consciousness? What if you could see the world from the Point of View of constantly writing programs, instead of seeing the world through the programs you have already written? Wouldn't that be a novel idea?"

"Yeah, that would be super, I guess, but is that possible?"

"Anything is possible. It is simply a matter of figuring out how to do it. In this case, you would have to slow down the brain wave frequencies you use for thinking. Or, in another way of talking about it, you would have to center your point of awareness deeper in the thinking machinery."

"Oh, I'm sure. Like I'm just going to dial in a slower thought wave, right?"

How quickly they forget. Let's see if he remembers with a slight nudge.

"You are also allowed to keep on doing what you have always done."

"But what if I don't like doing what I have always done?"

He does remember.

"Then I guess you'll have to trade that in on a newer model. It isn't all that hard. There is a model which says that for each year in your childhood you learn a brain wave frequency. I don't know if it's true or not but you can use it 'as though it were true' to begin to remember when you wrote which programs. For instance, tell me a memory you have as a child."

"Like what?"

"You were a kid?"

"Yeah."

"I kind of thought so."

"What do you mean?"

"What do I mean that you were a kid or what do I mean about remembering an event you had as a kid?"

"Okay. I remember going with my dad to an auction somewhere and that we stopped in this place and had the best French fries."

"See that wasn't so hard, now was it? The question is why do you remember that?"

"I don't know. I just remember it."

If this is anything like his other "significant" memories there is an iceberg lurking about in these waters.

"You may 'just' remember it, but there is something important for you wrapped up in that memory. How old were you when this happened?"

"I don't know. I wasn't very old, I don't think."

"So how old is 'not very, I don't think'?"

"Who knows? I guess I must have been in the first grade or maybe just about ready to go into the first grade, because the reason I was with my dad was that my mom was gone some place."

Uh oh, mom and dad have been going at it and little Bobby is caught in the middle. This iceberg is a whopper. I'll say one thing for this guy. When he pulls up a memory, it's a doozy. I need to maintain a Theta rhythm in my voice to help him hold the memory.

"Where had your mom gone to?"

"How should I know? I was just a little kid. I don't know, I guess they must have been fighting or something because I remember that the reason we had to eat French fries was because no one was home and when we left my mom was yelling at my dad. Well, they were both yelling I think, and we had to eat somewhere else and she wasn't going to be home or something. I think they were fighting is all."

"So how old were you?"

"I don't know. Somewhere around six, maybe. I was either in the first grade or I was about to go into the first grade because I had on these new shoes that I really thought were cool. They were, too."

So that's why he's got a rebellion issue with his dad. Mom's been feeding this thing since the kid was five or six years old. No wonder the soul has been forcing the issue.

"So, let's see. You were about six years old which would put you at the upper reaches of the Theta brain wave frequency. That would mean that you were still learning emotions, and your mom was mad at your dad. Do I have that about right?"

"I think there was more to this, but yeah. So?"

Let's just pull this out in the open and see what it looks like in the light of day.

"I'll bet your mom told your dad that she didn't have to do what he said. I'll bet that she said that she could do whatever she damn well pleased."

"I don't know if she told him that then or not, but I remember her saying that."

"I'll bet you do."

"What's that supposed to mean?"

"Well, that means great French fries or not, you won't do anything your dad tells you. I'll bet that you didn't even want to eat those French fries until he said you could go hungry or eat. I'll bet that you didn't eat the hamburger, either."

"How did you know about the hamburger? It looked awful."

"I'll bet it did."

"So what? Are you saying that is why I'm afraid of my dad?"

"No. But I'll bet that is why you do what you want and are afraid he'll find out."

"No way."

"See how useful other people's Points of View are? I just lent you mine and you saw what you have been using to define your world with for the last 30 years or so."

He needs to think about this one for a while. What he doesn't need is for me to go stomping around in this program making one or more parts more real than they already are. I need to practice Not Doing for a while. He needs to practice recapitulation for a while. I almost wish I could explain those two concepts to him right here and now, but they need to be presented in order.

Points to Consider:

1. Bob's attitude changed about his dad due to writing the program.
2. The teacher gave him third party substantiation for the programmed result.
3. The teacher told Bob that he can't see the color of his own eyes in order to show him that he can't see his own programming.
4. Bob then had to consider a new Point of View which is that his current programming may be limiting.
5. By borrowing the teacher's Point of View Bob was able to see why he is rebellious or "scared" of his dad.
6. Changing Points of View is the precursor to applying Harmony Function.
7. Bob got a glimpse of his childhood programming written by his mother and father by using a Point of View other than his own.
8. Shamans use the idea of changing Points of View in a much broader sense. They may actually move the very place they have always used to assemble the world which can result in a very different description of the world.

Chapter 3: Communications

"I know what 'it' means well enough, when I find a thing," said the duck,
"it's generally a frog or a worm."

— Lewis Carroll, *Alice in Wonderland*

As the Shaman progresses, masters programming and begins to notice that his view of the world has changed, he is nearly driven to tell others of his exploits. Indeed, part of the knowing process is Communication with others, but for the Shaman, Communication must be exact. The question is how to make Communication exact enough to accurately transmit the experiences he has. Communication is one place where the modern day Shaman has an advantage over his historical counterpart.

Because of research over the last century or so, we know more today about how Communication takes place and what it consists of than our forefathers ever could have. We have the privilege of being able to take advantage of studies which show how Communication takes place and what actions are necessary for the exchange of accurate information.

Communication takes place when one person who is in control of his beliefs, his sets of control programs, his programs and his conscious thoughts, transfers information to another person with the same set of controls in place. But that information has to be in a ready state in the second person for transfer to yet a third person who has those controls in place or Communication has yet to take place. In other words, if I tell you something, I haven't communicated until it is clear enough for you to tell that exact same thing to someone else. The other side of this coin is that if someone tells me something and I don't understand it well enough to explain it to another person, then I don't really understand or *know* what was said.

This idea is very important to Shamans. A measure of the success of their activities is the communication of ideas. If ideas are not communicated, the learning process is not complete. The process of learning from Delta affects the entire biocomputer. The problem is that it can take years for a single changed belief to filter up through the various levels of the thinking apparatus unless knowledge is made concrete through Communication. Even when Communication results in actual knowing, the thinking machinery can take many months to sort through a given change in belief. The Shaman deals with many changes of belief through adopting various Points of View or Assemblage Points. Therefore, accurate exchange of information with others is tantamount to the Shaman accumulating knowledge, and for the Shaman, knowledge is put to use as energy.

An example of knowledge becoming energy is what a Shaman does with a simple definition of equal opposites. In language, equal opposites are known as dichotomies. In other words mommy is the opposite of daddy, black is the opposite of white, up is the opposite of down, and good is the opposite of bad. To the Shaman, none of these statements are "true." To the Shaman these statements are convenient linguistic shortcuts. The Shaman knows that woman and man are not equal opposites, but are different expressions of humanity. He may also know that mommy is opposed to daddy, but that is a different story.

The same is true for the dichotomy of good and bad. The Shaman doesn't lose energy with those two thoughts. He may treat them as a duality, but not as a dichotomy. He knows that good is something that is to his advantage and bad is something that is not to his advantage. He doesn't waste time nor energy on trying to be good, for instance, because being good, to him, simply means that he is staying within the Agreements of his societal structure. He is "good" to his wife, he is "good" to his children, he is "good" to his friends, he is "good" to himself, and he is "good" at what he does, whether he is doing Shamanic things or other things. The Shaman may think it is "bad" to lie, for instance, because telling a lie would divide his thinking ability in half and he would lose energy. That certainly would be "bad" for him, but good and bad are not equal nor opposite for the Shaman. Hoarding energy and wasting energy is not equal nor opposite, either, and that is how the Shaman thinks.

For the Shaman to function in society, he must communicate. Therefore, Methods of Communication must be developed which allow the Shaman to report his findings without rendering him ineffective. There are two ideas which aid in Communication on any level. One idea is to speak of things in terms of their relativity and the other is to understand that all words are abstractions.

If we are to replace dichotomies, we must structure our language so there are no equal opposites. There would not be Right and Wrong, for instance. We could replace those two concepts with one thought which we could perhaps express as "advantageous." We could say that something was "right" in as much as it provided advantage or that a thing was "wrong" in as much as it was not advantageous. Advantageous would then become the scale and we would refer to positions on the scale as having more or less advantage. This is why we need to understand that the word is not the thing. Right and Wrong are abstractions. You cannot break out your measuring tape and size up either concept. You can't quantify right or wrong. Yet we all use the words every day. But, since right and wrong can't be quantified, they must exist, like beauty, in the eye of the beholder. This means that they are *believed* to be real or are abstract. What right is for me and what right is for someone else is very likely to be different sets.

Right and wrong are common everyday concepts which everyone uses, but if you ask as many as five questions designed to get someone to tell you how they know that something is right or wrong, you are likely to evoke an angry response. We don't really know how we know something is right or wrong, we *believe* it to be right or wrong. The reason is that we can't actually measure something that is abstract; and right and wrong is as abstract as it gets.

If we have trouble differentiating between abstract belief and reality in common concepts such as right and wrong, how would anyone communicate about completely unknown concepts such as events connected with Shamanism? In order to know how you know, one has to have the actual experience. If you actually experience something then it is no longer in the realm of belief nor is it abstract. You can then explain how you know what you know within the limits of that experiential reality.

There is an axiom that states, "Knowledge requires three events. First you must be told about something from an authoritarian or an authoritative source. You must then have the experience. Then you must obtain third party substantiation. Then you know."

Let's take the concept of writing a program designed to do something for you. Does that really work? According to the axiom, you can't know until someone tells you how to write one, you write it and someone else says, "How did you accomplish that?" You would then know how to explain the concept to someone else and would, by definition, then know how you know.

Some events in the Shamanic experience are much more complicated than writing a program. How do you get third party substantiation for a common experience for those born to the Office of Shaman such as having Dreams about impending events or simply knowing the best way to obtain Agreement with difficult individuals? Obviously, Agreements concerning "off the wall" experiences would have to be obtained from other people with similar experiences. This takes time.

Let's say that an individual receives information concerning a belief he holds as real which changes the nature of that belief. That belief could be about having Dreams which seem to portend events which seem to come to pass. The individual may have spent his life believing that the dreams were nothing more than cause and effect reactions. If he were to receive information later in life that such dreams were common to a particular type of Shaman and that those Shamans were collectively known as Dreamers, then he would be tempted to change the way he *believed* about those dreams and what do to with them. But the change in belief would necessitate changing certain emotional sets of programs controlling other programs, which would change an even broader base of programs, which would change even the logic used to consider the dreams.

All this mental activity could, again, take some time. It wouldn't be necessary to think about the changes while they were occurring because changing the belief starts the process, but the process will take time. However, communicating about the event with others who can "understand" it can *time bind* the process. To *time bind* means that a process which normally takes lots of time doesn't, because the normal time is bound together in some kind of common experience.

Clarification:

> *Time binding* is simply the process by which one person bundles up his experiences and shares the whole bundle with another. A good example might be that of an older brother or sister explaining to a younger sibling how to do something. The older kid can usually remember the various pieces of information that he had to learn in order to accomplish a given task. It is common to see the older sibling explaining all the parts in sequence so that the younger sibling can quickly grasp the concept. As we grow older we sometimes lose the ability to remember all the component parts of a piece of knowledge. With just a little practice we can remember how to do it. It is through this process of *time binding* that we can share experiences and speed up the learning curve of even complicated experiences.

Once we consider the process of *time binding* as an activity of Communication, then we must consider the effect of communicative activity for and to the Shaman. It would certainly be true that the Shaman would view any communication as a deliberate act. Since Communication would be a deliberate act for the Shaman then it would follow that the Shaman would see Communication as an exchange of energy. If that is true and the Shaman would incorporate any communication into himself so that Communication could be transmitted to another individual, the Shaman would necessarily consider the effect of any communication on his being. If the effect of a given communication would be debilitating in any fashion then the Shaman would be nearly forced to take exception to that communication. In other words, he would have to disagree with that communication.

Since the Shaman views Communication as an energy exchange he must make every effort to gain energy through his communication. If, for instance, he were to be successful in *time binding* experiences for another individual he would be due an energy "payment" from that individual. He would have saved that person perhaps many years of trial and error. Those years have a value that could be measured in energy expenditure and the Shaman would be the recipient of some of the energy. The exchange takes place at a non-conscious level and is a natural result of *time binding*.

It is hard to know if the apparent energy is actually energy or if it is nothing more than a type of learning which results in the Shaman understanding how to employ that learned or acquired knowledge as power to be used to whatever ends. Once the Shaman understands that *time binding* is a deliberate act and that a deliberate act results in energy or power he will soon be searching for other deliberate acts of communication which will have the same results. As he accumulates energy or power he will find that his Point of View necessarily changes. In some individuals the change of Point of View will change so much that he will begin to assemble other entire world descriptions which are known as a Movement of the Assemblage Point.

In some few individuals, the change can take place in a matter of seconds. In most individuals it may take anywhere from a few months to years. With the individuals who experience a Movement of the Assemblage Point in a matter of seconds, the change seems to actually take place in the energy body or aura. The same thing happens for those which require more time. Although a Movement of the Assemblage Point can be facilitated by another Shaman it can also be accomplished more or less by the individual.

The trick in a change of this magnitude is to be able to maintain equilibrium. To experience monumental change and at the same time not be engulfed by wishes for how things once were or feelings of inadequacy is the mark of a Shaman with energy to spare. Not everyone born to the Office can cope with changes in his life which demand a new type of attention. Many cannot conceptualize how to employ new-found ideas and the excess of energy which accompanies the change of even small beliefs, much less changes of entire belief systems. For those who can accommodate sweeping change, the need to employ that energy is tantamount to life itself.

If the goal is to communicate about beliefs from a place in the mind which controls belief, then the means of that communication is to consider the beliefs which one holds about things that appear real to the self. The charisma of communicating about beliefs is to allow others to believe as they must and to allow oneself the same privilege. One would be oriented toward knowing the soul's view of the world. One would eliminate nonfunctional beliefs about real things and assimilate the suspension of disbelief. One's impulses would be to believe in order to create new realities. One's needs would be to maintain equilibrium. The possibilities of changing lifestyles will accelerate the mental processes. The form of Communication will utilize third party substantiation to verify real concepts. The substance of Communication will change how reality is perceived.

Some things to do in order to better understand Communication

Everyone talks to each other. Try communicating an abstract idea that does not concern a movie, a book, or any common religious or political belief. The idea cannot be about yourself, but it must be something that you understand. It may be necessary to begin with an outline of the points that you wish to communicate. In the communication, avoid the use of any dichotomies. Make note of all questions about your communication because those questions indicate where you were less than prepared.

Wait three days and check on how the communication was received. Don't worry if there are harsh statements about the nature of your communication because even harsh statements indicate that the communication was a success.

If you receive feedback that indicates Agreement with the communication try it again with someone else. Repeat.

Another communication homework would be to *time bind*. This will consist of explaining a process to someone so that they will take less time to learn the process. You will be able to observe the effect of the communication in the way they adjust to the process. This should be a daily activity. Each time you communicate about a process you should be more efficient, which can be measured by how long it takes each new individual to learn it.

Each time after you communicate and get feedback on the success or failure of your communication make a note about your personal energy. How do you feel about yourself, in other words? Do you feel "on top of the world?" Do you feel drained or listless? Then notice how other people react to you. When you feel that your communication was a success do other people seem to "like" you better? Keeping a notebook about these events can be useful.

Points to Consider:

1. Communication is a deliberate act.
2. Communication depends on understanding that the word is not the thing.
3. Communication must have third party substantiation to take place.
4. Because communication accomplishes things, the Shaman can "collect" energy through communication.
5. Changing Points of View facilitates Communication.
6. Actual communication is concerned with reality.
7. Dichotomies are not real.
8. In actual communication, consciousness is the observer and the soul is the operator; the reverse order is illogical.
9. The soul is real.
10. "Soulful" communication may result in such a radical shift of how the Shaman views the world that the world itself may seem to change.

Story Chapter III

Bob has stopped by a couple of times. The last time he was here, he talked at length about the event when his mom and dad were arguing. He actually accomplished a pretty good recapitulation and all on his own. The most important part is that he has recognized he wrote a program back then that was not necessarily to his advantage. He has even taken the time to write a Goals/Means program to counteract some of that event.

For all his goofiness, I actually have to admire the kid some days. I wouldn't want him to know that. I might have to use some heavy tactics with him yet.

The next item on the agenda for Bob is Communication. This is always a heavy topic and I want to overload him quickly so that he has to nearly sit in a stupor and listen. I doubt that will actually happen, but I do need to walk him as deep into his thinking machinery as I dare.

"Hey Bob, how's it going?"

"Pretty good. I've been thinking about this idea of using other people's Points of View to see my own. I'm not so sure that it works the way you say, though."

"Really? Why is that?"

"Well, if you actually use someone else's Point of View you have to be like they are. I don't think that is such a good idea."

"Bob, I have to tell you a couple of things here. You may like some parts of this more than you like other parts."

"Oh boy, here it comes."

"The part that you may like is that it's true that you have to be like the other person to a degree and the part that you may not like is that is how you learn other Points of View."

"But I don't want to be someone else. I want to be me."

"Bob, you can take my word on this, you are definitely you."

"If I take on someone else's Point of View, then I will be that person, won't I?"

"In some ways, maybe. But the idea is to understand who 'you' are, not to be someone else."

"I don't understand this, then."

"Probably not. Look, why do you think I am taking the time to talk to you about any of this?"

"Because of my overwhelming charm and good looks?"

"That's a consideration, but not a motivation."

"Then what is the motivation?"

"I have to."

"You have to? Did my dad talk you into this?"

"No, but I don't have a choice. You see, a while back someone took the time to talk to me about these things, and once he did, then I had to take the time to tell someone else just so I could be sure that I understood what he said."

"What? You don't listen so good?"

"I listen pretty well, but listening isn't enough. If I can't explain what I know to someone else then I really don't know it."

"Oh, so I'm like your guinea pig."

"No. It's that Communication hasn't taken place in *me* until I can explain what I've heard to someone else."

"You haven't ever explained this to anyone before?"

"Sure I have. But that doesn't mean that I communicated with them. They may have explained it to someone else but they may not have, either. I'm pretty sure that many people even understood perfectly well what the communication was about, but may not have been able to share it with someone else. In any case, I owe it to my benefactor to tell you what I learned from him."

"Do I know your 'benefactor'?"

"No you don't, and even if you did, it is not because of you that I owe it to him. I owe the explanation I'm giving to you because he communicated with me."

"So why me? Why not someone or anyone else?"

"Because you came to me and asked me to talk to you."

This one is going to throw the kid for a loop. He's still having problems with the idea of the soul. Walk softly here.

"I didn't ask you to talk to me about this."

"Well, you actually did. A part of you knows that I know things you need to learn, so you came to me to find out about those things. I never argue with whatever that power is. I always do what it tells me. So do you, but you just aren't aware of that yet."

"What 'power' are you talking about?"

"Well, the common name is the soul."

"My soul told you to talk to me?"

"That's a little simplistic, but we could reduce it to that."

"So when did this take place?"

"When you asked me why you were afraid of your dad."

"I asked you about that. Why do you think my 'soul' asked you?"

"I have more practice at Communication than you do."

"I communicate pretty well. I've never had any problems for a number of years now, believe it or not."

"I know that's what you think, but I use a different set to define Communication than you do."

"Well, that's obvious."

"It isn't as obvious as you think, I'm afraid. When you think about communicating you think about being conscious, or maybe a more accurate word would be 'aware', of talking. You even direct your talking to other people who think about it the same way you do. I, on the other hand, think about Communication as something that takes place at the deepest levels possible. The way I think about Communication, if it doesn't take place at those levels, then it is nothing more than babble. To me, Communication means that, for lack of a better term at this point, souls talk to each other."

"Are you kidding me?"

The idea of the soul really represents something frightening for this guy. It isn't going to make any difference for this conversation, but I'll have to wrestle the fear out into the open sooner or later.

"No, I'm not kidding. Let me ask you a couple of questions. The Church talks about saving souls, right?"

"Right."

"What does that mean? Does it mean that some little part of your heart is going to heaven? Does it mean that your spirit is going to heaven? What do you think it means?"

"I don't know, not really."

"Well let's, for the sake of this argument, say that we are all souls like the Church says. Where is this soul we are supposed to be? Is it bigger than a breadbox? Can you measure it? Is it part of our life?"

"I guess it is, but that's religious talk."

"Well I don't buy that. I think the soul is an integral part of who we are. I think that the soul is present in all the people and I think the soul expresses all the time. The trouble is that we have this thing called consciousness which seems to be kind of jealous. At least that is a way of talking about the event. I don't really know if jealousy is the right word, but let's say that there appears to be a conflict between the two parts of our self. There is the possibility that there isn't really any type of conflict at all, but that the soul just doesn't think that most of us are quite ready for prime time."

"Do you really think the soul *thinks*?"

I wonder why this idea represents a fear.

"Of course. I don't think it thinks the same way consciousness thinks, though. Not only that, I think it acts through our bodies too. I think that the soul communicates through the body. In fact, I think the body is an instrument of Communication for the soul. That would mean that talking to yourself would be contrary to logic. If you are talking to yourself then who is doing the talking and who is doing the listening? If the soul does the talking, then does the consciousness listen?"

"I still think that is all a bunch of religious bunk."

Okay, so you have to defend talking to yourself. Let's see if you know anything about communicating.

"Look, you are *all* hung up on the word. The word ain't the thing. You hear the word "soul" and you think, 'Oh that's a churchy word and I don't want to have anything to do with anything churchy, so I can't think about *that* word.' What a crock! The word only points at the thing. The way you think about words is like someone pointing at a sunset and you saying, 'But that's in the west and I can't look in the west.' I'm not sure, but I'm pretty sure that thinking like that doesn't put your good looks and overwhelming charm in a good light."

"Wait a minute. Are you saying that this isn't a table?"

Bob! You remembered about the table. I thought you missed that.

"Kind of. Table is a word. The word is not the thing, although it points to the thing. The thing can be defined with words, and word description can be extremely accurate, but the word or words are just words. The thing would exist with or without the word or words. Do you think a mountain or a tree is dependent on the word 'mountain' or 'tree'? I don't think so. I think trees existed before there was ever a word for them. I think the same thing is true about the soul. I don't think it is dependent on anyone's description or word for it. I think it existed before there was a word to point in its direction."

"Wow, this is heavy, dude."

"Oh give me a break. You're the one telling me how well you communicate, remember? I mean you certainly think about all this before you open your mouth, right? Hell, you haven't even had any problems communicating for a number of years now."

"It isn't that, it's that what if you're wrong about this? I mean, I'm not afraid of going to hell or anything, but this is deep shit, man. You're talking about stuff that preachers should be talking about and stuff."

So… You do believe in the soul. You're even afraid of going to hell. If that's true then why does the mere mention of the word "soul" put you into a panic?

"Bobby, Bobby, Bobby! You worry about the strangest things. You're telling me that to think about the soul is evil or at the very least wrong. Could you define 'wrong', Bob?"

"I'm not saying that it is wrong to talk about it, but…"

Nope. He hasn't thought about Communicating. He's not even aware that he uses words that he doesn't understand. His idea about believing in something and mine are a lot different. I'll have to bury this in his subconscious so I'd better pay careful attention to modulating my voice so that I elicit a Delta or low Theta response.

"Can you define 'wrong', Bob?"

"You mean right now?"

"No, I mean tomorrow. Of course I mean right now. You can define 'wrong' can't you? You are using the word."

"Well…wrong is something that is bad, I guess."

"Could you define the word 'bad'?"

"Yeah, bad is something that is not good."

"'Bad' and 'not good' is the same?"

"Well, you know, God will get you if you're bad, you know."

"No, I don't know. Explain that to me, please."

"I don't know! Something that is bad is bad. Why do you want to know what bad is? You're the one talking about all this."

"You can't explain it, can you?"

"I can explain it. I just don't have the words is all."

"You can't explain a word you are using?"

"Didn't you just say that the word is not the thing?"

"Why yes, I did. I didn't think you were paying attention."

"I pay attention just fine, but you're using my own words against me."

"I'm not, but it wouldn't be hard to do, that's for sure. Okay, I'm going to let you up. Ready?"

"Ready for what?"

"There are two parts to this so you have to pay very close attention, okay?"

"I pay attention just fine."

Here it comes, Bob. Slow down the voice and watch his eyes. Don't let him go to sleep, but keep him on the edge of the subconscious.

"Of course you do. The first part is that you think that 'wrong' is the opposite of 'right.' It isn't. To think about wrong being the opposite of right would be like thinking that one-inch is the opposite of 12 inches. One inch isn't as long as 12 inches but the two measurements are not the opposite of each other. The second part is that you believe in wrong and right. You don't know what they are, but you do believe in what they are. What do you think, that telling lies was all right until God wrote the Ten Commandments? After Moses came down from the mountain, then all of a sudden it was wrong to lie? That doesn't make sense, now does it?"

"No… Telling lies before that would have been wrong, too."

Got him below the threshold of consciousness or he would be arguing.

"Really? So you're telling me what? That God was pissed because everybody was telling a bunch of untruths so he added that one to the list? I don't buy it. I think that telling lies is a dumb way to use the brain. I think that committing adultery is a dumb way to get along with your neighbor. I think that it is dumb not to honor thy father and mother because if you don't honor them you can't learn from their mistakes. I think wrong and dumb are about the same."

"I don't know."

"That's true. So, tell me. If you're so good at communication, why haven't you thought about all this?"

"Who knows?"

"Well, if the body is an instrument of Communication for the soul, don't you think it would be wise to understand what Communication actually is?

"If that's true, it would be."

"That's what I like about you, Bob."

"What's that?"

"You never give up."

"What's that supposed to mean?"

"I've been talking to you about some simple things you believe in. You can't explain why you believe in them but you treat those things as real. What if you had to explain about things that you found to be complicated, what would you do? Cop out? Would you do the homework to be able to explain those things to other people? If not, how would you know that you know? Didn't I tell you at the beginning of this conversation that I have to explain things to you so that I am sure that I know what I think I know?"

"You might have."

"I assure you I did. The reason I told you that, if you remember, was that I had no choice but to *communicate* with your soul. I owe it to you to give you a clear explanation about how Communication takes place so that your soul can communicate with other souls in the easiest form possible. Why should you have to go through all the trouble I went through to learn what I know? You will probably go through a lot of it the same as I did, but if I explain the process of Communication to you then maybe you can go through it a little easier."

"What makes you think I'm ever going to communicate with anyone's soul?"

"What makes you think there is a choice available to you? Do you think you can un-have this experience? Bob, you have started on a journey and the reality is that you don't have any choices any more about whether you go or not. The only choice you have now is about how well you make the trip."

Good. He doesn't have anything to say. The brain needs to have this program in place so that the soul has an avenue of Communication. This information needs to be programmed at the deepest level possible. I doubt that he will even be able to access this information for several months, maybe longer. By the time he can access it, the soul will be using it. I always worry about this because in one way it is deception. But I am talking with the soul, not with consciousness. There is no deception on that level.

Points to Consider:

1. Bob had considered what changing his Point of View would accomplish.
2. The teacher undermined the right/wrong dichotomy early in the communication so that Bob couldn't use right or wrong to defend his current Point of View concerning the soul.
3. By undermining 'right' and 'wrong', the teacher "gave" Bob the energy to consider the idea of Communication.
4. Since Bob seems to be concerned that the soul is a concept reserved for church use only, the teacher used the Ten Commandments to illustrate Bob's current understanding of his own abstractions.
5. The teacher introduced the idea of consciousness being the observer and the soul being the computer operator by appealing to Bob's sense of self-worth and maybe even his rebellion.
6. It was necessary for the teacher to push Bob through the lesson so that he (Bob) couldn't defend his current Point of View.
7. It may have been deceptive for the teacher to leave out parts of the explanation, but to the teacher, the soul was the beneficiary of the Communication and, therefore, the lesson.

Chapter 4: Difference

"Don't ask me what I think of you
I might not give the answer that you want me to."

— Fleetwood Mac, *Oh Well*, Lyrics by Peter Green

As the Shaman learns to communicate and to know how he knows about things, he begins to notice something. Not everyone he tries to communicate with is interested in his experiences, nor are they capable of understanding how he sees things so much differently than he once did. Alas, they have never had the desire to program themselves. They are content to continue on with the herd. They have the same Point of View they have always had and are quite satisfied to keep it firmly in place. When they talk, they talk about themselves and are not remotely interested in communicating; they are simply interested in telling. The moment the Shaman born to his Office first notices this phenomenon is the point of no return. The Shaman has seen the Difference between what he once was, and what he has become.

No one can see what they're looking with. I can't see the color of my eyes without the help of a mirror and I have never met anyone who could. It is just as difficult to see our own programming and we use it as much as we use our eyes to perceive. Even if we know it is there we can't see it while we are looking at the world with it. This is the reason that the Shaman endeavors to take on other belief systems or Points of View different from his own. While he looks at the world through a new or different belief system or takes on another Point of View, he can for that period of time see the Differences between his normal belief system or Point of View and the new set.

Two things are accomplished by this ploy. First, the Shaman learns that it is possible to actually change the world. The world doesn't really change, but for the Shaman it might as well have changed because he is seeing things he never saw before. He is having new experiences in the world and it is not the same world he has always described. At times, the world he sees is so different that he must question if the experiences he knows he has had can even be possible. They certainly were not possible in the world he has always known or believed he knew.

The second thing that is accomplished is that the Shaman begins to see, from another Point of View, the world the majority of people see. It is a world of their own making, made to accommodate their desires, fears, pain, anger and he sees it as folly. If he actually can see the folly in the world he recently left, then he has to admit that the world he is presently seeing contains the same or similar folly. The difference is that, once seen, he can begin to control the folly. To *control folly* appears to be magical in the world he is leaving. Once the Shaman sees that Difference, he knows he can never go back.

Clarification:

> *Controlled Folly* is an interesting term. To the Shaman it is utter folly to consider that he can control anything or even hope to control anything with the programming he brings with him from childhood much less to allow that programming to control his actions while he blithely observes the world from his Beta or conscious thinking. As the Shaman begins to take on other Points of View and takes control of his programming and communication he is nearly forced to consider the idea that all of his new found "knowledge" must also be folly. The best he can hope for is to control that folly. In other words, rather than be swept away by the folly, he can begin to control how the folly flows and thereby develop the ability to *control folly*.

One of those obvious but overlooked facts about seeing things is that we can only see Differences. That's why camouflage works. When the eye doesn't discern a difference, it doesn't register anything as having been seen. If you look at a white sheet of paper, you don't see anything. There is nothing to see. If you make some squiggles on that sheet of paper, as with a Rorschach test, then the brain will begin to sort through its banks of forms and pull one out that is similar to what it perceives those squiggles to be. The funny thing is that different people will "identify" those squiggles differently. The same "identification" process occurs for nearly any new information. We try to fit it into pigeonholes which already exist. In other words, we try to perceive it as not being different. If it isn't different then we don't have to attend to anything.

We try to change any information outside of our experience so that it becomes something we already know. In some ways, we could consider this informational sorting to be a little lazy on our part, but if we already know something similar isn't a threat and we throw new information into the "similar" or "already known" bin, then we don't have stress about it. However, this action can be detrimental. It can actually prevent us from learning. When a Shaman is presented with information which threatens his existing belief system he will immediately attempt to see if the new data will give him the opportunity to discover a new Point of View. To the Shaman, new and different information is an opportunity. To ordinary people it is a threat.

The only way we can understand new information is if we can see a difference between what we already know and the new information. For this to actually occur, we have to relate what we know to the new data. The Shaman uses a ploy which is similar, but not quite the same. The Shaman adopts new Points of View and new belief systems in order to see what he actually knows and what he is learning. This has been called "moving the Assemblage Point."

Clarification:

The idea of seeing things from another Point of View can be thought of in two ways. One way is simpler. Simply adopting another Point of View is nothing more or less than seeing a given topic in another way. There is a sliding scale of complexity, however, in seeing different Points of View. For instance, if one was to contemplate the difference between labor and management, it would be relatively simple to see that labor wants more money and management doesn't want to pay it. If labor were to hinge the desire for more money on greater productivity, then labor would be changing to a management Point of View.

There are more complex issues which could be considered in this matter, obviously. The most complex Points of View to adopt are concerned with perceived reality. Nearly all of us think of our reality as being fixed in place and not at all open to interpretation. This is an error. For instance, in the United States it seems that the logic which permits the invasion of Iraq is nothing more or less than self-defense. In other parts of the world there exists a logic that views the attack on Iraq as arrogant. It is unlikely that either Point of View is correct, but if either or both sides were to accept that other Point of View as if true, then a new Point of View would be available to both sides.

If changing Points of View could redefine political or even religious belief in reality, could it be true that even the very fabric of what we "normally" see as the real world is also plastic? What if we could also see and experience the real world through Dreaming, for example? In other words, what if the human experience of the Dream State was actually part of the waking world? The immediate answer to that question is almost always, "No Way!" Yet, if someone could assemble the world just a little differently, then that Dream State could be as real as it is for the Aboriginal People of Australia. That would constitute a Movement of the Assemblage Point, not just a change of a Point of View and would be much more complicated, indeed.

Moving the Assemblage Point is an apt name for the event because it describes what occurs when we adopt someone else's Point of View or their belief system. We see or assemble things from a different perspective. If we change our Point of View, then all the programs connected to the old or regular Point of View, including memory, also have to change to accommodate how we assemble the world we are now seeing. One way to think about changing Points of View is to consider it as though one were a general-purpose computer which can switch from one task to another with very little time lost in reprogramming.

In real life, however, there is a decided lack of motivation to stray out of our cozy, personal, hard won system of beliefs. Only the Shaman seeks out and tries on new beliefs as though he were changing suits of clothes. The Shaman is driven to discover how to assemble the world through ever more complex systems. He needs to include as many ideas in his worldview as possible so that he can more accurately describe the differences he encounters.

The Shaman is trying to connect with the soul, or the Other, if you prefer. He is exploring the depths of his own thinking and he can't see what he is looking with without a mirror. The only mirror available to him is different ways of assembling his world. He can't talk to his friends about what he is experiencing because they are experiencing the world he is leaving. He virtually has no one to confide in. All he has left are the worlds he can assemble.

As the Shaman moves his awareness deeper and deeper into his own mind, he will experience assembling his world through Alpha, which will not be all that different from the Beta world. The Alpha world is more laid back. It is calmer and often quite sensual. The problem with this world is that it is held in place by strong emotions which emanate from Theta programs. Some of those emotions have to do with sexual relations, some have to do with unresolved issues with parents, some have to do with traumatic childhood events and some have to do with rage or even a sense of inadequacy. Some emotions are nearly benign but all emotions have the ability to move the body. A Shaman who is locked in Alpha will program himself and others whenever he opens his mouth with whatever emotions are locked away in Theta, whether they work well or not. He himself will soon find that he is caught in an endless loop of playing out those emotions. The only way out of the trap is through the trap.

The Shaman deals with the emotions as though they were a trap. One can get caught in emotional loops because "excitation causes interlock." If an emotion is particularly strong then it will excite the brain, causing the brain to interlock with the cause of the excitation. Generally, this is another person. If someone says something which makes us "mad" we tend to blame that person. It is better to realize that "mad" is self-generated. The Shaman experiences the emotion and then examines himself to see why the emotion is there to begin with.

The Shaman will soon find that he needs to begin to look at the world through his Theta programming. The Theta world is volatile. In some ways it is void of feeling and in some ways it is nothing but feeling. Angry outbursts are as common as snuggly, huggy needs. It's like being three years old all over again except for one small detail. The Shaman is a grown adult and must act accordingly. Pragmatism needs to be programmed into Theta as quickly as possible. A Shaman locked in Theta will be programming others with whatever he believes to be true in his Delta programming. That the belief may not be true for anyone else only causes confusion in himself and others, but because he states his case so strongly he can easily sway others to his belief system. This is a dangerous passage for a Shaman. The power he feels is seductive. This is not actual power, but it has the feel of power and everywhere the Shaman looks he sees others who are lauding his accomplishments. Some Shamans never progress beyond this point. This type of Shaman is prone to surround himself with others who proclaim him to be the "fairest of them all."

Clarification:

Contrary to popular belief, one person's emotions can be felt by other people. They are all the time. It is interesting to note, at this juncture, that crowds can be caught in a collective emotion and each individual in the crowd can be affected so that he will act as the crowd acts even though he normally would never do such things. One of the factors that causes this type of behavior is the overall emotion of the crowd. We notice the crowd-induced actions because they are not the norm. However, we do not notice that the same type of event is constantly occurring.

We are all affected by our own and by other people's emotions at all times. This describes a type of subliminal programming that is below the threshold of awareness. Anyone who can master his emotional state will have a subliminal programming effect on those he contacts. We all talk about the leader who imbues his colleagues with positive attitudes. We all recognize the sports figure who "wins" the game with his emotional set, but we almost never acknowledge the emotional effect we have on those who surround us.

The Shaman who masters his emotions will, without any covert thought, affect those with whom he comes in contact through his emotional set. Since that set will be other than "normal", then the Shaman will influence others to his way of thinking. This defines an obligation of the Shaman to ascertain that his emotional set is based in carefully considered beliefs about what he knows real to be.

If the Shaman can progress to assembling his world through Delta thinking, he will find himself at first in a dream-like state. It is a state where any idea could become real. Yet logical thought is not a strong part of Delta and applying logic to Delta thinking seems to be an oxymoron. In Delta, any belief encountered can be easily accepted. Sobriety, practicality, and pragmatic action can be believed, too. Applying these qualities to belief can be daunting, especially if the Shaman cannot examine his central beliefs concerning what he thinks is real. In some ways, a Shaman exploring Delta can seem to be terribly wishy-washy. He may not be able to effectively program himself, although when he speaks he will have a devastating effect on those who listen. The most common effect on the listeners is that he changes their beliefs without their permission and this will evoke a sometimes-violent reaction in the programmed. In short, we could say that Delta is a quagmire even though its exploration is an absolute necessity.

Clarification:

Moving awareness to any brain wave frequency causes the body to "vibrate" at that frequency. For example, if we move awareness to Alpha, then we speak in an Alpha rhythm, walk in an Alpha rhythm, think in an Alpha rhythm and affect others at an Alpha rhythm. This may not be noticed by other people because they may put that Alpha rhythm in their "similar bin" and assume that what they are experiencing is "known." Moving awareness to Delta rhythms means that the practitioner is not only "vibrating" at Delta, he is also causing those around him to "vibrate" at Delta rhythms. This can be devastating to someone who is not prepared for the effects of such "vibrations." For example, because the voice of the practitioner is "vibrating" at a Delta rhythm then a listener will "vibrate" right along with his voice. This is more difficult to place in the "similar bin." If the practitioner were to have changed his Point of View about commonly held beliefs, then he could excite that belief in the listener. A Shaman doesn't have the right to excite other's beliefs without their permission. Therefore the practicing Shaman must be "invisible" to those whom he communicates with so as not to inadvertently change their system of beliefs. If he is asked about his Point of View, then the Shaman has carte blanche to "vibrate" to his heart's content. That doesn't mean that he won't evoke the same response, but in this instance he has been asked for his Point of View.

For the Shaman who can pass through the rigors of self-exploration, there are many Assemblage Points available which do not seem to be connected to the thinking machinery at all. One description which is useful in understanding this phenomenon is Self-Meta-Programmer. One definition of Meta could be, "from above or behind." In other words, the Shaman would be controlling his actions from above or behind the brain. There are also those who say that there is an actual point of light in the energy body or aura which is located high up on the aura above the shoulder blades. I offer this thought so that a model can be constructed as to how this can work.

It seems in actual practice that the "out of the brain" control center is something like a type of sub-harmonic. There is a method of tuning stringed instruments where you can touch a string so that the note it is sounding is cut in parts. If two strings are sounding a single note and one string is a little out of tune a sound will appear which is between the strings and not on the either string at all. The sound between the strings makes a sound which can be described as a "wah...wah...wah." As the turning of one string to the other approaches perfection, the "wah...wah" sound gets longer in duration until it disappears altogether. It is still there, but it is no longer noticeable. A Shaman who is operating from the Self-Meta-programmer, or who is in control of the point from which he assembles the world, will be invisible to his fellow man because there will be no notable difference in his behavior. He will leave no tracks.

Clarification:

Until the Shaman reaches a certain control over how he assembles his world, he is a bit out of tune. That out of tune-ness gives him away to other people, as it were. Unless he has dominion over his programming all the way through the Delta level, then he is being driven by programming that is "foreign" to him or which comes from somewhere other than his own experiences. The programming may be from mom and dad or teachers or even his own childhood *perceptions* of what programming should be. Until he can adopt other

Points of View at will, he will program other people to his old Point of View. He may not intend to program anyone else, but the strength of the "vibrations" from slower brain wave frequencies change other peoples programming at a subliminal level. When a Shaman is in control of his programming and can adopt other Points of View at will, then his communication can be so integrated to the programming of another person that the other person won't, or perhaps can't, notice any difference between his own vibrations and those of the Shaman. The Shaman, therefore, would leave no tracks in the other person's mind.

The Shaman is careful to either tell someone he is affecting a programming change in that person or he will affect the change so carefully that the person in whom the programming has been altered will never be aware that he himself didn't rewrite the program. Either of these maneuvers requires skill and honesty. The Shaman must be doubly careful if he is dealing with someone who is considering entering the path of Shaman and with a Shaman with less skill. Both individuals deserve to know everything that is being done so they can choose whether or not to participate.

Some things to do to better understand "Differences"

If it doesn't make a Difference, it doesn't matter. Have at least one communication every day that makes a Difference. In other words change something for someone every day. This could be as simple as saying that the clerk at the hamburger joint is doing a good job or that the teller at the bank is always so helpful. These are people who experience a lot of negativity every day. Why not make a Difference and give them something positive?

A common problem for many people is the inability to think for themselves. It seems that this type of person must have validation in order to do anything. They will ask repeatedly about how other people view their actions. When a Shaman is confronted with such a person he will often make a Difference by refusing to validate the value of the person, but will validate that person's ability to decide for himself. Anyone can "be nice" and say that even hair-brained ideas are "interesting." The Shaman cannot agree with that reality so he finds a way to make a Difference.

When a Shaman encounters a belief system which is exclusionary in nature he will also encounter words and actions which are rarely in sync. For instance, if a "belief system" states that it is necessary for an outside individual to join the "belief club" or be excluded from that club, then thought and action are not integrated from the Supra-Self-Meta-Programmer through to logic. An exclusionary "belief system" must be an extension of ME. It makes no Difference simply because it cannot accept other Points of View. In other words, such a belief system doesn't change anything in the world.

Clarification:

There are certain religious sects which demand that any individual who wishes to be part of the sect take on an exclusion belief which states that those outside the sect are so different that they cannot be trusted even for regular conversation. These sects or "belief clubs" are populated by people who deem themselves to be better or even purer than others. The basis of this pureness or better-ness seems to always be rooted in the members of the club accepting some sort of belief. Those who cannot or will not accept the defining belief are excluded from the club. Any exclusionary belief must logically make the believer different from other people. Since we are all humans who believe in order to make things real, then the question which arises from the exclusionary belief is why would anyone think that a logical thought would make them better than someone who finds error in that thought?

If the belief of the sect were to change reality in some measurably beneficial way, then wouldn't any reasonable human want to include himself in that system of belief? Why would anyone be excluded? The only reason for excluding other people would be if the stated belief would only result in self-aggrandizement. For instance, if I say that I believe that I pray to the great god Pan and because of my prayers I am healthy, wealthy and wise, but if you don't pray to Pan then you are the worst type of person, I am hardly changing any reality. I am simply making myself great in my own eyes. My exclusionary belief, therefore, is nothing more than me, me, me.

Yet the Shaman must interact with many individuals who hold exclusionary belief systems. The fact that he is a Shaman indicates that he is to make a Difference both in and for the earth where he lives and which provides substance for his very life. If he overlooks the actions of people with exclusionary belief systems, will he make a Difference? If the Shaman is to make a Difference, what, specifically, would that Difference be? If necessary, write it down and post it on your refrigerator.

Points to Consider:

1. The Shaman seeks to note Differences between his current programming/set of beliefs and other programming/sets of belief in order to accumulate energy.
2. The Shaman seeks to explore his own emotions and beliefs in real things so he can avail himself of other emotions and beliefs in real things.
3. The Shaman is most interested in the Difference between consciousness as the computer operator and the Supra-Self-Meta-Programmer, soul or Other as the computer operator.
4. The Shaman uses his knowledge gained through observing Differences to make himself invisible to non-Shamans.
5. The Shaman seeks to know his own programming in its entirety through observing Differences in Points of View.

6. Observing Differences is a Shamanic tool which will show the Shaman exactly what he does and exactly how he does it.
7. Therefore the Shaman strives to "Make a Difference" in the world.
8. The Difference to be made by the Shaman is always related to the spirit, soul, Other, or Supra-Self-Meta-Programmer, since all of these words refer to the same "thing".
9. Since the Other, or whatever word one wishes to use, is "above and behind" the brain/programming, the Shaman clears a path through his programming so the Other can express.
10. One art of the Shaman is to clear that path for other people while leaving none of his programming behind. In other words, the Shaman makes a Difference without calling attention to himself or the difference.

Story Chapter IV

Poor Bob. He is going through a bad time. He's been to talk to his sister, I think, or maybe his sister-in-law. He tried to explain about programming himself and was met with a polite, "That's interesting." Of course, he also had to try to explain how to communicate from the soul and met with some comments which were not as polite and I'm pretty sure not as interested.

He is coming along pretty well, but doesn't know it. It will soon be time for him to ask about what he is learning. I don't know if he is aware that there is a system here or not. I don't think he knows, even though he is past the point of no return. He is actually pretty adept. He thinks about the things I tell him and he tries to put them to use. He has done pretty well at changing Points of View, although adopting a new Assemblage Point is still out of reach for him. I haven't talked with him about different brain wave frequencies and that is probably the next thing I need to do. He has been able to achieve Alpha frequencies on his own, more or less, but he doesn't understand what he is doing.

He has been doing pretty well with new information. Once in a while he fights about it or defends his existing position, but overall he has done well. He has the most trouble with defending his position, I think. Most people do, and I shouldn't really be too hard on him for acting like a normal human being, but I do get after him on that issue simply because he needs to let it go. When he finally does accept new information, then he doesn't waste much time going through and changing the programming to accommodate the new belief. That's a little unusual. Maybe that's why I like this guy. I'd better be careful not to let him know that, though, he's liable to get too complacent.

"Hey, Teach."

"I thought we discussed that. Didn't I tell you about that?"

"What do you want me to call you?"

"By my name. What else?"

"But I'm learning lots of things from you. I should call you something."

"You just think you're learning things. You haven't even gotten in the ball park as a spectator yet."

"What do you mean?"

"See there. What did I just tell you?"

"Okay, define 'ball park.'"

Bob is slowly beginning to adapt to what he thinks it is I want from him. I do want this type of response, but what I see is that slowly but surely, his soul is beginning to communicate.

"Bob, have you ever heard of brain wave frequencies?"

"Maybe."

"You either have or you haven't."

"I've heard of them, but I don't know diddly about them."

"Your communication skills are improving, did I mention that?"

"Several times."

"It's worth repeating. There are four major brain waves and you have been accessing two of them rather well. You started out with one and you have been touching the other one every now and then."

"I have?"

"Nearly everyone uses Beta which is the fastest one and the one where logic seems to exist. We all use the next slowest one when we fall asleep. In fact, we use all the frequencies when we sleep. You have been using Alpha a lot when we talk. Some of the reason for that is that I am asking you questions and giving you information about programming and other things that kind of force you to use slower thinking patterns just to understand the subject."

"Sometimes my head hurts after one of your sessions."

"Poor baby."

"Serious."

"Do me a favor. Stand over by that window and look outside. Now tell me what color your eyes are in that light."

"What?"

"Am I stuttering again?"

"No, I heard you, but why are you asking me what color my eyes are?"

"Can't you see what color they are?"

"No. We've done this before and I still can't see the color of my eyes."

Sorry about repeating myself, Bob, but I need you to think about this some more.

"No one can see what they are looking with. You think you are pretty smart being able to write programs for yourself and all, but did you ever think about a program which can control sets of programs or about a program which can control sets of programs which control sets of programs?"

"Say what? I don't think I got that one."

"You've learned how to write programs. But there are programs which control whole sets of programs and there are other, even more complicated, programs which control those programs. When you wrote the program to give your dad respect, that was just a simple program. Behind the respect issue is a program which controls sets of actions or responses with your dad. This program might even control how you act with any adult male, for instance. Now that would be a set of programs, don't you think?"

"That it would. Are you telling me to write a program to correct how I deal with adult males?"

It's time to slow the voice cadence down and begin to lower him down into Theta. He needs to be as slow as possible for this. We've been over some of this material before, but that doesn't mean that it is all in one place yet.

"No, I am telling you that such programs exist. At the same time I am asking you if you are aware of such programming in yourself?"

"No and no, I'm guessing here, but I would say not."

"I would concur. Not only am I telling you that there may be a program which controls how you deal with any adult male, but I am also telling you that there may be a program which virtually defines what 'adult male' means to you. That would be an even more far reaching program, yeah?"

"Oh, yeah."

"Okay. We could say, in a very general way or as a way of talking about this subject, that the program you wrote to help you give your dad respect is an Alpha program. I don't mean that it is the top dog, in this case, but that it relates to Alpha brain waves. Understand?"

You should be registering Alpha, Bob. I don't want to mark it for you, but you are slipping away from your normal   conscious thought.

"I guess so. I don't have any idea about what an Alpha brain wave is, but if you say so then I'll accept it as so. For now, anyway."

"Great. So, the program which controls how you deal with any adult male could very well be embedded in your Theta brain wave frequencies. Normally when we talk about Theta programming we talk about it in terms of emotion. Generally, we describe emotions with single words. We say things like, 'I'm mad.' Or, 'I'm sad.' Or, 'I'm stoked.' Think about that. If you say that you're 'stoked' about something, then the 'stoked' feeling or emotion in this case permeates everything you do while you are 'stoked.' In other words, being stoked controls sets of programs. Understand?"

"Okay."

I need to steer clear of anything that is too emotional now because he is already in mid-Theta. If anyone saw him at this moment, they would think he's catatonic.

"Now then, what type of program could allow or control being 'stoked'?"

"I really don't know. When I'm stoked, I'm just stoked is all."

"Let me try this another way. Ready? Here comes. Have you ever seen a green cat with yellow polka dots?"

"No."

"Are you sure?"

"Yes. I'm sure."

"So you know what you know and you know what you don't know. Is that true?"

"I know I've never seen a green cat with yellow polka dots."

"Could you tell me what allows you to be 'stoked'?"

"I just feel good is all."

"So why don't you 'feel good is all' all the time?"

"Sometimes I don't feel good, I guess."

"What allows you to 'don't feel good, I guess' instead of 'stoked'?"

"I don't know. What allows me to?"

"It's what you believe real to be."

"I don't need to believe in something that is real."

"You don't? Are laws real?"

"Of course, and I don't need to believe in them."

"Of course you don't. So what does a law taste like?"

"You can't taste a law."

"Right. You can measure it, though."

"You can measure what it does."

"You can? What's the biggest one you ever measured?"

"Well, I never measured a law."

"Wow! You didn't? You have seen laws, though, right?"

"Yeah. I've seen laws."

"How big were the ones you saw?"

"They were on paper."

"They were? Could you pet them? When they got older did they go outside by themselves?"

"Okay. What's your point?"

"My point is that you believe in laws. They are abstract. That means that while they are real and they affect us, they exist solely because we believe in them. That also means that they don't exist without our belief in them."

"And that proves what?"

It's going to take you a long time to bring this point to consciousness. Not only will it take a long time, you will have to try over and over again to make your perception of what I'm about to tell you fit the world you know.

"It doesn't prove anything, but it does point at something. It points at the idea of belief making something real. That would be a program which controls sets of programs which control sets of programs. I wonder what you believe an adult male is."

"I *really* don't know."

"Ooo, Bob made a funny. Okay, look. Adult males, like laws, exist no matter what you believe about them. However, what you believe about them affects your *perception* about what they do and don't do. Your *perception* about adult males is an abstraction which you treat as real. If you were to change your belief about adult males, you would also change how you *perceive* them. If you changed how you believed about 'stoked' you would change everything that permeates you when you are 'stoked'. Some things might stay the same, but there would be a difference."

"Like the difference with my dad, right?"

"You got it."

"So are you telling me to write a program about how I believe about my dad?"

"And just when I was ready to start bragging on you, too. No. I am not telling you to write a program about how you *believe* about your dad. I am telling you that you *believe* in lots and lots of things and what you *believe* about those things affects how you see them. In fact, because you *believe* those things you treat what you *believe* as though it were actually real. I might add that most of what you *believe* probably doesn't have a speck of support in actual reality, but that won't change how you treat those things unless you discover what you *believe* and why you *believe* it."

"So am I weird or what?"

"No, you are a normal human being who hasn't read the directions."

"I'm a guy and we aren't supposed to read the directions."

"That's true, but when you can't put it together then maybe the directions will give you a clue about how the thing works."

"Okay, I don't think I believe in laws or about how I deal with my dad or any other guy, but let's say you are right. Doesn't everybody believe in laws or about how they deal with their dad? I mean what's the big deal?"

Go over this carefully, Bob. There are lots more pieces here than you think. Of course, you don't have much experience in manipulating ideas at this pace. So, I have to let you have your head.

"The big deal is that you *believe* and that act of belief empowers you to treat what you *believe* as 'real.' In fact, when you *believe* in something it may as well be real."

"Well, that's simple enough. Why the whole song and dance to say that?"

"Because you can't see what you're looking with. I have to show you a difference in order for you to see what I'm saying."

"What difference are you showing me?"

"I see laws as abstractions. You see laws as real. We are both right, but laws can't exist unless the populace believes in them. And that is precisely the catch."

"I still don't see the difference you claim to be showing me."

Everyone gets at least one check.

"Okay, let me ask it. Maybe you can see it that way. Do we see the idea of laws the same way?"

"No."

"What is the difference in how we see them?"

"You see them as something people have to believe in for them to work. I see them as real."

"Very good. In the English language we call that a difference."

"Okay. I get it."

"Great. Ready for a real difference?"

"I don't know, but I have this funny feeling I'm about to hear it anyway."

"You have that right. Here comes. Who is it that *believes*?"

"I do."

"Of course you do. But do you suppose that there is a part of 'you' which does the *believing*?"

"I don't know."

"Well, I submit that it is the soul which does or at least should do the *believing* in real things. That's why you need to communicate from the soul, because the soul is the part of 'you' which makes the reality you see."

"If that's true then what are you actually telling me?"

"What I'm actually telling you is that you are a special person who was born to an Office."

"You know, talking to you takes me to some pretty weird spaces. So what Office was I born to?"

"You were born to the Office of Shaman."

"Get out of Dodge."

"To use your phrase, 'Serious'."

"What if I don't want to be born to the Office of Shaman?"

"You have the right to walk away and never deal with any of this again. That's the easy stuff. The harder-to-accept stuff is that if you actually see the difference between how you think and how 'normal' people think, you won't be able to walk away."

"What do you mean?"

"You have been learning some concepts which are basic to the activities which Shamans perform. That doesn't mean that you have become a Shaman, just that you now have been exposed to some Shamanic concepts. If you continue to learn this set of information, you won't be able to return to what you once were. At this point, you still are what you have always been. Just a guy with a curious streak who likes to talk to lots of people who have different opinions than his."

"Are you saying that if I continue to talk with you I'm going to be trapped into becoming a Shaman?"

"No, but I am telling you that I can't continue to tell you about the things I know unless you are sure you want to know. Some of the ideas that I know about can take years to understand. Not only that, they require experiences to back them up. This type of information isn't for everybody and I don't want you to continue with this line of conversations unless you are sure you are willing to pay whatever price to get this information inside of you so that it is useful. That doesn't mean that I can't continue to talk to you, it just means that I can't talk to you about this stuff unless you really want to know about it."

"What if I want to know more?"
"Then you need to ask."

This is an important passage for Bob. I have to check to see if I'm right about his soul bringing him around to see me. I have to tell him what this means and I have to drive his awareness down into his being so that he can actually comprehend the concepts. There isn't any other method to accomplish all this unless his Assemblage Point moves. I've never seen anyone comprehend any of this from the consciousness programmed from childhood. I don't know if this is fair or not. In the long run, it doesn't make much difference because if the information is not something he is looking for, he'll simply disappear. I doubt that's going to happen.

Points to Consider:

1. The action of the teacher is to *time bind* at least one passage from consciousness to the soul for Bob or from the soul to consciousness.
2. The teacher presents Bob with different ways (Differences) to observe common ideas.
3. The teacher is establishing the method for Bob to eventually understand what his Specific Function is in the world of Shamanism.
4. Bob can't understand what the teacher is doing at this time because he still lacks a good deal of information.
5. The teacher gives Bob the opportunity to disengage from the communication because if Bob-the-soul is not attuned to the line of communication being presented, Bob as body, mind and soul won't return.
6. If Bob returns, then by his actions he will agree to continue the communication.
7. It was, therefore, important for the teacher to open one passage between Beta consciousness and Delta belief in order to know without any doubt what Bob's next action means.
8. The teacher, in order to be fair with Bob, had to make sure that he told Bob why he was communicating and what he based his need to communicate on. So he told Bob that he owed the Communication to his benefactor and he told Bob that he considered Bob to have been born to the Office of Shaman.
9. The teacher crafted his Communication with Bob in such a way that Bob, by his own logic, would have little choice but to agree with the differences being presented while guiding Bob to rewrite his programming.
10. The teacher left no programming tracks, yet Bob has a new program which he, himself, wrote.
11. A difference has been achieved.

Chapter 5: Not Doing

"I was going to the store for a pack of cigarettes,
but I'll go to Seattle if you want to."

— Tom Waits

A rite of passage on the Shamanic journey is when the Shaman gains control of his own programming. If he can snap his fingers in rhythm to the different brain wave frequencies, for instance, he knows he has understood the content of those frequencies or at least some of what they do. This is an important step because it signifies that the Shaman has spent some considerable time and energy on the process of reprogramming himself. The control of programming will be noticeable to the Shaman as a "removed from the normal rat race" ability to communicate. He will, by this time, have the ability to watch Communications unfold. He will be thinking from the slower brain wave frequencies.

Clarification:

For the novice, brain wave frequencies will be a mystery. It takes some time and practice to become familiar with what different brain wave frequencies do. As experience is gained, the rhythm of each frequency becomes apparent. Certain types of thoughts belong with each brain wave set and, because of this, the adept will soon find that those rhythms are recognizable and will ring in his head as though he were listening to a metronome.

As an individual learns to access what can be termed as slower thinking patterns, connections with Dreams, and psychic phenomenon, he may be challenged as to what can be done with his talents. The trick is to balance normal activities with Not Doing. Not Doing is the method used to allow time for the brain to catch up with the change in beliefs. Not Doing is a phrase which has been used before, but it is a very accurate description of the event.

Not Doing is in reality an activity. It is the shadow of doing. Not Doing is not sloth and perhaps is best described as the activity of stalking or hunting for the true nature of anything. If you leave your house and forget to bring something with you, instead of turning around and going back to get it, go on to your destination to find out what it is that your soul is telling you or wants you to learn. If your significant other wants to go to Mom's for the weekend, go. Who knows what you might learn. You never know from where the spirit will send you a communiqué. Accept all invitations for Agreement which are not contrary to your central beliefs. They will take you to places you would never go on your own. You will have new experiences and, through those experiences, you will pass through the hardening fires of profound self-examination because you will be following the dictates of the spirit. This is the nature of Not Doing.

For most people, knowledge doesn't come in a flash of light. It is a slow, steady process that involves patience. Lots of patience. It is the nature of knowledge to come to those who seek it in quiet undulations. It is shy and reveals itself slowly without fanfare. It comes in a steady, inexorable, undeniable manner. Those it chooses cannot change their destiny, even if they could muster up the desire to do so. Knowledge will find those it wants and teach its lessons without respect to readiness. Knowledge is a terrible and wonderful master. Do not resist its touch. Allow Not Doing to aid the accumulation of knowledge.

As knowledge accumulates, patterns emerge in the Shaman's activities. A byproduct of Not Doing is an increase in energy. Increased energy often expresses itself in recurring opportunities to demonstrate a talent pertaining to the Shaman. Some people will find that reading cards or tea leaves give them the needed method to interact with other people. Some people find that massage or a relationship with healing plants is the preferred method of interaction. Still others will consider teaching, whether traditional subjects or some form of Shamanism, preferential. Some will become mental health workers or even 12 step facilitators. Others will find fulfillment as salesmen or small business operators. In all cases, what the emerging Shaman will accomplish will be essentially the art of Agreement.

Clarification:

Increasing energy is a term which comes up from time to time in any discussion about Shamanic activity. It is difficult to explain exactly how energy is increased. In one way the increase in energy could be considered as mental. As the programming is streamlined, there is a proportional streamlining of thought sequences. This is often perceived as an increase in energy, as it may well be.

There is another aspect to increased energy which is connected to the effect the Shaman has on those with whom he comes in contact. He certainly has an energetic effect on others due to lowering his brain wave frequencies because the act of lowering his frequencies tends to lower the frequencies of those around him. Yet it is more likely that the effect is multiplied by the Points of View that the Shaman uses to communicate. The Communication seems to result in *time binding* for other individuals and *time binding* seems to free energy for both the Shaman and the other individual.

There is a third aspect to increased energy at work here as well. This third idea is connected to the healing abilities of the Shaman. It could be that because of his own inner explorations he is able to subliminally bring more healthy attitudes to others, but it is more likely that because his emotions are under his domination that he "vibrates" more strongly than others.

The card reader may agree with his client that life can and should be better.

He may even propose methods the client can follow which will actually make his life better. The healer will agree that his clients should feel better and help them achieve that better feeling. Teachers will agree with their students to learn the things they wish to learn. The mental health workers will offer the Agreement of less stressful programming. The salesmen and business operators will offer Agreement to a wide range of clients that their products or services will work better than the ones now employed. No matter what expression of Shamanism sticks, the Shaman is always involved with forging Agreements. He may Agree to disagree or he may Agree to uplifting things or he may Agree to base things, but he will be dealing in Agreements.

Agreements have always been at the center of the Shaman's bag of tricks. A Shaman went to the "underworld" or some such to obtain the Agreement of the Spirit of the Bison for a good bison hunt, or talked with the rain god to ensure lots of rain, or communed with the recently departed to know what revenge they wanted for their untimely demise. Sometimes the Agreements were permissions, sometimes they were instructions and sometimes they were payments, but they were always an Agreement of some variety or another. It has always been the work of the Shaman to understand and wield the machinery of Agreement whether that Agreement was for an individual, a tribe, or a larger social group.

The problem with getting Agreements from entities which are spiritual in nature, such as the spirit of the Bison, is that regular people couldn't verify that the Agreement was made. As a consequence, the Shamans of days gone by had to shroud their activities in mystery. The mystery was necessary because the Agreement wasn't with some spiritual entity, it was actually with the people of the tribe. Remember that the Shaman was the most educated individual of his social grouping. He actually did know things that regular people didn't know. He knew because of the rigors of his training and regular people couldn't grasp those concepts because they hadn't gone through the training process. As a consequence of the difference in educational levels, the Shamanic secrets had to be closely guarded. Those secrets could not be revealed to others, lest the secrets lose their power.

Guarding the secret of Agreement was a Not Doing of the tribal Shaman. Sharing that secret would have meant that the tribal Bubba wouldn't have had the necessary respect for the dictates of the Shaman, nor for the Shaman himself. That the respect was held in place by fear of that spirit of the Bison may have been because fear was all Tribal Bubba could wrap his mind around. The Shaman, by the Not Doing of guarding secrets, offered Tribal Bubba an Agreement to eat during the winter by utilizing fear as a motivator. To Tribal Bubba, that was an offer he couldn't refuse.

If the education level of today's Bubbas were equal to Tribal Bubba, we would be talking here of the spirit of the computer chip or the spirit of the canned baked beans. Fortunately, folks today have a higher level of education.

But the Not Doing of imbuing Shamanic activities with mystery or guarding them is still a valid ploy. In a 12-step program for recovering alcoholics, the newly initiated cannot possibly understand the benefit of the 12 steps, but by attending meetings with other folks going through the same struggles, he can experience two aspects of mystery. First, he must accept by faith, not knowledge, that the mysterious 12 steps will work. Then he can join a social group where Agreement makes the 12-step process real and he can start down the long, long road to recovery.

In some ways, we could say that the Not Doing of telling the truth is mystery. For example, if we were in a room full of people discussing subatomic particles we just might not understand what they were saying. If we were to ask, they might say that subatomic particles are little bitty pieces of energy which follow a kind of dance around bigger little bitty pieces of energy. We would have to accept the mystery of the little bitty pieces of energy because we don't have the educational background for understanding subatomic particles. In this example, "little bitty pieces of energy" is actually the truth, but is not expansive enough to remove the mystery, yet it is the truth.

Any small business operator knows that an asset of his business is good will. Good will is a mysterious commodity, but if we were to break it down to its simplest form we could say that it is the Agreement that the community holds with the business, but to the businessman, good will is an asset. The Tarot reader makes a show of letting the client shuffle the deck and then deals out the mysterious cards that tell him that the client is suffering from a lack of understanding of his true nature or that his business is on the cusp of going to the next level. If the cards don't actually say anything, then we might have to assume that the reader is offering the client an Agreement to feel better about his condition in life. The masseuse pushes here and there, cracks a joint or two and the client experiences the mystery of massage and Agrees that he is cured of an aching back or sore knee. All of these examples have something in common. Each practitioner is a type of Shaman and each Shaman offers an Agreement which makes something real. Each Shaman manipulates a certain mystery as a catalyst which allows other people to believe in something that becomes real.

The Shaman accomplishes this feat through the art of Not Doing. In the course of our day-to-day lives we tend to be constantly active. The problem is that much of the time our activities serve to reprogram our current and personal Point of View. We sometimes spend a great deal of energy "proving" our Points of View to be "true" or "real." The Shaman uses Not Doing to break his reprogramming cycle. Breaking the reprogramming frees the energy that was used to hold the Point of View in place. The Shaman, by this time, must know that any Point of View is nothing more than a description of the world. The Shaman knows that in terms of complete world description, one Point of View is not better than another. In other words there is virtually no Difference between one Point of View and another.

The Shaman uses his freed energy to observe the endless programming loops in other people. As he recognizes the patterns of the loops, he can insert Agreements in the loops which may actually cut the loop. This Shamanic activity is simply not possible without the practice of Not Doing. It is Not Doing which frees the energy necessary to observe and communicate at the exactly appropriate moment. If the Communication is well crafted, then an Agreement is reached and a new reality is observed. It may well be that nothing in a broader scope of world activity has been changed, but it is true that for the Agreement holders the world description has changed and that change may as well have changed the world.

Not Doing is an integral part of the Shaman's bag of tricks. It allows him to bring the spirit, soul, and "slower" thinking processes up out of the "other than conscious" to be applied to the world in terms of Agreement. As the Shaman forges Agreements, he affects the *perception* of reality for himself and for those with whom he forges the Agreements. The change in *perception* of reality occurs because the Shaman sees his own programming from the perspective of the soul. Anyone with whom he can agree will be affected by his perspective. They may dismiss his perspective as something they want or don't want but they must make a decision about his perspective. If they Agree with him, they must necessarily Agree with his perspective. Since his perspective is anchored in his knowledge about the spirit or soul, they, too, will forge a relationship with the part of themselves which they consider to be spirit or soul. They may never be able to forge the same relation with the spirit or soul which the Shaman enjoys, but his Agreement will forever alter how they think and how they perceive their world. In other words, they will, through the act of believing, make a new or different reality and so will the Shaman.

If the goal is to practice Not Doing, then the means of Not Doing is to find the shadow of the do. The charisma of Not Doing is to allow spirit to be a part of any activity. The orientation of Not Doing is to develop patience. To Not Do we would eliminate frenzied activity for the sake of doing something. To assimilate Not Doing we would forge Agreements to make new ideas become real. The impulse of Not Doing is to incite belief through emotional motivators. The need of Not Doing is mystery. The possibilities of Not Doing are catalytic methods of motivation. The form of Not Doing is to forge Agreements. The substance of Not Doing is to forge new realities for others.

Some things to do to better understand "Not Doing"

Listening or accepting is the Not Doing of defending an existing Point of View. If an action must be defended then it was ill conceived or is related to a type of importance. Defense of actions include not only actions which are harmful, but also actions which are helpful. At least once a day listen and accept a compliment or a criticism without defending anything. Just listen and say thank you.

Some things are best left as a mystery. It may be better to allow your life history to fall into the category of mystery. To repeat your version of your life history to anyone who will listen does not accumulate energy. Ignoring invitations to recount your life history is the Not Doing of reprogramming your Point of View. Living life takes place in this moment. Yesterday and tomorrow is not a dichotomy. They are reference points in time. While yesterday affects what anyone thinks in this ever present now and the hopes for tomorrow should determine the trajectory of now, neither has a place in the deliberate actions of this instant. The mystery of this instant is the Not Doing of personal history. To the Shaman "now" lasts a long time.

Time is a matter of perspective. To the Other, time may not exist. The Not Doing of conscious or logical thought is allowing the Other to express through the body. The Shaman is not constrained by time to realize accomplishments. There is the lifelong now present in any endeavor. Don't rush to be on time. Be on time. Throw away your watch and include the Other in this instant. The Not Doing of learning is understanding.

Points to Consider:

1. In a way, Not Doing could be considered as the time needed to recharge the battery.
2. The Not Doing of mystery is simply telling the truth to the level the listener can comprehend.
3. The Not Doing of reality is belief.
4. Consciousness as the observer is the Not Doing of thought.
5. Not Doing teaches the Shaman the natural order of things including the natural order of the mind.
6. Not Doing is a fountain of energy for the Shaman.
7. Agreements may not be possible without Not Doing present in the life of a Shaman.

Story Chapter V

I haven't seen Bob for a while now. I wouldn't be surprised if he were to show up at any time, though. I'm sure he has been wrestling with himself about a lot of things. He doesn't know it, but he has actually been using the Shaman's ploy of Not Doing. I doubt that he has given even so much as a passing thought to the things I've talked to him about. That would be the correct thing to do because his thinking and belief system have been assaulted brutally during our conversations and he would need time to allow the thought processes to heal. The nice thing about that process is that it is painless and you don't know that it's happening.

Sometimes that process can take up to ten years or more to run its course. For me, it occurred in a matter of minutes. I'm not sure that I would wish that on anyone else because it sure did confuse me. For the longest time I thought that was the way it happened to everyone. Eventually I developed patience and realized that some folk take longer. I suspect that Bob will be one of those who take some time, but not all that much. He will be lucky in that regard.

I need to present Bob with the idea of Not Doing. This is a strange concept, in a way, because it has to be presented in stone sober consciousness. It teaches a subjective idea, yet it is given to consciousness as though it is almost a throw away idea, but it still has to be wrapped in mystery so that it takes on power.

"Well, look what the cat dragged in."

"Yeah, yeah. I've been busy. I went to see my folks, then I was at the beach for a while. I got a job over there, but it didn't work out. Now I'm back."

"It would appear. So, what's up?"

"Oh, nothing much, just thought I'd stop by and see what's up with you."

"Same old, same old."

"You been making people's heads hurt?"

"No, there haven't been too many folks by lately."

"When I was over at the beach I was talking to this guy who reminded me of you."

"Handsome dude, eh?"

"No. Well, he was at least as handsome as you, but he talked about a lot of the same shit."

"Really?"

"Yeah. Well, not really, but kind of."

"What kind of shit did he talk about?"

"He was into Indian religion or something."

"And...?"

"Well, he talked about some of the same things, kind of."

"He told you that you could only see Differences?"

"No, not that kind of stuff. I don't know. I kind of thought of you when I was listening to him talk is all."

"I'm touched, deeply touched."

"Give me a break. He didn't really talk about any of the same stuff, but the way he talked about it was the way you talk about things sometimes."

"Oh?"

"It's just that when he was talking, I could remember things you and I talked about."

"Like what?"

"I don't know. I can't remember now."

"Do you know why you can't remember?"

"Because I forgot?"

"Maybe. And maybe because that information is stored in a different Assemblage Point."

"A different what?"

"A different Assemblage Point. Whenever I have talked with you, I have pretty much made you think about things in a different way. It's not that I forced you to think one way or another, yet I did. One way to think about that event is to say that I lent you an Assemblage Point to look at the world in a certain way. Remember in the Goals/Means program the part about Charisma? I told you that it could be thought of as the attitude of approach? Well, I have presented you with lots of information that is new to you and in order for you to 'see' it you have to look at the world from a different angle, as it were."

"Not as it were. You always make me look at things from so many different angles I feel like I'm playing Twister again. The only difference is that there aren't any cute girls to accidentally bump up against."

He's there now. Let's use the cute girls to mark the conscious Beta conversation we were having and he'll see Not Doing as a new Point of View or a move of the Assemblage Point. Logic will accept the idea as though it has been there all along and will be thoroughly confused about applying it. He'll sort it all out eventually.

"When you played Twister all you did was bump up against girls?"

"Well, there was this one time..."

"Okay, I already have too much information."

"She was really fine, though."

Now this has the right feel of consciousness to use for presenting Not Doing. I'll remember this feeling while using it to present the concept of Not Doing.

"I'll take your word on that. So, you figure that you haven't been really doing anything with what we've talked about for the last few months, eh?"

"Not really. Like I said, whenever I talked with this one dude I kind of remembered some of what we talked about."

"Well, I have some news for you. What you were doing is called Not Doing."

"I wasn't just out on the beach every day. I worked, but sometimes at night I would go over to this dude's place and we'd talk for hours."

"Yeah, that's called Not Doing."

"Am I missing something here?"

Yep. Logically you can't accomplish anything by Not Doing it. But already consciousness is trying to put Not Doing to work. Insidious ploy, using a Beta construct to teach a Delta thought process. Don't you just love it?

Maybe. Not Doing is a tool Shamans use to buy time and other things."

"What things do they buy with it?"

"Let's just say for now that they buy time with Not Doing."

"How does this work?"

Consciousness is fairly chomping at the bit to put this one to work. No energy expenditure and it's a useful activity. Something for nothing. Well, not quite.

"Well, you've been over at the beach letting your programming catch up to what you've learned. You probably even had some experiences that 'proved' that one piece of information or another worked a certain way for you. You could say that you were practicing Not Doing while you were over at the beach."

"Okay, what did I accomplish?"

"I'd say that you must have changed some basic beliefs you held during the time we talked. You may not have changed them very much, but you changed something. That change precipitated changes in the programs which control sets of programs. If you remember, that would be emotional changes probably located in the Theta brain wave frequency. Then the programs changed in order to accommodate the change in the emotional sets. Those changes probably occurred in the Alpha brain wave frequencies. Finally the way you actually think in consciousness changed."

"Hey, you know what?"

"What?"

"When I was talking with that dude I remember a couple of times when I was saying things that I didn't really know I knew. At first it scared the hell out of me, but it was like I had these complete thoughts about how the things he was talking about worked."

"Wow. You surprised yourself, did you?"

"Yeah, kinda."

"Let me ask you something. Have you ever walked out of your house and forgotten something you were supposed to take with you?"

"I hate that. I'm always going back to get something or another."

"The next time that happens, continue on. You never know what ˉˉˉˉ ˉˉˉ[1] is trying to tell you."

"Are you trying to tell me that my 'soul' is making me forget the mail?"

Ooo. Consciousness is a little miffed that this Not Doing may be a soul event. Appease the boy's reason a little and all is well.

"No, I am flat telling you that is the case."

"Come on. You just got done telling me that I spent several months letting my brain work out the changes I've had in what I believe. Now you are telling me that my 'soul' makes me forget things on the spur of the moment?"

"Who says it is on the spur of the moment?"

"What do you mean?"

"Aren't you a creature of habit?"

"Not that much."

"Not how much?"

"I'm not so predictable that I do things at the same time every day or every week."

"You're not?"

"No! I'm not."

"You know, I once knew this guy that worked for the phone company. He told me one time that it is amazing how punctual people are. Do you know that people make phone calls every day at almost exactly the same time? This guy worked in the billing office and he said that from month to month the same times would show up on bills for calls. For instance, in an office a guy would call out every day at 9:22 in the morning, every morning. But you are different, right?"

"I certainly hope so."

"Let me assure you that you aren't. I hope you become unpredictable, but at this point I'd say that is something you may aspire to one day."

"Yes sir, Mr. Gloom and Doom. Thanks for the vote of confidence."

"Think nothing of it."

"You really think I'm that predictable?"

Yes, I do think you are that predictable. But that would be too much of a blow at this point.

"I think your soul is trying to tell you something. I don't know if it's about predictability or not. Why don't you leave the stuff in the house and find out?"

"You know what? My head's starting to hurt."

"Poor baby."

"You don't have any pity on me at all, do you?"

"No. Why should I? If I'm easy on you, you'll never learn."

"What is it that I am learning, anyway?"

"You are learning the ways of a Shaman."

"Why do I want to learn that, again?"

"Because you were born to the Office of Shaman. I've known that since you first started coming around here and asking questions. Of all the places you could be right now or any time you've been here, why did you end up here?"

"I don't know. I just like coming by and shooting the shit every once in a while."

Oh, Bob. You can't still be thinking that this is all mere coincidence.

"Of course you do. Why aren't you still at the beach shooting the shit with the dude?"

"He didn't really know what he was talking about."

"And I do?"

"I don't know if you are full of shit or not. I do know that you make me think about things. Sometimes you make me think about things that I don't really want to think about until after I talk with you. Then I think about them a lot."

"Oh, stop. You make me feel so special."

"I mean it. Sometimes when you tell me things I can't get them out of my head for a couple of days. Then sometimes I can't remember a thing."

"That's good. Whenever you hear a new idea or a belief changes, it is best to not talk about it for at least nine days. That is another Not Doing you can practice."

"So you really take this Shaman thing on, don't you?"

"No. I gave all that up a long time ago."

"It doesn't look like you gave it up."

"I don't suppose it does, but for me, I function like a regular old guy most of the time. Whenever I need to talk to someone, then the soul takes over and the regular me is on hold until I've said what that person needs to hear. I don't suppose that any of that makes sense to you at this point, but that is the nature of being a Shaman."

"It doesn't really sound that weird. Sometimes when I was talking to the dude at the beach it was like something else took control and I was talking about stuff I didn't know I knew."

Okay, let's just reach back down there one more time and tie all this together.

"Shamans call that something else the Other."

"That's a good name for it."

Yes it is. Using the word "soul", especially for you, is nearly misleading. The word "Other" is more nearly accurate. The Other is really another part of us and a part that is rarely allowed to express. Those who can naturally use the Other to express really should be set apart to their Office. I wish there were another word for "Shaman." That would make this whole process have more meaning. Still, we are limited by the language we use and that is part of the process.

Points to Consider:

1. The teacher told Bob about Not Doing as though it was a common concept.
2. But he tied it to the Other.
3. The teacher suggested that Bob practice Not Doing through promoting common forgetfulness as a teaching tool of the Other.
4. The teacher lauded Bob for using Not Doing at the beach.
5. Bob now considers Not Doing as part of a natural order, which it is.
6. Bob will now be able to observe what he does specifically through Not Doing.
7. Bob also has used Not Doing to allow the Other to express ideas and thoughts which Bob was not aware of having.

Chapter 6: Honesty

"A friend is someone who tells you when you err."

— Anonymous

The greatest challenge of communicating is having the courage to say something that is, without doubt, going to upset someone. If the Shaman tells the truth, he can face the likelihood that no matter what he says, someone is going to be upset. This is a dilemma, but the alternative is to agree with untruths. If the Shaman is going to be honest with himself and with others, then he may not Agree to perpetuate untruthfulness in himself. This makes it difficult to communicate with those who wish to have his Agreement about solving problems because they may not enjoy honest communication.

Honesty with one's self is hard. Honesty with others is harder. We all guard secrets which we think that only we know. These secrets can destroy us. We may guard secrets about who we really are, or what makes us cry, what we enjoy, or even what we fear and these secrets are our little lies to ourselves and to others. When we humans learned to lie, we began to divide the amount of thinking machinery available to problem solving. It is honesty which we must reclaim in order to progress on the path of knowledge.

One aspect of honesty, or dishonesty as the case may be, which is particularly debilitating, is blame. Blame is a convenient method of not looking at something real. Part of the reason we all like to blame others so much is that we often do not understand the truth about an instance and, rather than discover the truth, we simply blame a nearby patsy and kid ourselves about what actually transpired. This type of event does not define honesty.

Blame is debilitating because we cannot learn from the event, nor does blame make maximum use of the thinking apparatus. If we are presented with an opportunity to learn and we take the blame shortcut, we waste a perfectly good thought which could easily serve us for the rest of our life. The worst part of blame is that it prevents us from dealing with the real world. For instance, if someone steps into a hole in a sidewalk on a city street, the common reaction would be to blame the city. "If the hole wasn't there I wouldn't have stepped in it," we say. That part is true, but it does not allow for us to be responsible for our actions. The truth of the matter is that we didn't see the hole and we did a dumb thing by stepping into it. It is not necessarily our fault nor is it the fault of the city that we weren't paying attention to where we were walking. Assigning fault won't fix clumsiness and if we blame someone else for our lack of attention, then we have failed to learn to watch where we are going.

This is a silly example, but it points to the type of honesty a Shaman must practice. At times, an individual may have a program which was learned in childhood. The program may not have worked then and still doesn't, but until it is recognized and changed it will continue to run our life. Some childhood programs are easy to recognize. No one thinks there is really a Santa Claus and no one holds on to that thought for a lifetime. We are likely to think that mom or dad tried to control our life, however. Until we become adults, mom and dad do control our lives within certain limits. When we become adults, we need to understand that the reason we survived childhood was the result of that control. Many people carry anger on into adulthood concerning the control that mom and dad were obligated to exercise. Such anger can be hidden from an individual because he uses it to look at the world. It is part of his description of the world to think that he is still being controlled and that individual may be confused as to why he erupts in anger over seemingly innocent encounters. It takes Brutal Honesty to identify and eradicate such long-term programming.

It is only through honesty and, at times, only Brutal Honesty, that we can realize the truth of our experiences. We must take care that we don't enjoy the brutality more than the honesty, particularly when we are dealing with programming in others. It is a fact of the Shaman's life that he will deal with programming in other people. It is the only way he can hone the skills necessary to look deeply into his own programming. To deal with programming in others, the Shaman will, from time to time, have to say things which the other person will not like. The Shaman has to be Brutally Honest about some issues or he will be a sidelined spectator who simply watches the world go by.

Clarification:

Brutal Honesty is a term which seems to some folks to be too, well... brutal. Some people would like to have only a modicum of honesty. Certainly a little honesty is much better than no honesty at all, but that level of honesty simply won't serve the Shaman. While considering the way to present this concept, several terms were considered. Merciless Honesty would have been another choice, for instance.

The problem here is that the honesty required is actually more like the honesty of the lion. Food to the lion is food. It doesn't make any difference to the lion if the food is gazelle, water buffalo, or missionary. It doesn't make any difference if the gazelle has been a good gazelle or if the missionary is a pious meal. To the lion, fresh meat is fresh meat.

To make this concept more nearly personal, we need to consider it from the stand point of our life and death. At the end of our life we will have the reality of how we lived. If we have made a difference with our life, then we will continue to affect future generations. If we have practiced politically correct honesty, we will leave behind a politically correct effect. If we have practiced socially acceptable honesty, we will leave behind a socially acceptable effect. If we have employed the type of honesty called for here, then we will leave behind an uncompromising effect.

If anyone feels that the term Brutal Honesty is too stringent, then please coin a term which means the same thing for you. The word is not the thing. In this case, the words used have been chosen to point in the direction of the event. It is the event, not the word, which carries the power.

Programming exists which carries painful memories. Most of the time, remembered pain is more perception than reality. In other words, let's say that an individual experienced an event when he was in first grade or at a family reunion during early childhood. The individual may not have understood anything about what was going on, but he heard people laugh. The laughter wasn't directed at him, but if he thought it was and related the laughter to an action he was performing at the time, it could cause a painful memory. The pain may be all perception, but the program written during that event could still be running and would still be controlling action. To the individual with that memory, the pain is real and if the pain is even lightly touched, defense mechanisms can go into effect. Defense mechanisms such as blame can be activated so the pain isn't experienced again.

As the Shaman examines his own painful programming, he develops the tendency to be callous with pain. He tends to view painful memories as commonplace events which are necessary to eliminate. He also tends to forget the first time he experienced a painful memory when he encounters painful memories in others. It is at this juncture that the Shaman's true character makes itself known. If he can develop kindness with his fellow man while he deals with their pain, then he will progress on toward knowledge. Yet kindness is sometimes terrible to those it visits. For some people the greatest kindness is to show them the brutal truth, but the brutal truth can be painful and some people cannot accept that kind of truth without blaming the messenger.

For example, it is obvious that an honest parent wouldn't allow a child to cross a busy street by himself. That parent would certainly not allow his child to play on the same street. But would an honest friend tell that same parent that their cocaine use is more dangerous to the child than allowing him to cross the busy street? Would he tell a father that resolving problems with his wife is necessary for the child's well-being?

Honesty extends beyond this point. The Shaman owes honesty to those he councils. Yet he also owes honesty to himself. The crux of this issue has to do with what has been called energy. There is a strength involved with streamlining programming through honesty and that strength could certainly be called energy. Whether that strength can be converted to energy is a question which each individual needs to answer for himself. But should that father begin to resolve his problems with his wife, then hasn't the child's whole life been changed? Is there energy in this equation for the child? Would the father have more energy? Would the mother? Would the friend who dared be brutally honest have more energy?

If a Shaman or anyone else wishes to be honest with those around him as well as himself, then he has to find a way around the Agreements which other people want for their pet programs and general dishonesty. How can the Shaman agree that a particular foible is unavoidable? How can he agree that a lie in any form is an acceptable substitute for reality? If he stands against the lie, won't he alienate those he wishes to aid? The truth is often a frightening prospect and a Shaman may not have time to appropriately deal with an individual who actually asks for his help. The father may be so incensed that the Shaman was honest that the situation escalates too rapidly for reason. The only option left to protect the child may be blunt, well-crafted statements which the father has to deal with at another time. The father must love the child even if he becomes angry at the moment about the truth of his situation. The blunt statement may evoke anger at the time, but in a few days or weeks, the truth may weigh heavily enough that the father will have to accept it.

Added to this dilemma is the idea that the Shaman is often forced to wrap his activities in a shroud of mystery. In the days of the Tribal Shaman, he really couldn't talk with Tribal Bubba directly about programming, for instance, because neither one had the language which would describe programming. Was the Tribal Shaman fudging the truth when he told Tribal Bubba that he had to follow the warrior's path? If today's Shaman told our present day Bubba that he had to follow the warrior's path, would present day Bubba understand any better than Tribal Bubba would have understood the concept of writing programs to effect self-improvement? If today's Shaman faced having to talk to the wayward father, would he be able to explain the probable path of events for the child or would he have to wrap his statements in a cloak of mystery?

Today's Shaman may have less need for mystery than the Tribal Shaman, but if today's Shaman is to be believed or trusted, then he must craft responses that allow him to deny Agreements with falsehoods and at the same time court the time necessary for any other individual to work his way through his programming so that he can arrive at the truth on his own. At times, the only method available to today's Shaman is to resist negativity so hard that those to whom he directs his resistance interlock with his statements and demonstrate that interlock as anger, sustained anger. "I'll never talk to you again" anger.

A true statement is, "Excitation causes interlock." Some people like their negative programs. They will defend those programs to the death, it seems. They are often very proud of that programming and will do everything they can to defend their own self-destruction. Sometimes a Shaman has no alternative but to excite such a program and "make" the individual "mad." The longer the individual talks to himself about why he is "mad" the more likely he is to resolve the issue. He will still be "mad" at the Shaman, but the self-destruction will fade away. This is a dangerous ploy, but can be very effective. The question is if the Shaman owes that much to the person. He may or he may not. It is certain that he owes himself the ability to look in the mirror in the morning and like what he sees.

The withdrawal of Agreement from a program will effectively cause its demise. It may take a good deal of time to pass away, but it will go. In between time, it will be struggling for survival and, like all living things, it won't go peacefully into that dark night. But the most important reason for honesty for the Shaman is that he, in the course of his work, will go into places in his mind or in his spirit that will be indistinguishable from hallucination. It is common, for instance, for Shamans to see energy lines on the surface of the earth. If no one else can see those lines, does that mean that the Shaman is hallucinating? Only the Shaman knows the answer to this. To tell the difference between a hallucination and an actual, reliable event requires an honesty which is well beyond simple morality. This is an honesty honed to ruthlessness. The Shaman must apply this type of honesty to his personal experiences. Without this extreme honesty, the Shaman will lack the loving caring born of the realization that, "There, but for the grace of God go I."

Honesty is the only kindness any individual can offer. Anything less than honesty perpetuates pain and misery. This is not a popular concept, but kindness requires that it be presented here. A Shaman, because of his honest kindness, cannot allow himself to be swayed by popular ideas and must remain true to himself. As he strives to alleviate pain and misery in himself, he will be nearly forced to alleviate pain and misery in others.

Things to do to better understand "Brutal Honesty"

Differences and Brutal Honesty are closely related. They are both subjective ideas which we control, more or less, with objective or conscious thought. A major Difference is that every time we tell a lie, there is a moment of decision which passes through consciousness. Even though we consciously note Differences, we can allow subjective or other-than-conscious thought to override the noted Difference.

Tell a lie or perpetuate an unfounded or untrue rumor. Even if you are questioned about the veracity of the untruth insist that it is, "How you heard it." Continue in this vein for nine days. At the end of the nine days go back to everyone to whom you told the lie and straighten it out. In other words, tell the truth, but the whole truth. Note the Difference in you when you lie and when you tell the truth. Don't defend the lie or your reason for telling the lie. This should allow you to recognize the pain that someone else feels when they tell a lie and are caught in it.

Choose an acquaintance who is "kidding himself" about something important in his life. Make sure that you understand the nature of the situation. Then, using a third party example, explain how unfortunate the situation is for the third party. An example might be someone who is racist. You would tell a story of someone in a different race who is racist and how that person's racism negatively affects his quality of life. Allow the acquaintance nine days to mull over the import of your story. Check in on the acquaintance to see if the story had the desired effect. If it didn't, tell the story again, but this time use the acquaintance as the principal character, then duck. The alternative to ducking is perpetuating racism in you and your acquaintance. If you don't *disagree* with racism, then you must *agree* with it. That's as Brutally Honest as it gets.

Racism is, obviously, an extreme example and even though cheating on a spouse isn't perceived as such an extreme social problem as racism, the Shaman would have little choice but to *disagree* with either action. The reason for disagreeing with either action is the same. Both actions are socially unacceptable and cannot be allowed in the Shaman's life.

Here's a situation from real life. Work this out using a pro and con tally sheet. You as Shaman or concerned citizen, as you wish, encounter a Midwest farmer. Some five to seven years before you meet the farmer he fell on hard times and had to go down to the local widget factory to earn money to pay the mortgage. He was good at making widgets because the particular widgets he was making are large and he can use his knowledge of heavy equipment to understand the widget making process.

However, due to his independent farmer mentality, he soon finds himself at odds with the shop foreman. The nature of the conflict is that the farmer comes a good distance to work and is often "late" due to his responsibilities back on the farm. He works late many nights to make up for his tardiness but, try as the farmer might, the foreman just doesn't think that the farmer is a "team player." The farmer, of course, notices the cold shoulder he gets from the foreman and begins to be a bit aggressive and even abusive toward the foreman. The foreman, of course, takes his case to Management, who reviews the work record of the farmer and finds that his efforts are causing an increase in widget production. Management sides with the farmer and chides the foreman for not solving his "farmer problem" long ago. The foreman, now dutifully chastised and with his grandiose feelings hurt, begins to take any and every opportunity to make life difficult for the farmer. The farmer provides the foreman with many opportunities.

This situation continues for about 18 months until the farmer develops chronic lower back pain. The farmer soon goes to his doctor and the doctor tells him the pain is due to the movement he makes down at the widget factory. The farmer takes the doctors written opinion back to the factory and presents it to the foreman and states that he (the farmer) expects that the widget company insurance carrier compensate him for lost wages. The insurance carrier soon sends the farmer to their bank of doctors to determine if the farmer is telling the truth about the pain or not. The insurance doctors can't find anything physically wrong with the farmer, but do acknowledge that he is suffering from severe and chronic lower back pain. They order an operation. It fails to alleviate the pain. They order another one with the same results.

In the meantime the widget factory management realizes that they are open to a lawsuit from the farmer and hire their own lawyers. Their problem is: What if the farmer decides to sue them for the actions of the foreman? The foreman followed company procedure with the farmer and couldn't allow everyone the same latitude as the farmer. The insurance company sent their lawyers to investigate the farmer and the widget company. The whole thing was getting a bit expensive for everyone involved.

About this time you, as Shaman, are introduced to the farmer. You have three conversations with him while he sits in a rocking chair in his kitchen. You notice that movement can produce excruciating pain for the man, but you also notice that every time he talks of the widget factory he does two things. The first is that he states that the foreman, "just wouldn't listen." When he mentions this he lowers his left shoulder. He then follows that statement with, "I just wanted to do a good job and get out of debt." As he says this, he lowers his right shoulder. During your three interviews with the farmer you hear these two statements back to back perhaps 30 times. After the third or fourth such statement you also notice that he has to stop and ask his wife for some of his pain medicine.

It is obvious to you that he is reprogramming the event over and over. You also notice that his pain seems to be connected to the reprogramming event because each time he lowers a shoulder he tenses his back. That tension never seems to be relaxed in any of your conversations. What do you do? You can see that the only solution is to put the farmer and the foreman together to talk through their differences. Still... there are the lawyers and there are the doctors and there are the millions of dollars already spent on operations and legal fees. Those lawyers aren't likely to cotton to the spirit of the owl or giving the farmer peyote. Those doctors don't even want to know that the operations weren't necessary. The widget company management doesn't want to run the risk of the farmer getting even more ammunition against the foreman. So what do you do? The solution to this problem actually required Brutal Honesty.

The actual solution to the farmer's physical problem took place in the break room of the widget factory. The farmer, the foreman and the Shaman were present. After the bile was expressed by the farmer and the foreman, the Shaman asked them both if he could state what he saw as the problem. They both agreed. The Shaman stated that neither man was correct nor was either man wrong. He said that the foreman had a job to do and part of his job was to make sure people came to work on time. He said that the farmer didn't have the factory work ethic, but that he was a hard worker just trying to keep his farm by doing the best he could. Then he shut up. The foreman agreed that the Shaman had essentially stated his position. The farmer then released his pent up frustration while stating that he understood that the foreman's job was to enforce work time, but that he had spent his life in the field working until he was done. He said that he never thought about how a factory had to operate.

In fact, he had thought that the factory workers were lazy and that the foreman encouraged them to be lazy. Both men had other things to say, but nearly all of it was in the same vein.

A month later the farmer was loading hay in his fields.

Points to Consider:

1. Honesty cultivates empathy.
2. Honesty, like charity, begins at home.
3. Honesty cannot be taught.
4. The greatest kindness to oneself is Brutal Honesty.
5. The Shaman must possess honesty in order to progress on his path of knowledge. Without it he will never be able to discern reality from hallucination.
6. A common activity for the Shaman and nearly anyone else is Agreement. To actually Agree with another person requires a special type of honesty. It is an honesty of kindness and an honesty of protection which must be enacted ruthlessly by both parties to the Agreement. An Empathy, if you will.

Story Chapter VI

I have to talk to Bob about honesty. It isn't that he is a habitual liar, it's that he kids himself a lot. He lives in a world where kidding yourself is the norm. It's accept-able in that world, but it is not acceptable in the world he's beginning to inhabit.

I've noticed that Bob doesn't ever talk about his mother. I'm betting that this is a subject that he has hidden away somewhere and will require a good deal of intensity to get him to actually bring up those memories and talk about them. Since he doesn't have a steady girlfriend and he isn't gay, there is something about his relationship with his mom that he needs to look at.

It's good that this subject matter is about a woman. Honesty of the nature he needs to learn is feminine in nature. I call this type of honesty Brutal. Brutal Honesty gets right down to the nitty-gritties and looks at things the way they actually are. It isn't polite, it doesn't care about how anyone feels and it bares the soul. In short, it is Brutal. It will feel that way to Bob and it may hurt his feelings some. That can't be helped. This is a step that he will have to repeat many times in his journey and a step that everyone who is born to the Office of Shaman must repeat. It is a necessary part of the learning process.

"Bob, I notice you don't talk much about your mom. Why is that?"
"I don't remember my mom very well. She took off when I was little."
"Where did she take off to?"
"She lives somewhere out west. Arizona, I think."
"Do you talk to her much?"
"I don't ever talk to her."

Three questions and already the fight or flee Programming is in evidence.

"Why is that?"
"She took off, I didn't."

This is well defended and encased in thick walls.

"So?"
"What kind of bitch would take off and leave her kids?"

Bitch? That's a heavy word to use to describe anyone's mom. I need to be gentle with this for a couple more questions, at least. See if I can coax the story out before he runs.

"I don't know, but it doesn't sound like you have the whole story, maybe."
"I have all the story I need to have."
"Oh, boy."
"What's that mean, 'Oh, boy'?"
"It means that you are probably kidding yourself about a bunch of things. That's what it means."

"So what do you think I'm kidding myself about?"

"What's the 'all the story you need to have'?"

"She took off. She left my dad, my sister and I and took off for Arizona. What kind of woman would do that to her kids? Where was she when I had to talk to my sister every night about where she was? Where was she when my sister cried herself to sleep every night? The bitch just took off and left us to fend for ourselves. That's all the story I need. Why?"

"You seem to be a tad defensive about these questions."

"I'm not defensive. I'm just being honest."

My dear old daddy used to say not to look a gift horse in the mouth. I'll need to put a good deal of pressure on honest here, but since we're dealing with adages, strike while the iron is hot.

"Right. If you're being honest, cows can fly."

"What do you know about it? Did you wake up every night crying for your mom? I did until I wised up."

"You wised up, did you? Exactly how did you wise up?"

"One day it dawned on me that the bitch wasn't worth wasting my time on. That's how I wised up."

"So how old were you when you 'wised up'?"

"I don't know. Maybe seven or eight."

Okay, Bob, here it comes. This won't hurt much but you have to take a look at what you are saying.

"Christ. You are allowing yourself to be run by a seven or eight year old? I would agree that when you were seven or eight, that was a pretty good way to face a situation you couldn't understand, but you're grown now."

"Well, she's still a bitch."

He accepted part of it. That's good. Now let me try to be the good guy for a little while. Keep the cadence at about three cycles per second.

"What if you made a mistake way back when you were seven or eight? What if you decided without having all the facts? What if she had reason to leave?"

"What reason could she have had to just take off and leave us like that?"

There's the voice of that betrayed little eight year old. That little guy didn't have anyone to take his side when his mom left. He thought that she would support his rebellion towards his dad and then she up and left. Keep it slow and give that little guy some help.

"Well, I can think of a bunch of reasons."

"Yeah, well none of them will change how I feel about her."

Let's see if some real facts will help the little guy make the transition to adult.

"Yeah. Are you aware that the human brain is hard-wired in certain ways that we really can't escape? Take a woman for instance. A woman will die to protect her children because she is hard-wired that way. So you're telling me your mom is hard-wired in a different manner, is that right?"

"I don't know how she's hard-wired and I don't want to know."

"You know what I think? I think you are flat out lying. I think you want to know everything there is to know about your mom, but you are afraid to ask."

"I told you! I don't need to know anything about that bitch!"

Let's close this thing right here before he programs it all again. Keep it really slow.

"You may not need to know, but you *want* to know."

"Look! This isn't any of your business, so why don't you just butt out?"

I can't let him try to scare me off no matter how hurt he is. I can pull rank on an eight year old. Let's do that and paint the mom as a long-suffering saint. Eight year olds like that.

"Look yourself. You're going to hear this whether you want to or not. You are so full of shit about this that even I can't believe it. Do you actually believe that your mother never shed a tear about not being able to see you? Or are you too filled with your hate to even consider that one?"

"I don't have to consider anything just because you say."

Rank is good. Now let's bring this into the present. I need to push pretty hard because eight year olds respond to that.

"What are you going to tell me next, 'Eat shit and die'? I don't care about all your anger. If you want to lie to yourself, that's your right but I don't want any part of it. Your mama loves you simply because she's your mama. If you're not big enough to deal with that, God help you because I sure as hell won't. I don't know what the circumstances were that she felt she had to leave, but I'm sure you know more about it than you are allowing yourself to look at."

"I don't have to look at nothing. She left and that's it."

A few more sobs won't hurt. That was a heavy hit for a little guy. Too bad he didn't have anyone to help him out back then.

"Is that why you don't have a steady girlfriend or a wife? You afraid that if you had one she'd leave just like your mama did?"

"That's not any of your business."

Maybe not, but you need to have this brought up to real time. Besides, the subject at hand is Brutal Honesty. As much as this memory hurts you, you absolutely have to have this tool in your arsenal. The grass really will be greener on the other side of this fence.

"Yes, it is. I only deal with honesty. If you can't get honest with yourself about something as important as this is to you, then you can't be honest about anything."

"So what? I'm just supposed to forget it?"

Enough tears, now. It's time to get to the heart of this issue. I'll need to keep up the pressure so he doesn't regress.

"You're not *supposed* to do anything. Unless you want to keep on acting like an eight year old. That looks like it's working well, don't you think?"

"It works okay for me."

Keep it slow and keep it intense.

"Oh, yeah. Here you are all growed up and just pitchin' a bitch 'cause your mama left you. You don't have a real relationship with *any* woman because you're afraid you might get your feelings hurt again. That's working really well. You're just doing great."

That got to the heart of the matter. He's been wondering about this one for his entire adult life. He couldn't even bear to look at it. Keep it really slow and ease him through it.

"What, the cat got your tongue? Look, all this anger about something that happened when you were seven or eight doesn't make a whole lot of sense. If you're serious about what it is you're learning, you need to be brutally honest. Not with me, but with yourself. You can't afford to be carrying this kind of baggage around on your shoulders. Now you can be as angry with me for telling you this as you want to be. I don't care. If it helps you out to get angry at me, then go for it.

"But before you run off, I want to tell you a story. When I was a little kid, my grandfather died. Actually, both my grandfathers died within a few months of one another. I took it pretty hard. One day I was sitting in class and didn't make it to the bathroom in time. I was, naturally, chagrined even though I didn't know the word at the time. When I came back from the lavatory, I was sitting at my desk looking out the window. I could see the field where my grandfather last cut hay. As I sat there lost in my sad, sad memory, my teacher called my name. 'How many grandfathers do you have?' she asked. 'Two,' I answered. 'No,' she said, 'you don't have any.'

"Oh, how I hated that woman. I cut her off from any Communication. I didn't even want to see the ground she walked on. But you know what? I never had trouble making it to the john after that. It took lots of years before I realized what a kindness she had done for me that day. The shame is that I never had the chance to thank her for her Brutal Honesty. She saved me from years of pain and misery with that one statement. She was the only friend I had. No one else had the courage to tell me the truth.

"Now you can take what I'm telling you about your mom and be mad at me for as long as you need to. I owe that to that teacher. But Hotdog, you need to find a better way to describe those events that are haunting you. I suggest that you get on the phone, talk to your mother and clear this up. That is if you're man enough to do it. If you're not, then keep on hating the woman. But if you can't handle this one way or another then I'm off you for life. Go on home and think about this. If you get it handled come on back and we'll talk about it some more. The choice is yours."

Too bad I had to be so tough on the guy, but he's been caught in a war between his mom and dad for many, many years. It has nearly paralyzed him. I don't know what they fought about and I don't want to know. They both used the kids as weapons, though. She would encourage Bob and probably his sister to rebel against their dad so he would suffer. He would be long suffering himself so he could show her how wrong she was. So she took off and left him with two rebellious children who he dutifully raised in spite of their rebellion. Bob seems to have gotten the worst of the deal. He has been a good boy for his mom and rebelled against his dad for all these years. It is strange behavior for someone who is so angry with the very person with whom he holds the rebellion Agreement. But then I shouldn't be surprised. Once a program is written it becomes the rule of our life until it is recognized and changed. Sometimes Brutal Honesty is the only method for recognition.

Points to Consider:

1. Bob was suffering with a program which had been written in childhood.
2. The teacher was honest with Bob in spite of Bob's full range of emotional defenses.
3. The teacher empathized with Bob's pain.
4. The teacher met each of Bob's emotional outbursts with equal strength.
5. Bob recognized the program and stopped defending it long enough to get another description or Point of View.
6. Brutal Honesty is not for the weak of spirit.
7. Without the mirror of honesty and another Point of View, Bob may never have recognized his program.
8. Excitation causes interlock and Bob was interlocked with this program because of his childhood fear.
9. The interlock was very strong and to break the interlock required that the teacher be as honest with himself as he was with Bob.
10. Bob was born to the Office of Shaman and, as Shaman, he cannot allow childhood fear to rule his life.

Chapter 7: Direct Knowing

*"You got to be careful if you don't know where you're going
because you might not get there."*

— Yogi Berra

When most people think of Shamans, they probably have an image of some half naked, ugly guy, a fur loin cloth tied around the waist with a leather thong, buffalo horns sprouting from his head, a peace pipe in one hand, a rattle in the other and blowing smoke in four directions over the body of some hapless soul gravely wounded in a clash with a Saber Toothed Tiger. An image, by the way, that most modern day Shamans have done little to dispel. Most of today's Shamans are looking for the path back to the way things used to be. They may be hoping to find some lost Spirit of the Bison wandering around looking for a home. To be Brutally Honest, they would do well to begin looking within, but not for any lost spirits.

There is a certain romance in harking back to yesteryear when things were simpler. It may very well be true from a romantic Point of View, but we don't live in yesteryear. We live here and now. If we practice Brutal Honesty with ourselves, then we must come to the conclusion that we cannot solve today's problems with yesterday's solutions. There are no answers in searching for the Lost Spirit of the Bison or the Lost Spirit of the Owl or any other lost spirit. Those are lost spirits and they were lost for a reason. They are no longer part of our world.

What the modern day Shaman really needs to find is how he knows what he knows. There is a difference between reading something, then saying that we know it because we read it, and experiencing something. There is no substitute for experience. It is an integral part of knowledge. Without experience, we cannot actually "know" anything. Perhaps it is better to say that the brain doesn't actually "know". "Knowledge" without experience must be defined as common belief. Therefore the first delineation a Shaman makes concerning knowledge is between what he knows and what he believes.

Clarification:

The word 'belief' is used in this text in many ways. Some beliefs are deliberate and some are not. When the Shaman 'believes', it is hoped that he is deliberate in his belief. Some of the beliefs which we as humans utilize are foisted on us by our own lackadaisical or peripheral thoughts and others come from early childhood Programming. The word 'belief' here refers to a rather casual act of acceptance which becomes a belief, for all practical intents and purposes.

Belief, as considered in this text, does not refer to the act of "accepting" a religious tenet as though true. It refers to a function of Delta brain waves. Another way of stating this thought would be that the word belief as used in this text refers to the things we learn as babies about how the world functions. For example, a baby who is learning to walk sometimes finds himself under a table. The baby learns that the underside of tables "really" have "really" hard obstacles. If the baby doesn't "really" pay attention he will bump his head on those "really" hard obstacles and it will "really" hurt. In other words, the baby learns that the table is "real" and must "really" exist. The baby therefore learns to treat the table as "real" or he continues to bump his head. Most babies learn to believe the "reality" of the table. There may be problems with other "real" things that babies learn to believe.

Actual knowledge exists only after three conditions have been met. First, an authoritarian or authoritative source shares information about an issue. Second, the issue is experienced. Third, substantiation is acquired about the experience from a third party. This is a prerequisite for any knowledge related to our common thinking machinery. A classical example is a baby learning to talk. Mom and Dad say to the baby over and over again, "chair, chair, chair." The baby then experiences chair. Baby crawls under the chair, licks the back of the chair, sits in the chair, climbs up on the chair, turns the chair over, walks by pushing the chair, and one day says, "Chair." Big brother or sister then says, "Hey, Mom, baby said 'Chair.'" Baby then *knows* "chair." All knowledge acquisition follows this same pattern. Without these three steps being fulfilled we don't *know*, we believe, or perhaps it is better to say that we don't know, but we kid ourselves into believing we know.

However, within the Shamanic experience there is also Direct Knowing, but the problem with this concept is that it can be a lot like making stuff up. To know and know how you know is the defining factor for what you know. For instance, if I ask if you have ever seen a purple cat with yellow polka dots, you are able to say, "No." If I ask if you have ever seen a black and white cat, you are able to say, "Yes." This is a silly example perhaps, but it points at a very important fact, which is that we all know what we know and what we don't know. Still, the Shaman deals with a set of information which is outside this defined set of knowledge. How is this possible?

A common myth is that Direct Knowing is a type of psychic phenomena which can be employed to pick the winning lottery numbers for next week's Tri State drawing. It isn't. Direct Knowing is a result of using all the tools in the previous chapters to sort out the things we think we know from the things we know and the things we believe. Once this is done, we have an inventory of what we know, what we think, and what we believe. This sorting act is called *recapitulation* in some Shamanic circles. Sorting through the memory for this inventory requires solitude and dedication. It is sometimes necessary to sort through the memory time and time again in order to achieve enough clarity to differentiate between what we ourselves know, think and believe and what we were taught or conditioned to know, think and believe. This is why it is important to know *and* know how we know the information used in a given program. The steps are to remember who told us a particular thing, to remember when we had the experience and then remember who agreed that the experience was real.

Clarification:

> Direct Knowing is accomplished by utilizing energy reclaimed through employing the other tools. It is an expression of what a Shaman does. Different Shamans will employ Direct Knowing in different ways. How any given Shaman employs Direct Knowing is a result of personal preference. The purpose of this passage is to *time bind* the steps of the process.

All this is a platform for understanding what constitutes information which comes to us from other sources. Other sources can include Dreams or savant-like flashes of understanding. The déjà vu experience is common to many people. This occurs when we are in a real life situation and something about the situation feels as though we have Dreamed the events previously. The Shaman may experience such an event as déjà vu or may even go into a Dream state during the event and get direct knowledge about what is occurring, but through a real time Dream. Often the Shaman will claim that his knowledge is a result of applied logic, but even he knows that is a smoke screen. In reality, this type of knowing is not applied logic; it is the result of Direct Knowing.

There is another type of Direct Knowing which is common to the Shamanic experience. In this type of Direct Knowing, the Shaman suddenly is aware of something in a manner which has no apparent connection to his experiences. There are two models which lend themselves to understanding this type of event. One model would say that the Shaman has a flash of genius. The other model would say that the Shaman has a savant "understanding" of what is pertinent. There is a scene in the movie *Rainman* where a box of matches falls on the floor and Dustin Hoffman's autistic character says that there were 432 matches which fell. This is a Hollywood example of a savant-like "knowing."

In either type of Direct Knowing, the Shaman would be hard pressed to explain how he knows what he knows at that moment. It is likely that both types of Direct Knowing are common to all humans, but because of the terrible weight of unresolved Programming, we cannot afford to be aware of the importance of these flashes of insight. Only the Shaman who has had the time and commitment necessary to sort through his experiences and tested his knowledge with others will have sufficient awareness to recognize Direct Knowing for what it is.

There are those who will say that this type of information comes from the soul or Other. There is certainly a good argument to be made in support of this claim. It is a model which requires but a little faith to accept and may be the best explanation available. Yet it is true that the Shaman will experience Direct Knowing, but only at the cost of *recapitulation*. Unless an individual has dedicated himself to the daunting task of *recapitulation* he can never be sure if his "flashes of insight" are a result of Direct Knowing or are the result of convenient hallucination.

To accomplish the *recapitulation* necessary to differentiate between having an active imagination and Direct Knowing requires the understanding of how Programming works for a given individual, understanding what Points of View have been changed, mastering Communication, understanding what Programming is used to view the world, disconnecting the internal dialog through Not Doing and being Brutally Honest with oneself. Without this rigorous self-examination of the Programming we use to look at the world, we cannot possibly know what we know. If we do not know what we know then how can we be sure about what is imagination and what is Direct Knowing?

For those born to the Office of Shaman, there are only two options for behavior. One is to take advantage of the talent he has and pay whatever price is necessary to accomplish the level of Shamanism he can with the tools he can understand. The other option is to ignore his talents and do nothing with them. This would be like a person being born with musical talent then studying for years to perfect that talent. Even though it would seem that anyone would opt to take advantage of his talents, the price is simply too heavy for many. What these skills actually are, as opposed to what one would assume them to be, are quite different. To someone without experience, Direct Knowing appears to be something on the order of a flash of knowledge which foretells the future. To someone with experience, Direct Knowing is a solution to a problem which does not seem to be connected to anything that individual knows. The future is rarely involved other than as a result of current Programming.

The same could be said of Programming, Not Doing, or any other of the tools we have covered. The shaman must be a paragon of sobriety and practicality. Hoped-for events such as seeing an aura do not occur with a sudden insight. It may occur, but first all the steps of learning must be completed and all the Shamanic tools must be utilized. Small realizations must be built on so that further realizations can occur. There is no piece of knowledge which one can learn which will cause all the pieces of the puzzle to fall magically into the proper order.

Within this thought is the idea of *suspending disbelief*. Most of us hear of Shamanic feats such as Direct Knowing and take the position that this cannot happen. This is an act of disbelief. It is logical in our culture to take such a position, but the Shaman must *suspend disbelief* in order to know how he knows what is possible and what is not possible for him. The problem which plagues logic is how it can be possible to accomplish "magical" feats. To the Shaman, magic is for the uninitiated and has nothing to do with the practical application of his knowledge. Shamans cannot "do" magic. They can do amazing things depending on how their energy and Programming are configured, but the application of Shamanic tools is nothing more or less than a practical approach to learning how to think about thinking.

Clarification:

There are times in any Shaman's life when Direct Knowing comes unbidden to the awareness of the Shaman. Disbelieving is no protection at this juncture. It is necessary for the Shaman, therefore, to suspend the act of disbelieving. Anyone can opt to not believe something, but it requires special knowledge to deliberately suspend disbelief while utilizing Not Doing to accumulate the understanding which results in a new Point of View or a new definition of real. In a struggle for his life, the Shaman must use his lifetime of discipline to Know Directly what he should do. Direct Knowing must be cultivated for these times. Direct Knowing is funded by the utilization of the other tools discussed in previous chapters. It is wise to maintain an energy "fund" to energize Direct Knowing. It is sometimes an energy drain to not believe something that is real like Direct Knowing.

Some things to do to understand "Direct Knowing"

Do you remember playing pretend games as a child? One kid would say that the fort was at such and such a boundary and then another kid would say that the river was at another place and a third kid would say that inside the fort was a house. Maybe nothing was visible, but every kid who played at the fort that day would add things and know where everything was whether there was something to mark that thing or not. Direct Knowing feels a lot like those pretend games. The Difference is that it isn't pretend.

One way to recover that feeling is to imagine the solution to a problem. Let's say that the problem is how your boss thinks about you. There is nothing about his interaction with you to tell you what he thinks, but you have the "feeling" that he doesn't like you. At this point you have nothing that can tell you anything. However, if you were to "imagine" what his problems might be, you could begin to "deduce" what his true attitude toward you is. If you were to "imagine" that he probably has to produce a certain amount of work to keep his boss happy and if you were to "imagine" that he has to keep peace in the work place family then you could "imagine" how you fit into his life. This is a simple exercise that anyone can accomplish.

So let's say that the problem is that you know how your boss thinks about you because your boss tells you that he simply doesn't like you, but you like the job. Now the problem is a bit more complicated. In this example you would treat your boss as though he were an enemy to be defeated. How would you defeat him? You could discover what he likes in terms of coffee in the morning, the type of sandwich he likes at lunch and cover for him when he is doing something that is against company policy. This would appease him perhaps, but it would also make you less than you may wish to be.

This time you need to imagine where his weaknesses are and why, precisely, that he doesn't "like" you. If he doesn't like you because of your work habits, then you must change them. If he doesn't like you for personal reasons, then you have the option of using his dislike of you against him and to your advantage. You would "imagine" what has caused him to think out of the natural order. You will "know" what that deviance is because he will have told you when he told you why he didn't like you. That thing is his weakness. It is something that he fears. Imagine how to use that fear to defeat him. All the Programming, Point of View, Communication, Difference, Not Doing, and Brutal Honesty skills will have to be used. Your task, if you choose to accept it, will be to defeat the tyrant by "imagining" how to use his weakness against him.

The Shaman often is faced with communicating with other people concerning all manner of subjects. A Shaman who has some mastery over Direct Knowing will be faced with the problem of other people who refuse to believe that his way of thinking is valid. His task is to find the program component that will *suspend disbelief* for that person long enough to insert the information that someone may need. Generally, the Shaman has only one shot at accomplishing this task. Try talking to an individual who "believes" in science. The task is to "Know Directly" what program component will *suspend* his *disbelief* long enough to get him to be Brutally Honest about the existence of the Other. Hint: Knowing how you know is a prerequisite.

Points to Consider:

1. Direct Knowing is an experience common to many, many people.
2. Direct Knowing for the Shaman is accomplished by study, *recapitulation* and accepting the natural order of thought.
3. Direct Knowing is a precursor to Intuition.
4. Direct Knowing may "feel" as though it is a logical process or a Dream, but when information which comes through Direct Knowing is examined, the logical "deductions" or Dreamed event has no exact placement.
5. Memory can play tricks. Keeping notes on things which seem to be Direct Knowing can help sort through memory misplacements.
6. *Suspending Disbelief* is an integral part of Direct Knowing.
7. Anyone can "not believe"; it takes no special skills at all.
8. To the Shaman, the world is a mysterious place and the things which are possible have no limit. That includes the things which are possible in the Human Being.

Story Chapter VII

I hadn't seen Bob for several months. I had heard that he got a job doing something with welfare which required him to counsel parents or check on them somehow. That would be in keeping with his Shamanic bent and it has, no doubt, given him a chance to apply some of the knowledge he is accumulating.

He was pretty angry about the whole thing with his mom. I knew he would be and I still feel bad that sometimes the only way to get through stuff like that is to break the walls down. I'm sure there are those who would say that breaking walls down is not as kind as they would like, but I am not interested in being kind in this case. I am interested in seeing if Bob has the mettle to become a Shaman. Even though I wish it could be gentler, I know better. If Bob has any chance at becoming a Shaman, then he will deal with things a lot harder on him than giving his mom a call.

One problem that Bob still has is that he can't see enough of the picture. It isn't time yet to reveal the whole picture to him but he is about ready for another piece of the puzzle. By now, he has had time to put some of what he has learned to use. He is accumulating experience and his experience is allowing him to begin to know how he knows.

"So how's your mom?"

"You never miss a beat, do you?"

I have to check to see what we can talk about, Bob.

"Not with you."

"Actually, she's fine. I went to see her a couple of months ago. Before you say anything, her side of things is a lot different than I imagined."

"Somehow I'm not surprised."

"Well, I was."

"Good for you. So, what brings you over here? I thought you'd be busy with your new job."

"Actually, it is what's going on at work that I want to talk to you about."

This is something new. He's asking a question about what is going on in his life. Cleaning things up with his mom has freed up lots of circuitry.

"What's going on? Can't get along with your boss?"

"No, I get along with him just fine. It's what's going on with me when I talk to people."

"What goes on when you talk to people?"

"Well, you know that I have to go to talk with kids and their parents about what is going on in the family. We get reports from neighbors or other family members and I have to go check it out."

"That makes sense. You would be a good man for that job."

"That's the thing. I'm great at it, but I don't know how I figure things out sometimes."

Oh, the Other is beginning to make itself known. No wonder he's spooked. He still doesn't have his issue with the Other resolved.

"You're a smart guy, why shouldn't you be able to figure things out?"

"It's how I figure things out that bothers me."

"So do I have to play twenty questions or are you going to give me some hints?"

"Okay, it's like when I go to see these families sometimes I know what the problem is way before they ever give me enough information."

Direct Knowing can be unsettling, that's for sure. I think I need to start slowing this conversation down. Maybe mid-Alpha will make him feel better for now.

"And the problem is?"

"I don't know how I come up with the information."

"You come all the way out here just for that?"

"Yes, I did. It's very disturbing."

"Why are you so disturbed about this?"

"There isn't any way I should be able to know these things and I'm pretty sure it's connected to what you have been telling me."

"Well, I'm afraid I don't know nothin' 'bout welfare chil'un an' their families."

"I'm not talking about that."

"Well, what is it that you are talking about?"

"How can I know or be aware or whatever it is about things before I know about them?"

"It's simple. You're beginning to develop Direct Knowing."

"You mean I'm becoming psychic?"

"I suppose, in a way, but that would be the sideshow explanation. Direct Knowing is something else. It is more of a tool than simply being psychic. Direct Knowing is connected to the soul. Some folks think that Direct Knowing is actually a moment when the soul pops up and tells us things. But to accept this explanation you'll have to suspend your disbelief about the soul, I'm afraid."

I should have covered suspending disbelief before this, but that can't be helped now. I don't think he will actually be able to wrap his mind around the idea. I'm going to drop him down into low Theta or high Delta to see if I can find a way to talk about this. Direct Knowing, like Not Doing, should be presented to stone sober consciousness. It is actually about the deep subconscious, but reason needs to be appeased or this will drive the kid nuts.

"Believe it or not, I'm not having as much difficulty with that as I used to."

"That's good, but I didn't hear that you say you understood."

"Well, I've thought about this a lot and it could be possible."

"That's good, but I didn't hear that you say you understood."

"This whole thing about the soul talking is just a little hard to swallow."

Okay, I have him past his fear, but reason is not happy about the soul jumping up and taking control.

"Yes it is, at least it is from your perspective. But you're still having trouble with this, right?"

"Well, not really."

"You're still having trouble with this or you wouldn't be here talking to me about it."

"Okay, there has to be another explanation. This whole thing about the soul is just too religious. I don't know if I can buy that."

It isn't about religion at all, but he doesn't have the tools to see that yet. Just keep it slow and see how he reacts to alternative explanations.

"Fair enough, let's say that what happens is that your dead ancestors or your guardian angel tells you these things. That make you feel better?"

"Come on. Don't mess with me. Tell me the truth."

The truth is that the Other is beginning to make itself felt in your life. Don't get too worried here, Bob.

"I told you the truth and you didn't like that so I'll tell you a lie and see if you like that better."

"When did you tell me the truth?"

"Just now. I told you that the soul is the one who lets you know about things, but you don't like that explanation. What is it you think you want to hear then?"

"You really believe in the soul stuff?"

"No, I know that is what happens."

"How do you know?"

"Ah! The right question. I know what happens for you because it is what happens for me."

"But how do you know it is the soul?"

"Because I spend time slowed down as far as I can be. Sometimes I think I actually make it to Delta brain wave frequencies, and when I do, I pay attention to the difference in how I 'talk' to myself. I, personally, don't favor the word 'soul.' I prefer the word 'Other'. But a rose by any other name, and so on."

"You really think those 'insights' come from the soul?"

"Do you have a better explanation?"

"That is circular reasoning."

"Maybe. But if the information doesn't come to you through regular thinking processes, then how else would it come to you?"

"I don't know."

Reason has him by the tail on this. He's down here in Theta-land, so I'll give him some reasonable explanations. I'll use the memory for the twister girls as the frequency to explain this. That might feel good enough for reason to be happy.

"Okay. Consider this. You've been sorting out a lot of old unresolved programs. You've been to see your mom and realized that things you thought were real weren't quite as real as you thought, right? You've been trying to give your dad some respect and that was essentially the same thing. As a result of just these two things, you've been freeing up a lot of circuitry. On top of that, you've been involved with a lot of families who, no doubt, had many, many experiences in common with you and your family. You may not have taken those things to the same destructive level as they have, but the important part is that you have a chance to look at lots of your own Programming in relation to theirs. Isn't that about the size of it?"

"That it is."

"Okay, maybe what's happening for you is that you are becoming an interpersonal relationship savant. If you don't like that one, then maybe you could say that you are a family relationship genius. It doesn't really make a bit of difference what you call it because you will have more and more experiences like these as you continue to clean out your own Programming."

From the look on his face I got some of it, but reason still isn't happy with having to move into the spare bedroom.

"You mean that it's going to get worse?"

"I don't know if worse is the word I would use. You will have more 'flashes of insight', if you will."

"I don't know if I want that to happen or not."

"I don't know if you want that to happen or not, either. Let me ask you something here. Why is it that you are so scared of the concept of the soul?"

"I'm not scared of the concept; I just have trouble accepting that what you're saying could be possible."

"From where I'm looking at this, you're scared of the whole concept."

"No, I'm not."

"Right. I'll tell you what. Why don't you practice a little *recapitulation*? That would give you a chance to go back over some parts of your life and see if you can't find out where your 'uneasiness' lies in relation to the term soul."

"You're so diplomatic."

"Uh huh. Do you understand the word *recapitulation*?"

"Not really."

"I didn't think so. What you do is to find some place which will afford you a minimum of sensory input. Then you make a list of significant events in your life. You start with one and you consider all the aspects of that event. You try to find out why you remember it, for instance. You try to remember how you felt and why. You relive it as much as possible and if it is still having an effect on you, change it so that it has the effect now that you want it to."

"What do you mean by 'minimum sensory input'?"

"Traditionally, that meant that you would go into a small, dark, quiet room where no one would interrupt you. You would see nothing but the walls of the room, sit on a chair, and remember the things on your list until you work your way through each item."

"Wow, that sounds like loads of laughs."

"It can be if you have lived a funny life, I suppose."

"Let me get this straight. You want me to sit on a chair for hours in a small, unlit room remembering significant events in my life?"

"I didn't say that."

"What did you say, then?"

"I said that was the traditional method of *recapitulation*."

"There's another way?"

"Yeah."

"Okay, what's the other way?"

"You could find a physical isolation tank and use that for your *recapitulation*."

"I've heard of those. In fact, I spent an hour in one, one time."

"Good for you."

"I didn't like it much because I got bored."

"Well, take your list and pick an item on it, then get in a tank and remember it. I doubt you'll be bored."

"How do you know?"

"I've spent a few hours in a tank."

"How many is a few?"

"Oh, I don't know, let's just say a lot. I can assure you that I was an emotional wreck afterwards. But then I tend to overdo things and take them beyond their limits just to find out. I wouldn't suggest that for you."

"But you're telling me to do a *recapitulation* in a tank."

"Yes, I am."

"So how is this going to help me when I know things about families that I don't have reason to know?"

"As I see it, you have two options. One is to accept that you are who you are and make the best of that and the other is to put your tail between your legs and run."

"Well, I'm not going to run."

"It's too late anyway."

"You are so encouraging."

"I just can't help myself. You are still going to have to suspend your disbelief. You need to take your unbelief or disbelief or whatever you want to call it and put it on the shelf for a while. Maybe six months or so, to start. If you find after that time you still need it, then take it down and put it back in place."

"What am I supposed to 'un-believe'?"

"Nothing. I'm simply asking you to suspend your disbelief. In other words, any damn fool can say I don't believe in this or I don't believe in that, but to deliberately put all that foolishness aside and see what you can see is an eye opening experience. You really shouldn't miss that."

What a weight is bearing down on Bob. It's terrible to realize that you're all alone and no one can help you. It is a necessary leg of the journey, but even that realization is small comfort.

Points to Consider:

1. Bob has progressed on his own to Direct Knowing.
2. That means that he has been applying all the other tools from Programming to changing Points of View to Not Doing to Being Honest with himself.
3. As a result, he has gone from reacting emotionally to acting deliberately.
4. Although it would be hard to imagine that Bob could admit it, he has placed himself in a position to use what he has been learning and to experience different Points of View by accepting his current job.
5. The Other is beginning to take control in his life.
6. The realization that consciousness may not be the only part of the "mind" that can or does "think" or supply information can be disconcerting at first.
7. Curbing the tendency to not believe it is possible may be the only comfort.

Chapter 8: Seeing

"Don't tell me 'bout your law and order
I'm trying to turn this water to wine."

— The Eagles, *On the Border*

As the Shaman begins to explore the numerous ways he can assemble the world, he encounters ways of helping others. One of the first methods anyone stumbles on is healing. Healing is certainly an art and there are those who invest a significant portion of their lives and daddy's money in learning to do it as well as it can be done. That does not mean that their methods are the only methods which can work, but it does mean that someone without their expertise had better be very, very sure about what he is doing.

For many Shamans, healing plants, massage and cleaning auras become convenient outlets for their talents. Others progress on and begin to manipulate the energy around the body to effect healing. The main difference between those who stop at plants and massage, and those who manipulate energy is the ability to move the Assemblage Point to a position which allows seeing or visualizing the aura or energy body. Both types of Shaman probably visualize or are aware at some level the energy which surrounds the body, but acute awareness of that body is necessary to manipulate energy. Some people refer to this acute awareness as Seeing.

Seeing isn't a tool, per se, but it comes as a result of using all the tools described thus far. Perhaps it is better to say that Seeing is an acquired ability which is employed by Shamans who have reached a certain threshold of understanding. Other tools such as Programming, Changing Points of View, Communicating, Making Differences, Brutal Honesty, Not Doing, and Direct Knowing can all be put to use by nearly anyone. Direct Knowing is the possible exception because it requires considerable preparation. Seeing is not the result of preparation. It is the result of accumulated knowledge.

Seeing includes many ideas and applications. Shamans *see* energy lines on the earth which in the Celtic tradition are called Ley lines and Dod lines. In the Chinese tradition they are called White Tiger lines and Dragon lines. Shamans *see* beneficial places on the earth. Shamans *see* the energy of the body. Shamans *see* the connection between people. Shamans *see* the bad energy some people send to others. Shamans *see* the way to correct those energies so that no one is harmed. Shamans *see* Programming in others and in themselves. Shamans *see* hidden events. The list of things Shamans *see* goes on and on but suffice it to say that Seeing includes many ideas and applications.

Seeing has been described as a visual event that does not include looking. It feels as though the eyes are involved, but it may be that it is nothing more or less than an extremely trustworthy or, perhaps, believable dayDream. Using the word dayDream to describe Seeing may be misleading, but someone who is new to this idea needs to have something familiar to compare the idea with, especially when trying to visualize the aura. Nearly every fledgling Shaman tries and tries to see auras. They will squint their eyes and strain to no avail. The reason is that Seeing requires a certain discipline which comes only after applying the tools.

Different Shamans from around the world ascribe different characteristics to the aura. They are all talking about the same thing, and the differences must be attributed to different ways of talking about a common event. Indian mystics and Tibetan Buddhists *see* the aura as lines of energy. Mexican Shamans *see* the aura as a luminous egg. South American Shamans *see* the aura with wheels of energy. In all cases, the Shaman or mystic is Seeing something which we collectively call an aura. That they all describe it somewhat differently denotes different belief structures as opposed to different things.

The most important part of the aura for healers and other types of Shamans are the Chakras. For healers, the Chakra set includes the Chakras in the hands. These Chakras are used by healers to impart energy, to absorb energy and to equalize energy. Some few Shamans even use the mouth for these same operations. There is always the question about how effective such ministrations actually are. It depends greatly on whether the Shaman has control of his energies and whether the person being healed wants to change. If the Shaman is only trying, then the results are very much less than effective. If the Shaman is actually in control of his energy, but the person being healed would rather die than change, the results are going to be less than effective. Every once in a while both parties are in Agreement for the healing to take place. The effect of this relationship is very effective, indeed.

Shamans who use medicinal plants and harvest them find the auras around plants to be very instructive. A plant with a large aura is powerful. The color of the aura will tell the Shaman the use for the plant. Some plants are useful for cleaning the nettles of life from an aura. Plant Shamans will know which ones will work for this type of operation. Other Shamans use smoke to *see*. Still others use sound. It doesn't matter what sense a Shaman uses to arrive at his non-ordinary sensory input, but it does matter that he learns to trust himself. Maybe all this is nothing more than using the brain in inventive ways and maybe it is a different slice of the reality pie. After all is said and done, all sensory input is a matter of interpretation. It is what we do with the sensory input that counts, not how we collect it.

For many Shamans, the ability to *see* is translated in the brain to familiar images. There are some who say that Seeing in terms of familiar images indicates that there is still work to be done. This may or may not be true. Because Seeing is a necessary step in the development of the Shaman, it may be more important to take Seeing as it comes rather than striving for perfection. There are many of today's Shamans who use this type of Seeing to great effect. For instance, there are many practicing seers who seem to see images of problems or of the future and so on.

Some of those who claim to be seers but have not mastered other tools would have to be somewhat suspect, especially those who seem to go on fishing expeditions in order to "see" problems in a given subjects life. However, it is also true that in order to make sense of the jumble of visual images which seers sometimes must sort through, it may be necessary to ask questions to know which images pertain to a given problem. There are those who seem to have a connection with Seeing in a manner which suggests a natural talent. Yet, it is difficult to give trust to anyone who does not exhibit Brutal Honesty in himself, for instance, for an individual who cannot accept other Points of View. Even if Seeing is a "talent" for such an individual, it would be nearly impossible for him to know how he knows because it would be highly unlikely to have completed a *recapitulation*.

There are many Shamanic disciplines practiced throughout the world. Some claim saints as the source of their power. Some claim spirits of one nature or another as the source of their power. Others claim different forms of deities as their source of power. There are even those who claim angels. Each discipline is constructed to support the source of power as described by that discipline. Because there are so many different "sources" of power, it is most likely that the name of the source is not the actual source. It is more likely that the seers in a given discipline have adopted a name for the source as a convenience. Since nearly every discipline claims some sort of spiritual entity as their source of power, it would probably be more nearly accurate to say that while the source of power may, indeed, be spiritual in nature, it is not likely that it is any given or named entity. It may be that Edgar Cayce's description of some sort of shared human memory would be more nearly correct.

Cayce claimed that he drew from the Akashic Records. Bear in mind that some of Cayce's claims are difficult, at best, to substantiate. For example, DNA testing has demonstrated that modern man dates from about 60,000 years ago. While there were other branches of the human family tree which date back well before that time, it is difficult to substantiate Cayce's claim that man is much older. Still, the idea of some sort of race memory may not be as far-fetched as it would seem. There does seem to be evidence of some kind of interconnectivity between people.

It doesn't really change anything to rename Seeing in any way which is convenient because each seer must find his own method for explaining what he *sees* to himself. If he can grasp an explanation which makes sense to him, then others may agree or not. The proof will be highly personal in any event. The idea is to apply as much discipline as possible to the Dreamlike images which come to all Shamans at one time or another.

The reason that the Shaman who can visualize a model of the energy body makes a good healer is that he *sees* the difference between an ordered natural state and a state which is out of order. With practice, he may note dark areas in the energy which tell him where there are problems in the actual body. This is not replacement for a doctor's care. It is an aid. There is a natural order to things and we all know what that order should be even if we don't follow it. A Shaman skilled in Seeing the natural order will immediately know where the order has been interrupted and know what to do to restore the natural order.

We sometimes refer to this type of recognition as "plain old horse-sense." There is an element of "horse-sense" involved with this practice of Shamanism, but it is more than common sense. It is common sense to understand that if you keep doing the same thing while expecting different results, you are a practicing Looney. Yet it is something else to be able to know why someone is doing the same things and craft an Agreement for a different course which is acceptable to the other person. Back in the days of Tribal Bubba, charting the natural order was a very learned accomplishment. Tribal Bubba may not have had the wherewithal to understand that his wife was jealous of his philandering ways. Tribal Bubba wouldn't have understood the word, much less the action. But the Tribal Shaman could have told Bubba that his food would be warmer and his wife would bear more sons if only he were to go to a thermal spring early each morning and bring a deer's stomach full of hot water home so that the Spirit of the Water Vapors would soften his dearly beloved's brow. Tribal Bubba would have fulfilled his mission, his dearly beloved would have wondered what got into the boy and the Tribal Shaman would have been considered to be a powerful Magician.

It is hard to sell the idea of the Spirit of the Water Vapors in today's market. The idea would have to be repackaged for our present day Bubba. Today's Bubba is much more educated and he knows that there is no such thing as the Spirit of the Water Vapors, but he will agree that if he doesn't want his Sweetness and Light to divorce him and take half of everything including the pick-up, he will have to try a little tenderness. That today's Shaman has to repackage his presentation is part of his art, but he can still *see* the natural order of things.

Some things to do to better understand "Seeing"

A common application of Seeing is seeing the human aura. There is an exercise to learn this art. You start by imagining that you are inside a rectangular tube which extends down below your feet by the length of your body and above your head the same distance. You take this imaginary tube and bend the lower part up and the upper part down so that you can join them in front of your solar plexus. Once the two ends are joined, you disconnect one end and give it a half turn, then rejoin the tube so it is complete. Now imagine that there is a green colored flow of energy passing through the tube. The energy starts at your feet and moves up through your body, then comes out your head and makes the half turn inside the tube where it joins in front of your solar plexus before it starts all over again coming up through your feet. This is a wonderful exercise in that it aids the person trying to *see* to begin to visualize what he wants to perceive. It has the added benefit of amplifying the energy needed to heal himself and others.

The tube forms a Mobius band which is a one-sided, three-dimensional object. You can make one with a piece of paper by simply cutting a strip of paper about one inch wide and eight inches long. Don't fold the paper but gently join the two ends together by giving one end a half turn. Trace the sides. You will find that there is only one side and it goes all around the paper. In fact, there is only one side or edge to the object. If you cut the paper in two by sticking a pair of scissors in the middle of the band and cut along the curve, you will find that you end up with a figure eight. If you cut it in thirds, you will end up with two Mobius bands. One will be the same size as the original and one will form a figure eight. There are those who say that this is how cells divide.

A further exercise is to imagine the figure eight as an energy flow between you and someone else. You may find that the person you pick to encircle with your imaginary figure eight energy flow will suddenly begin to deal with you more closely. A healing exercise is to imagine the Mobius band of another person with a part of his body held in the energy turn. For instance, if a person has an upset stomach, then you would imagine his stomach in the turn being washed green as the energy flows around and around the Mobius band. If you can imagine many, many tubes going around and around your body you would begin to get the idea of how the energy body functions.

Points to Consider:

1. It may be that every human being on the planet has the ability to *see*.
2. The thing that sets the Shaman apart from every other human is his discipline or his knowledge.
3. Power is most likely nothing more than applied knowledge.
4. There is a spiritual aspect to human nature.
5. The Shaman attends to that spiritual aspect.
6. Seeing is most assuredly connected to the spiritual aspect of humanity.
7. It may be desirable to assign certain attributes of Shamanic activity to spiritual beings which are "greater" than man.
8. Humans do not seem to be capable of maintaining honesty in the face of even seeming power.
9. Pragmatic discipline seems even harder to maintain.
10. Seeing may be the most seductive tool which a Shaman uses.

Story Chapter VIII

Bob has been to the tanks a few times and has begun his recapitulation. He is having some unexpected benefits or, from his standpoint, hallucinogenic experiences. The poor boy has begun to See. The first time it happened he actually saw the lines on the earth. I spent a couple of sessions with him just talking him down. He was sure he was having flashbacks. I don't know what he thought he was flashing back to, but he was a bit disturbed.

Since then he has focused his Seeing more on the people he is dealing with at work. Sometimes his insights are startling. He actually saw that one father was molesting his female children and stopped it. I guess the father was so scared that old Bob saw right through his BS that he got religion. Praise the Lord. I know he still doesn't understand Seeing but then there is a lot he still doesn't understand. The good news is that he Sees.

He came by one day not long ago and announced that he was terribly disturbed that one of his clients looked dark. A few days after that, the man died in an automobile accident. Bob was not pleasant to talk to. It shook him to the quick. I'm glad he had the experience but I could've passed on talking him through it.

"When I see how someone is, I want to tell them to stop doing whatever it is that is causing their problems. But every time I do, I just end up ticking them off. Why is that?"

"It's because you want to tell them directly."

"What's wrong with telling someone the truth? You told me the truth and even though I didn't like it at the time, I eventually learned from it."

"But you are a Shaman born to the Office and you're talking to Bubba and the Bride of Bubba. You need to put a little mystery around what you want them to know."

"How in the hell do I do that?"

"It's not as hard as it might seem. All you have to do is appease their reason."

"Appease their reason?"

"Yeah. When you are out there talking to folks who live in trailers and government housing about how they are supposed to be taking care of their kids, you *see* who they are, don't you?"

"Most of the time."

"So tell them a story that their reason will accept."

"What kind of story?"

"Oh, I don't know. You've talked with tarot card readers and such, haven't you?"

"Yeah."

"Well they almost always do that. They know better than to tell you that you have unresolved issues with your mother who passed away, so they tell you that the spirit of your mother is watching over you and that you should light a candle to her and ask her to help you find a job that will be better than flipping burgers down at Mickey D's. They don't tell a woman that she should treat her husband with a little respect so that he will treat her with respect. They tell her that her husband is thinking about leaving her and that she should ask a dearly departed loved one to intervene so that he changes his mind."

"I don't think I can lie to people like that."

It never bothered you before.

"Then tell them the truth and let them keep on doing what they are doing. Do you think they want to hear the truth? If you do, you're going to have some tough days down at the office. Of course, you are allowed to tell them the truth, too. The problem is how much of the truth can you tell them at one time? Can you tell them enough for them to understand why you think what they are doing is wrong or even disadvantageous? Is their attention span long enough to get what you are saying before they get angry? If it isn't then you may need to appease their reason with as much of the 'truth' as they can handle in this instance."

"Well, I can't lie to people."

He needs to slow down even more. Maybe it's time to explain some of who he is. As he clears more and more of his old garbage out of the way, his true nature as a Dreaming Shaman becomes more apparent. At first, I thought he was a Stalker because of how he used his energy to defend himself. It turned out all that was defensive maneuvers.

"So don't lie. Appease their reason instead. Sometimes people simply can't deal with the "truth" the way you are going to see it. You can certainly figure out a way to tell them the "truth" so that they can deal with it at their level. It isn't all that hard to do both things at the same time. Think about it like this for a minute or two. A few months ago, when you first started coming around could I have told you that your Alpha or even your Theta Programming needed a few adjustments?"

"No, I wouldn't have understood anything you were saying."

"Exactly. You didn't have the information that would have allowed you to understand what I was talking about, right?"

"Yeah."

"But I still had to 'tell you the truth' about a problem which was visible between you and your dad. So I told you to write a program to respect your dad. That was the truth, but yet it wasn't. The God's own truth was that you had to adjust some mid-level Theta Programming. It was also 'true' that you didn't respect your dad, even though it wasn't the Truth. Understand?"

"Kind of."

"Okay, this is the essence of Seeing. When you are talking to someone you have to be aware of the level of their ability to understand at that moment. You are trying to get them to understand a concept that may be more involved than any concept they currently understand. The onus is on you to find a level from which you can explain the concept. You have to be complete about it, but at the same time you may have to explain it in layers. It's kind of like building an onion one layer at a time. After enough layers, you have the Truth of the onion, but maybe there wasn't even one layer that was a 'true' onion."

"So you tell someone something that is true, but not necessarily The Truth."

"Yeah. You have to be able to *see* what they can deal with at the moment. You may be able to *see* that they can eventually wrap their mind around the whole concept, but at the same time you may be able to *see* that the subject is so new that an entire foundation needs to be laid to support the idea."

"So it's like what you are doing with me, right? You could *see* that I could eventually understand this thing about the Shaman, but because I didn't have enough information about the parts you've built a set of knowledge one piece at a time."

"Exactly. If I had started out by telling you that you need to *see*, for instance, it wouldn't have made any sense to you at all."

"Okay, I think I need to consider this a bit more, but it's a lot clearer than it was."

"You're really a pretty smart guy and I think you can do this without too much trouble. But now I think it's time for you to understand about something else, though. There are two basic types of Shaman. One is a Dreamer and the other is a Stalker. You are a Dreamer. You will always Dream better than you Stalk. That doesn't mean that you don't need to learn how to Stalk, though."

"What?"

"When you are out there talking to your 'clients' and you *see* what's going on in their lives, you are practicing Dreaming. There is much, much more to Dreaming than what you are doing at the moment, but we'll get to that as time allows. But for now, we need to talk about Stalking. You run out in your world of welfare recipients without a care in the world. In this respect, you are as careless as a kid with a gun. You're not even aware that you are in a fight for your life every time you encounter one of these 'clients.' You tend to think of yourself and not be aware that there are other forces at work about you. Tsk, tsk."

"I'm not careless."

"From where I look at things, you are. From where I look at things, you are much more concerned with being a good boy than you are with changing the behaviors of your 'clients'. 'I can't tell them lies.' So you put your life on the line for what? So you can go to heaven? So they will think well of you? I thought you were out there to make a difference with those people."

"I do make a difference."

"Yes, you do. But you are still more concerned about your appearance than in making a difference for them. You *see* what goes on in their lives and you think about how great you are that you can *see*. It irks you no end that they don't know what manner of greatness has passed through the portals of their trailer. Do you get them out of the trailer and out of the desperation that put them there in the first place? No, you don't. You simply scare them into being 'good little Indians.' If you were actually making a difference, you would craft what you say to them in such a way that they would be getting off welfare and getting a job and you wouldn't ever have to talk to them again."

The problem is that his ego is trying to claim what he is doing. It always has, so it's accustomed to taking credit. This is even more dangerous than talking to people about what he sees. Because he's so careless, he's liable to tell just anyone that he sees things in his head and therefore he knows. Add that carelessness to ego and you have someone trying to put out a fire with gasoline.

"That's pretty ambitious."

"Yes, it is. But then if you're not big enough to make that kind of a difference, then I'll just shut up."

"It isn't that I'm not big enough. It's that it isn't my job."

"Oh. You're not a human being."

"I'm human. I care."

"Of course you do. Just not enough to make an actual difference."

"That's not fair, and you know it. I'm out there every day. I see stuff that would make your hair stand on end and I do the best I can."

"Do you, now? You get them out of the trailer park?"

"No. That's not my job."

"Whose job is it?"

"I don't know."

"Oh?"

"I'm not supposed to counsel them about things like that. I'd get fired."

"I see. If you actually made a difference, then you wouldn't have a job. Do I have that right?"

"So what do you want me to do? Do you want me to be without a job in order to live up to some standard that you set for me?"

This is the problem with issues that pertain to both the conscious self and the Other. They have to be handled in Beta, but they pertain to Delta. If I take him down to Delta and simply program him, then he'll continue to use the now conscious Programming. If I don't program him, then I need to convince the conscious self that he's in danger. The danger is real, but he can't see it from consciousness. Let's see if I can cajole him past this.

"Remember that I'm not your dad. I'm asking you if you are big enough to make a difference. If you are, then job or no job, you will change realities for people. You need to understand that. It is what you were born to accomplish. But then I'm not talking about what you do while you are on the job."

"Okay, now you have me all confused."

"Thank you. I thought I was making perfect sense."

"If you are, I'm missing something."

"You're missing a lot, but that is for another conversation or two. For right now, let's just say that you aren't applying Shamanic tools to what you do. If you wanted to actually make a difference, then you would find a way to tell them so they don't suck all your energy up and leave you an empty shell. There is more of that happening than you think because every time you have Shamanic experiences with your clients you end up over here whining about how you don't understand this or that."

"I don't whine that much."

"That could be a matter of opinion. You don't even use your Dreaming skills to make a difference."

"How can a Dream make a difference for these people?"

"Haven't I told you about the Mobius strip?"

"Yes, you have. I *see* myself in a green stream of energy all the time."

"Good for you. Have you ever seen other people in a green stream of energy?"

"No."

"Why not?"

"I don't know. Why should I?"

"Because it helps them, that's why."

"It helps them?"

"Certainly. If you visualize other people in that same stream of energy, they get to feeling better about themselves. If you make that energy loop from them to other members of their family, then everyone gets to feeling better and they might even begin to get along."

"Why didn't you ever tell me that before?"

"I did."

"I didn't understand it, then."

"That's probably true."

"You mean if I visualize energy going around the members of the family, then they start to get better? How do you visualize that?"

"I don't know how you visualize it, but when I do it the energy makes a figure eight around each person. I first *see* lots of Mobius bands flowing around a person until the collective Mobius bands make up a ball or something similar. Then I *see* a piece of that energy make a loop that includes another person. Then that person cuts loose of some of his energy and amplifies the loop. If there are several people involved with an idea, then I include all of them."

"Does that work?"

"Why don't you try it and see?"

"So that would be using Dreaming, eh?

"Yep."

"So how does Stalking come into this?"

"When you first *see* someone as a Mobius band, it is often hard to *see* their energy as green. Sometimes it is the right color but really dull. Instead of it being a translucent green it is an olive green, for instance. Sometimes it is another color all together. Sometimes it is white, or gray, or red or some other color. There are times when you really don't want to change the color, but for your bunch I don't think you will do any harm if you keep it green.

"When you are trying to change the color, there is a part of you that knows why the color is wrong. A few days after you *see* the color and get it to change, then you will be able to tell them something that will appease their reason while changing some aspect of their Programming. Not only that, but what you need to talk to them about will just come welling up and you won't even know where it came from."

"You're Programming me again, aren't you?"

"Maybe a little, but I'm also telling you the truth. Of course if you don't want me to talk about this, I'll stop."

"No, no it's all right. But this sounds too simple."

"Well, it's easier to say than to do, if that's any consolation."

"So how does Stalking come into play?"

"The first rule of Stalking is to not enter into a battle unless it is worth risking your life on the outcome. When you begin to say what is welling up you need to decide before you open your mouth if this is something that is that important. If it isn't, then keep your mouth shut. If it is, give it all you got."

"So let me see if I have this straight. Before I go in to see my clients, I visualize these loops of energy running around each person in the family, then I'll be able to tell them how to get out of the trailer, as it were."

"Sort of. I think I would do the visualization stuff every day. But then I would do it before I go to sleep every night. If I were doing all this, which I'm not, I would *see* each one of my clients every day so that I could do the most good possible."

"So you're telling me to take my job home with me. That's great."

"Ooo, are we important folks or what? Yes, Bwana I take big cat. But Bwana, I take big cat between nine and five. If big cat come after da whistle blow, I come back tomorrow, maybe, if I am not otherwise occupied. Big cat heap big trouble, Bwana."

"I'm not like that."

"Well, you are like that in a way. I suspect that you see yourself as being kind of powerful, what with all this knowledge of Shamanism you possess and all."

"I don't know if powerful is the word, but I do think that I'm learning things that are not common."

"You are learning things that are not common, but you haven't considered that it is the learning that isn't common, not the things."

"Okay, say that again with more parts."

"All right. You've been learning about things that don't pertain just to a Shaman. Nearly anyone can accomplish any of the things we've talked about, even Seeing. What you have been learning is a particular way of arranging those things so that they can be used to your benefit."

"That's true."

"Because we've talked about these things in an order that might be connected to how they are stored in the brain, you have been able to sort through much of your own Programming. That sorting process has given you more circuitry to use for other thoughts. What you have learned so far is about how to order your thoughts and how to recognize events that might very well be common to anyone, even your clients."

"So I've been getting a little full of myself, huh?"

"I don't know if that is completely accurate, but maybe a little."

"I don't want to come off like a know-it-all."

"You don't. I think you just need to put some of this in perspective is all."

"That's fair."

"Look, this business about Seeing is an important tool. In some ways it means that you have ordered your thoughts to a great extent. But that doesn't mean that there isn't more that you can and will do. Being humble about your skills will keep you from driving yourself nuts."

"I think that maybe because all this is so new to me I sometimes get lost in what I know."

"That's a pretty accurate description. It might help you for a while to think about this as though it is something that is coming from some sort of higher power. I don't mean this in terms of God granting a special dispensation to you, but rather a sort of spiritual connection to the folks, if that makes any sense."

"In a way, it does. I've thought about something similar lots of times. I've always thought about it as though God singled me out though."

"I don't know about that because I think God is pretty busy and he appreciates anyone who helps themselves. But it is good sometimes to have some kind of greater-than-you entity to kind of keep you in line and humble at the same time."

"I think I can do that. So what you're saying is that even though I *see* things sometimes I shouldn't get too proud about that."

"Yeah, the world is a mysterious place and we simply don't know what or even who else inhabits this place with us. I'm pretty sure that we aren't the top dogs if you can imagine that."

"Even though I know that what you are saying is probably right, it is hard for me to wrap my mind around that idea."

"As your Seeing becomes more involved, you will probably have reason to revisit this conversation. Who knows, you may one day *see* other energy forms. There are many Shamans who report this type of experience and many of them claim that what they are Seeing are beings which are inorganic. You'll have to find your own way of describing what you *see* when and if that day comes."

Points to Consider:

1. Bob has arrived at a critical point in his development.
2. He has developed what seems to him to be a power.
3. Seeing is a tool, not a power.
4. Seeing is a tool which Shamans use to form Agreement.
5. One thing that Bob has learned is to allow consciousness "observer" status.
6. New ideas no longer elicit so much reaction from Bob; they are more likely to elicit contemplation.
7. The order that the tools were presented makes a Difference.

Introduction to Part II: The Concepts

The Office of Shaman has existed for thousands of generations and in thousands of cultures over the course of many thousands of years. The generations, cultural divergence and period of time through which Shamanism has endured should indicate that there would be a wide range of Shamanic practices. That is not the case. The question which must be addressed is how could there be a unified activity within such a wide divergence of educational and cultural concepts?

The answer lies in the symbolism of the first seven numbers. Remember that tribal Shamans were the most educated members of their social group. The realization that numbers existed represented the cutting edge of advanced technology of the day. At a time when speaking a word was considered to be an act of near creation, numbers represented powerful ideas, indeed. The concept of numbers and what they represented was a closely guarded Shamanic secret. Still, the concepts that the numbers represented had to be presented to the general populace.

In some ways, this presented a problem to the Shamans until they realized that they could present the concepts with symbolism and keep the idea which the numbers represented a secret. Some of those symbols are still very much visible. Good examples of those symbols are pyramids and sand paintings. The advantage of symbols was that they could be explained to any depth that suited the purposes of the Shaman. Even when the general populace learned to count and number things, the concepts that the numbers represented were still shown as symbols.

The concepts that the first seven numbers represent really hasn't changed in all the long years of Shamanic existence. The number one still represents unity. It always has and always will, no doubt. The number two still represents harmony. The number three still represents what one and two can do. The numbers have never changed, nor have the concepts which they represent. What did change were the ways the succeeding generations of Shamans applied the knowledge of the seven number concepts.

Consider that there are always two types of Shamans, which are the Dreamer Shaman and the Stalker Shaman. These two types of Shaman apply the concepts of Be One, Harmony, and Do in different ways. Within each type of Shaman, there are many, many ways of applying the concepts. It is not necessary to explore all the ways Shamanic concepts can be applied at this time. To begin, we need only examine the concepts themselves, but we need to be aware that the Office of Shaman does not have a formula for how those who fill the Office should fulfill their duties.

Clarification:

The terms Dreamer and Stalker are from another time. The idea of the Dreamer is not hard to grasp in modern English. What the Dreamer does is much more difficult to understand. In the simplest terms a Dreamer is one who utilizes Dreams in his everyday life. There isn't enough space here to address all the ways a Dreamer can utilize his Dreams.

The term Stalker is a little harder to understand. A Stalker, in modern English, is a predator. In our modern world, a Stalker is someone who practices his nefarious acts on celebrities. In this work, a Stalker is a type of Shaman. A Shaman who is a Stalker is one who utilizes techniques more often associated with trapping and hunting animals for food. There is a certain stealth and craftiness requisite in such activities. Other terms have been sought to describe this Shamanic activity, but none seem to be adequate to point in the proper direction. This is not simply the action of the hunter or trapper, but it represents the lone person fending for himself in an unfriendly environment. Study of the terrain, study of the prey, and understanding of both would be involved. The Stalker Shaman is almost so natural at his craft as to not need instruction.

For those born to the Office of Shaman, one of the first steps in claiming knowledge as power is to become familiar with the concepts of the first seven numbers. The tools which have been discussed up to this point in Part I are, in reality, simply aids to understanding those concepts. They are not ends in themselves. Using the tools releases energies, while the concepts harness or govern those energies. Once the energies are governed by the concepts, actual Shamanic activities can commence.

Points to Consider:

1. Those who hope to fill the Office of Shaman have always been educated people. That has not changed. Today's Shaman needs to have a broad educational base. Just as Tribal Shaman learned about his environment, so, too, must today's Shaman. The educational base of today's Shaman should include history, religion, philosophy and science. Of special interest would be subjects such as computer science, brain physiology and comparative religion.
2. There are actually 17 numbers/concepts which Shamans embrace. We only address seven at this time.
3. There isn't one thing to learn to fulfill the Office of Shaman, there are many things to learn. Each one is as important as another.
4. Each individual Shaman will apply the concepts according to the dictates of his movements of the Assemblage Point.
5. Shamanic energy is dependent on the use of the Shamanic tools. *All* the tools!
6. The following concepts govern those energies.

Introductory Story Part II

Bob has been working on actually helping his clients, but is finding that, more often than not, they really don't want help. This has concerned the boy, to be sure. It is a hard, but necessary lesson. I sympathize with him, but I can't show that at this point. He still doesn't have a structure to hang what he knows on and this needs to be rectified as soon as possible. Now if he will sit still for a bit I'll tell him. This part is going to be a lot harder for him than learning about the tools, although he does have the advantage of knowing about using the tools now.

I guess I should quit worrying about him. He'll just have to take his licks like everyone else. Even though this maneuver is a little dangerous, it will be one-on-one and I can monitor him pretty closely. Still, I always get nervous about taking someone deep into their subconscious for the first time. Folks have been known to find a reality they like and not come back, ever. This is hard to explain.

People rarely ever go into the same level of consciousness as the "teacher." They tend to stop just a bit short. In order to get Bob into the proper levels, I sometimes need to talk to him from the sub-harmonics of brain wave frequencies. In one way, you can think about this as though it were Beethoven being played with the accent on the second and fourth beats rather than the first and third beats. That would not really be accurate, but it points at the event. Let's just say that the rhythm of the voice is extremely slow.

"Bob, I think it's time to take the gloves off with you."

"What do you mean?"

"I mean it's time to start showing you some things that you'll need to know in order to stay in touch with reality as you continue down this path you're on."

"That sounds ominous."

"Well, I'm not telling you this so you can be your same old careless self. You are going to have to pay even better attention from this point on. Up until now, it hasn't mattered if you act like a careless little kid or not. Now it matters. You have gone past the point of no return and because of that you are either going to put all your energy into learning or there is a good chance that you'll end up a babbling idiot."

There really isn't much chance of that happening, but I'm talking to a hard-head and I absolutely need his undivided attention or he will waste years of time trying to sort through what he's going to get programmed with. There are times when that old 2 X 4 between the eyes is the only way to get through to the mule-headed. Bob may not be as mule-headed as I think, but I can't take any chances here.

"Do you understand?"

"Are you trying to scare me? If you are, you are doing a very good job."

Yes, I am trying to scare you and if I stopped talking long enough for you to look around down here you might run out of the house screaming. So you just keep focused on what I'm telling you.

"No, I'm not trying to scare you, but I do want your undivided attention. I don't need you dozing off, I don't need you telling me what I can and cannot tell you and I surely don't need you thinking that you understand what I am saying, nor what I am doing. I'll tell you exactly what I am doing and what I mean. If I say something, then that is what I mean and nothing else. If you try to assign meaning, you will succeed in confusing yourself for years. So your job is to listen, not assign meaning, okay?"

"Well, okay then. But it still sounds ominous."

"Do you know how hard it is to find a smartass?"

"What?"

"If this information was for smartasses I would be sitting down at Denny's talking to every Tom, Dick and Harry who came in. I don't need to talk to smartasses about this at all. If you can't pay attention, then go somewhere else."

"I can pay attention."

"Okay, but I won't even play this game with you from this point forward. If you aren't serious, I can't talk to you at all. It won't be fair to you and God knows you're going to have enough trouble with what I have to tell you if you are serious."

"Like I said, I'll pay attention."

"Then find a comfortable position. Take a deep breath and relax. When people like you first are exposed to this information, they often are dubious. This is good. They have almost always spent a good portion of their lives looking for what they are destined to find out. You are no exception. You tend to be skeptical of anything anyone says because you have heard lots of ways to make yourself better from people who may or may not know what you are trying to find.

"They may have perfectly good information, but that doesn't mean that it fits you. For instance, you tried TM, and although it helped you a lot, you weren't really satisfied that it addressed your needs. That doesn't mean that it isn't a good program or that it doesn't work, it means that it didn't fit you. You are looking for something else.

"What I'm going to tell you today is a kind of introduction to a system that you can use to think about lots of Shamanic activities. It is not a be-all nor is it a means to an end, per se. It is simply a method which will serve you as a ground while you explore the world you are entering. Do you understand so far?"

"I think so. But since I don't understand what you are getting at, I don't think I'm sure that I understand."

"Okay. Well, I'm going to introduce you to a system of belief over the next few sessions we have together so that you can hang the activities of being a Shaman up to look at and compare to what you have always thought. This doesn't mean that you should use this system to solve all your problems, but the system may help you in ways you can't, as yet, imagine.

"For instance, you're always surprised that I know where you are going with a thought before you think you have given me enough information to even know how you are thinking, right?"

"Yeah, kind of."

"The reason I know where you are going is because I am hanging this framework up to talk to you. You can't see the framework, but that doesn't mean that I don't. In fact, it means that I am watching what you do from how you interact within the framework."

"Well, I'd like to know what that framework is."

"All in good time, my man, all in good time. At this point, I'm only going to say that there are seven concepts involved. Each one builds a foundation for the next. I will give them to you one at a time in a linear mode the first time through. After you understand each one of the concepts as stand-alone ideas, I will show you how to stack them up to make a worldview."

"You can do this with seven concepts?"

"Yes."

"These must be some hellacious concepts."

"Maybe. But for me they are nothing more or less than practical ways of thinking. In some ways, we could say that these seven concepts are extremely logical thoughts about how anything is done. In other ways, we could say that these concepts are so complex that they only apply to Shamans. Both statements would be true. It all depends on your Point of View."

"Well, I don't understand."

"I don't expect you to at this point. The next time you drop by I'll tell you about the first concept, okay?"

"I don't have a choice, now, do I?

"Not really."

"Then I'll be back."

"Okay."

Points to Consider:

1. The teacher had to get Bob's permission to continue.
2. Bob Agreed to continue and showed that he understood that he was on a path that was answering a need he has.
3. The teacher wrapped the next set of information in a cloak of mystery.
4. The teacher explained how he was able to see what Bob was doing in terms of the coming information.
5. Bob would love to be able to put that knowledge to use.

Chapter 9: Be One Function

As a Shaman masters the tools of his Office, he begins to wonder about the application of the new thoughts he is beginning to generate. He is also beginning to *see* the world in a different light or from a new perspective. From that new perspective, he is faced with a dilemma. What to do with what he knows.

What exactly does he now believe? What exactly does he now know? By now, he has probably discarded the need for ritual and because of that he is probably questioning exactly what the Church is providing people. He probably is also doubting that sacrificed chickens will accomplish much even in a symbolic way. In the void which Moving the Assemblage Point causes, he is likely to find himself drifting without purpose. All the accomplishments of Shamans which he knows about seem petty or completely beyond his reach.

What he lacks is a system of belief which will accommodate the Shamanic experience and give purpose to his existence. It isn't likely that he will know how to construct such a belief system and because the oral tradition of Shamanism has nearly died off, he may find himself at odds with what he knows. So then he begins to realize that from the ashes of his past life there is arising a structure which can serve to ground him. This structure consists of seven concepts. Each concept is simple, yet has profound implications which is how any belief system must be. The problem is how to sort through these concepts and bring them to bear in the life of the Shaman.

The first concept a Shaman encounters on the path of knowledge is the Be One Function. This idea could be expressed as Being at One, Being One with Yourself, Others and the World, or Existing With One Mind. This concept pertains to all manner of unity and is the beginning of Shamanic learning.

Clarification:

> The statement, "This concept pertains to all manner of unity..." does not appear to be a command to do, but yet it is. It is a command to be at one in Programming, accepting other Points of View, Communication, Differences, Not Doing, Honesty, Direct Knowing and even in Seeing. To accomplish the Be One Function using all of these tools and with all of these tools is a major accomplishment.

In the days of hunting and gathering when people still wandered in small family groups, the first Shamans were born to their office. As the Shamans observed their world, the idea of the Be One Function became necessary. Those first Shamans applied the concept of the Be One Function to, perhaps, several families to make them a tribe. Being a tribe meant that there were more people to defend one another, that there were more people to work together to hunt bigger game, there were more people to work at gathering wild crops and there were more people to cause problems with one another. Those early Shamans had to make the Be One Function understandable to the newly formed tribes.

They had to conceive of a way to unite the tribe. As a consequence, those early Shamans conceived of the idea of teaching the people that they were One People. Ideas such as how a man behaves in battle, with big game, or with other tribes required that the men become warriors. Codes of conduct were devised so that the men didn't quarrel with one another, but applied their warrior bravery where it was needed on the hunt or in battle. Battle in either of these arenas was beneficial to the tribe. Even more beneficial to the tribe was the idea that the men and women had to be of one mind in order to triumph. When the men were of one mind, they worked together to kill more game. More game meant the tribe would survive the winter.

Those first Shamans soon realized how the Be One Function applied to the people was different from how the Shaman applied the same Function to himself. He had to think of the Be One Function as uniting body, mind and soul. He had to integrate the world he Dreamed with the world filled with snow, rain and other life threatening realities. He had to speak to his people about the things he Dreamed with Brutal Honesty. In short, his body became an instrument of Communication between the Dream world, spirit world, and the cold, hard world.

Clarification:

It may seem that Be One would be conflicted with the idea presented in the previous paragraph; however, everyday people do not strive to accomplish a connection with the Other. That is something that the Shaman does. The application of the Be One Function for a life directed by the Other is necessarily different than the application of the Be One Function for someone who sees the world from Beta or consciousness.

For someone who sees the world from consciousness only, the Be One Function applies to the world he sees as with his job, family, friends and so on. For someone who sees the world from the Other, the Be One Function applies to all that is included in consciousness and to that which pertains to the Other as well. It isn't possible for the consciousness-only individual to see from the Other, so the application of Be One must, perforce, be limited to what that individual can see.

The early Shamans were faced with how to keep their people fed and how to keep them unified so they could supply themselves with the stores to survive hard times. The Be One Function supplied the answers. If the Shaman was at one with the world he lived in, he could direct his people to where the game was, where shelter was, what to use for clothing, ways to store meat, methods of starting fire, what plants were good for which ailments and what the spirit said about any decision.

The problem was that the Shaman really had no one to talk to about all the things he was doing. He could have asked Tribal Bubba, I suppose, but Tribal Bubba didn't have all the same information that the Tribal Shaman had. Can you imagine? "Hey Bubba, this looks like a good place to camp, what do you think?" "I dunno. I'm thirsty. How much further do we have to go today?"

As a result of keeping his own counsel, the Tribal Shaman had to rely on signs from the one world he inhabited to speak to him. His one world included much more than the world in which Tribal Bubba lived. The tribe may have been looking for winter quarters, for instance, and came upon a cave which had all the attributes necessary for sustaining life through the time of snow. The Tribal Shaman would have had to consult with his one world to know if it was the right cave or not. If a Grizzly bear had come out of the cave, some Shamans may have declared it perfect because the totem of the tribe was the Spirit of the Grizzly. Other Shamans may have declared it a bad choice because their totem was the Spirit of the Deer and grizzlies and deer are mortal enemies. In either case, the Shaman would have had to stay consistent with his worldview or the Be One Function would not have been in effect. In other words, the Tribal Shaman had an obligation to his people and the complex world in which he lived to believe in the Be One Function as completely as he believed in his own body.

As time passed, our Tribal Shaman began to show his age. One day it dawned on him that he was going to have to find a replacement. The problem was that all possible candidates were named Tribal Bubba Jr. Now Jr. would have had all the raging hormones of any teenager along with a decided lack of education. How could the Tribal Shaman impart his years of knowledge to such an unlikely candidate? The tribal Shaman *saw* the way. He would introduce Jr. to the wonderful world of Programming. And so Programming became the tool for learning the Be One Function.

There was only one problem with Tribal Shaman's Seeing. The concept of Programming was still quite a ways off in the future. So, Tribal Shaman decided to call the action he was contemplating a Spirit Quest, or the Warriors Way, or some other mystical sounding thing. The actual action was Programming though. He told Jr. to sit down and find his spot on the ground. He told Jr. to Dream of the Spirit of the Deer and then asked where the deer was and what the deer told little Jr. If Jr. made something up, then Tribal Shaman sent him back to Dream it again. In other words, Tribal Shaman programmed Tribal Bubba Jr. to incorporate the Be One Function into his life until he *became* the Be One Function.

Clarification:

To become the Be One Function indicates that an individual has unified his beliefs, emotions, feelings and logic or consciousness. In the case of the Shaman, the set includes unifying the Other as well. This is no easy task. It requires the strongest kind of self-examination. However, the exercises for modern people to learn the Be One Function are not the same as they were for hunter/gatherer people. Finding your spot on the ground, for example, doesn't have the same meaning for modern people because we do not spend our time gathered in extended family groups living off the land. While we must still be at One with the world we live in, that world has changed and as a consequence of the change, the method of interaction with the world has also changed. It is for new generations of Shamans to redefine the exercises for Shamans-to-be to learn that at Oneness. This defines a Shamanic task.

Modern day Shamans don't often have a need to consult with the Spirit of the Deer or of the Wolf or Bear. They may have a need to commune with the Spirit of the Freeway or the Spirit of the Cell Phone, but then modern day Shamans also have the Spirit of the Church and the Spirit of the TV to Dream about, too. Modern day Shamans have to Be One with the world they live in just as much as the Tribal Shaman did. They live in a world where Being One with Church Doctrine and the Global Village is tantamount to life, for them. Their words, actions and beliefs must Be One. They must Be One with their humanity no matter what myths or models they choose to explain their actions. The Be One Function is as important in today's world as it has ever been.

The world that today's Shaman lives in is more complicated than the world of the Tribal Shaman. In that ancient world, talking about the Spirit of the Deer or whatever spirit was enough. In today's world, we have to Be One with the idea of the soul, with the idea of auras, with the idea of computers and with the idea of space exploration. We must still use the body as an instrument of Communication but our Communication must be more complex than the Communication of Tribal Shaman. We rarely have the time to go walk out in the woods and find our place of energy, but we must keep our own counsel and listen as carefully to the answers we receive from our one world as did Tribal Shaman. The wheel of time has turned and we live in a different world from that of our predecessor, but that does not mean we will learn a different set of knowledge about the Office to which we were born.

Something that all Shamans have always and will always have to accomplish is to unite their thoughts and actions as One. They will always have to Be One with their people, their world, their spirits, their energy, their beliefs, their family, their friends and the earth where they live. To believe this Oneness affects the entire physical structure of the body. To believe, and thus make real, this Oneness affects the entire mental structure of the brain. To believe this Oneness opens an avenue of Communication with the Other. To Be One is the first of seven gold rings in the life of the Shaman.

Another way of saying this is that the Shaman must be consistent with his thoughts, actions and beliefs. If the Shaman gives his word to accomplish something, then he has actually bet his life on that accomplishment. To the Shaman, giving his word involves body, mind and soul. Why would the

Shaman give his word if he were not committed throughout his whole being? If his life has any value at all, then he has no choice except to enter into the forthcoming accomplishment as though he were in a battle for his life. The Shaman must realize that his life is on the line when he gives his word because his word and his life must Be One. That is the nature of the Be One Function.

Clarification:

Some people may take exception to the phrase "betting their life" as it relates to their word. However, a large part of the energy or power of the tribal Shaman was directly related to this very idea. The tribal Shaman actually did bet his life and the life of his tribe on what he said. The tribal Shaman may have said things about how and where to find game or where to live during the winter. But the lives of his tribe hinged on his declarations. Would it not stand to reason that modern day Shamans would derive a large part of their energy or power in the same manner even if what they talked about was a different set?

Points to Consider:

1. Programming releases energy which the Be One Function governs.
2. The need for self-Programming always arises from internal conflicts where the Be One Function does not govern energies.
3. It is illogical to consider that the mind alone exists without considering the Other as part of our One Life.
4. The Shaman will strive to bring Unity to his people.
5. Part of the Shaman's Oneness is to replace himself.
6. A changing world requires new techniques even for Shamans.

Story Chapter IX

Here he comes. I just need to remember to put enough mumbo jumbo over this to get him to think about it as deeply as he needs to. The problem with some of these concepts is that they sound so simple that they go right over people's heads. I have to make sure this doesn't happen with Bob.

He has to see this at once as simple and the most complex idea he has ever encountered. Maybe I should light some candles and play some whale songs. Naw, he would be buying whale song tapes for the rest of his life and his house would always reek of candle wax. I just better play my best game.

"I see you made it."

"I told you I would and I always keep my word."

"Do you now?"

"Yes, I do."

He can't go into his self-importance here. I need to keep him just enough off balance that he doesn't know what's coming next.

"That's nice. Why don't you find a comfortable position? Now take a deep breath and relax. Take another deep breath and go deeper. I didn't tell you to close your eyes. I need you to be wide awake and alert."

"Whenever I do my relaxation exercises, I always close my eyes."

Bob, I'm sure your self-importance is on a roll. This isn't the time or place for that. I have to get you past this as quickly as possible or I'll be Programming you with self-importance at a very, very deep level. That really wouldn't be fair. It would be easier if logic hadn't developed the ability to talk to itself. But it has. Therefore, I need to get him to see what I am telling him from a brain wave frequency which is slower than the brain waves he uses for normal consciousness and I need to get him there quickly.

"You're not doing relaxation exercises now. You are about to learn the first of seven concepts in a belief system which Shamans use in their lives."

"There's nothing wrong with closing my eyes. I can pay attention with my eyes closed."

"Hey! What am I telling you?"

"My eyes are open, see?"

As I'm slowing him down and getting him under his normal conscious brain waves, I might as well take a few shots at troublesome Programming for the guy.

"Bob, you know that kind of thing is almost cute when you pull it with your daddy, but I ain't your daddy. It is not cute when you pull it here. I am in the process of putting you in a deep Programming state and you don't have the foggiest idea of what program is being written. You haven't even paid attention to the rhythm of my voice. Do you think that I need to go through the relaxation exercises to get you into these deep states? I've been putting you in these states since we began talking. You have rarely noticed that I have been setting programs all this time. Now I'm telling you what I am doing and I'm telling you to follow what I am saying. Are you sure you want to set the thought you have always had as the basis of what I'm Programming you with?"

"I didn't think about it that way."

"I know. You may really want to pay more careful attention to the things that are going on around you before you decide that you know something. The first concept I'm going to tell you about is the Be One Function. This is a strange idea, in a way, because it is simplicity itself and yet it is terribly profound. From the simple aspect, any individual can apply the Function in his life and benefit from the basic tenant. If a person, any person, is one thing in his life or does one thing in his life, he will become very, very good at that thing. This seems to be something everyone does, more or less. But it isn't. We all divide ourselves up into compartments and most often don't let the left hand know what the right hand is doing. We have family. We have work. We have sports. We have groups. In each aspect or facet of our life, we are essentially a different person. We are not One. You're like that, aren't you?"

"I don't think so."

But you are divided. Let's see if I can give you an example that will show this to you without embarrassing you.

"Oh? You're the same with your dad as you are with your boss at work?"

"No. My boss is one thing and my dad is something else."

"So you do live one life in front of your dad and live another in front of your boss."

"I don't think they are different lives."

"What would you call it, then? Different facets of your personality?"

"Perhaps, but I don't live different lives."

"From my perspective, you do."

"How can you say that?"

"I don't think you want me to answer exactly what you asked so I'll answer what I think you want to know. From where I think about Being One, you are terribly divided. For example, when you talk to your dad do you think excessively about how to accomplish what your boss wants you to do?"

"No."

"I didn't think so. You know, someone who is a musician hears music all the time. They can't escape, nor do they wish to escape from the music. That is who they are. Obviously, I'm talking about a musician here, not someone who simply plays an instrument. Those people are One with music. Are you like that with what you do?"

"No."

"No, you're not. From that perspective or Point of View you are terribly divided. Now don't get me wrong here, I don't think that you can be anything other than what you are at the moment. That doesn't mean that you don't have to address this and come to Be One with yourself and what you do, it only means that up until this point you haven't had the knowledge to be different than you are."

"I probably knew that I wasn't as focused as I should be."

"I'm not talking about focus. I'm talking about Be One Function. Don't confuse the comfortable familiarity of this with knowledge. What I'm saying rings down to you through the ages of Man. But it is knowledge which has not been available to you before this moment. The reason it has not been available is that you probably haven't been conscious at this level since you were a baby."

"I've been conscious for quite a while."

I've got to broach the subject of the Other, but I don't want to spook him here. He still has some issue with this subject that is unresolved.

"Not here, you haven't. At this level, you are within earshot of your very soul. Now let me think. Aren't you the guy who told me that you don't believe in the soul because the word reminds you of some kind of religious experience?"

"You are a cold, calculating bastard. You know that, don't you?"

That wasn't too bad. He's angry with me, not afraid of the word. That, I can deal with. Just a nudge about his carelessness should punch up enough guilt to keep him in line.

"Yes, I am. And you are still careless. Are you One with that part of yourself? Do you exercise that part of who you are when you talk with your dad or with your boss?

"No. How do you do that?"

"How are you doing that right now?"

"I'm not."

"Oh?"

"You are bringing this out of me. I'm not doing anything but listening."

So, he does recognize the Other. That's good. Too bad this memory won't be available to him tomorrow. He can't bring his awareness to focus on this frequency without help as yet.

"I see. So you're telling me that this part of you exists only when I'm talking to you. Do I have that right?"

"It exists all the time."

"Yes, it does. The Be One Function includes this part of you. This isn't a part that you can compartmentalize and still have the Be One Function working in your life. Be One includes the body, mind and soul."

"Shit."

I think that was an acknowledgment of recognition.

"Be careful what you program here. Let's consider something. What if the body is an instrument of Communication for the soul? What would be the function of the mind in this configuration?"

"What configuration?"

"If the body is the instrument of Communication for the soul, then what function would the mind have?"

"I'm not sure what you're asking."

"Wouldn't the mind then serve as an avenue of expression for the soul? Would the mind be, to use a word, subservient to the soul? Would it be dependent on the soul for direction?"

"If the body was an instrument of Communication for the soul, that would make sense."

Be careful. I wouldn't want you to commit.

"Yes, it would, wouldn't it? Then if that were the case, the Be One Function would indicate that we would have little choice but to follow the dictates of the soul. We would have to be that One thing. We would have to be soul as well as body and mind. But then that flies in the face of what you consider yourself to be, doesn't it?"

"Maybe what I have considered myself to be, but now I see things differently."

"You actually have that right. Now you can see this, but what about tomorrow? Are you sure you will be able to see this tomorrow?"

"Of course."

"No, you won't. Tomorrow you will not even be able to remember this conversation. Oh, you'll remember that we talked about Be One Function and you'll remember that the soul was involved in the conversation, but you won't be able to remember that the soul is the part of us that gives direction. It will even be harder to remember that direction is to be an instrument of Communication."

"Why do you say that?"

"Because it's true. There is a great deal of Programming between you as soul and you as regular you. That Programming must be attuned to this idea before you can put the idea of Be One including the soul to use. That tuning process may take years to accomplish. But I can assure you of one thing. It is on its way."

Considering how frightening the concept of the Other is for him, he handled this pretty well. He strayed a couple of times, but that is acceptable. Now I'll just have to wait and see how long it takes for the first vestiges of this idea to surface.

Points to Consider:

1. The teacher introduced Bob to the Be One Function by talking about the Other being part of his life.
2. The teacher used the Other to cloak what he was saying about the Be One Function.
3. Bob resisted the idea of the Other at work in him, but didn't notice that the subject of the visit was the Be One Function.
4. The teacher "set" the program in place without Bob noticing, although the teacher was Brutally Honest about what he was going to do.
5. The teacher even told Bob that he wouldn't remember the program tomorrow.
6. Using Programming to explain the Be One Function would be the appropriate action.
7. The teacher's ploy was to get Bob to come closer to understanding the Other at work in his life so he can observe the released energy of the program change being governed by the Be One Function.
8. It is appropriate to allow Bob to realize that the Function is governing energy on his own at a later date.
9. Not every Shaman would teach in this manner.

Chapter 10: Harmony Function

As the Shaman learns to put his life on the line with only his word, something else begins to occur. Through his Communication with others, he begins to find that there are some who wish to maintain open dialog with him. Through having an open dialog concerning his activities with someone else who perhaps is also a Shaman, the Shaman discovers that for either party to understand the points made by the other, they both have to examine the beliefs, Programming and thinking which make up a given point in each other.

The closest common experience we all have in our day to day lives that approximates this type of Communication is the struggle that newlyweds have as they try to adjust to each other. If the newly married man and woman ever hope to live together as man and wife, then all the parts of their lives will be subject to examination by both individuals. Each will necessarily have to change certain Points of View concerning how life is lived. Some things will be deemed as not important enough to bother with. Some things will need adjustment or the marriage will fail. This common event of two people finding a way to live together is actually the Harmony Function at work.

The life of a Shaman is decidedly more complex than that of a married couple. A Shaman can't get divorced from who he is. He has no choice but to live in Harmony with himself. Nor does a Shaman have a choice about living in Harmony with others. If the Shaman commits to living in Harmony with the Other, he puts his life on the line to achieve this accomplishment. Not many married people are that committed to living in Harmony.

And so it is that the second concept a Shaman encounters on the path of knowledge is the Harmony Function. There are other names which could be applied to this Function but the best is Harmony. You could call it Love Function but while the function includes sexual harmony, it is the harmonious part of love and sex which this Function addresses. The Be One Function is all about the One. The Harmony Function is all about Two. It addresses all of the multitude of ways Two interact.

When Tribal Shaman encountered other tribes and other Shamans, he began to consider the Harmony Function. It was necessary and it was good to have allies and others to help, especially with big game and wars. It was also a good idea to have friends in other tribes because all the Bubba Jr.'s from both tribes were checking out all the Bobby Sue Jr.'s from the other tribe and you know that all the Bubbas from both tribes were a bit concerned about the things that fathers still concern themselves with today.

So the two Tribal Shamans got together and hatched the plan that would allow the two tribes to become tribe-in-laws, as it were. This idea called for both tribes to act in Harmony for certain events. For instance, it was highly likely that the two tribes had somewhat different customs concerning who was available, how old they had to be in order to be available, what they should know to be available, what work was expected from those who were chosen and who should leave which tribe when a union was made. Then there was the issue of how the choices would be made and who would have the right to choose and how the one who chose could be turned down without causing mayhem. This may have all been decided at that first meeting of the tribes, but it is more likely that each Tribal Shaman had to go back to his people to perform rituals, Dream and do his Programming so that he could come up with a suitable plan.

The upstart was that each tribe had to adopt new Points of View to accommodate the new reality. This is why changing Points of View is the tool for understanding the Harmony Function. For the Harmony Function to be realized in an individual, he will first have to understand that his personal mythology is insufficient. He will then have to try his best to understand how another Point of View or mythology can work in another individual. Then he will have to adopt it until he understands how that new Point of View functions in him and how it changes his behavior.

When the Tribal Shaman took a look at Bubba Jr., the apprentice Shaman, he had to have a twinge of dissatisfaction. Bubba Jr. had been raised in an environment within the tribe which reinforced the Point of View he held. The Tribal Shaman tried to reason with Bubba Jr. to no avail. So the next time the two tribes got together, the two Tribal Shamans took Bubba Jr. off to one side and tried to get him to see first one then another way to look at an issue. I'm sure that those two Tribal Shamans were quite familiar with another aspect of the Harmony Function before they were done with Bubba Jr.: Patience.

Shamans need to have as many Points of View as possible. To Shamans, a Point of View is more inclusive than what we normally think. For this reason, Shamans call this change Moving the Assemblage Point because an individual assembles his entire worldview through one position. We often mistakenly call our Point of View "who we are". In reality, our mythology or worldview is a result of never straying from viewing the world through a mental lens which focuses only where we point the lens. Part of the reason is the Be One Function. Another part of the reason is that unless we are goaded into Moving the Assemblage Point, we will be lazy and really have no motivation to move our view of the world.

Clarification:

A Point of View is exactly what it sounds like. However, there are Points of View which cover shallow ideas and Points of View which cover much deeper and broader ideas. You could have a Point of View about a new acquaintance which could change as you get to know that individual and you could also have a Point of View about a political issue or even about a political party. There are other Points of View which cover a much broader scope altogether. Points of

View which alter a current definition of the world are called Movements of the Assemblage Point.

Let's say that a modern day Shaman is born into his Office in Pratt, Kansas. Pratt is not a particularly worldly place, but the good folks who live there are certainly aware of world events and demonstrate their knowledge down at the Grange and over at the Dew Drop Inn coffee house on a daily basis. Now our Shaman would be able to navigate through the Pratt community without any problems at all. He would, no doubt, consider himself to be somewhat adept at his office. Yet if we were to suddenly pick our guy up and deposit him in Guadalajara, Jalisco down in Central Mexico he just might have to change how he thought about everything he ever learned back in Pratt. Our guy would need a whole new set of beliefs, a whole new language and a whole new way of looking at the world. This example approximates what Shamans mean when they talk about Moving the Assemblage Point. Now, if our guy was really a Shaman, he would be able to make such a move without much trouble. A Shaman would put his life on the line to live in Harmony no matter where he landed.

In some Shamanic disciplines, apprentices are fed hallucinogenic plants such as peyote just to challenge their long held worldviews. There are other means. The best by far is for the budding Shaman to adopt the idea that his construct of the world is not god-like or even God given. To realize this thought, the new Shaman must allow for the right of any individual to construct a worldview. That worldview may not agree with the Shaman's worldview, but that individual does have the right to see the world any way he chooses. Shamans who are involved with healing and convincing must take this position or they will be ineffective.

Today's Shaman must be very much aware of this concept. He must live with a wide variety of worldviews. He cannot challenge them or the holders of those worldviews may take exception to his challenge. He must allow the Harmony Function full sway in his life.

Occasionally, there are people who feel as though the Harmony Function is a part of Shamanic knowledge which does not pertain to them. They wish to form one-sided agreements, or be in control of others, or show their power through "black magic." These people will never understand the Shamanic Way. They are doomed to be shadows of what could have been. Their energy is false and their ways are weak. The Shaman who allows the Harmony Function to rule his life will progress beyond this point and develop energy and power that the "black magician" will never realize.

There is no worldview or system of belief so complete or sacrosanct that it is without fault. This includes the Shaman's multitude of Assemblage Points. The world is a mysterious place. It holds secrets that we may never understand and although we may never understand them, we must endeavor to live in

Harmony with those secrets.

Clarification:

The idea that no worldview or system of belief is so complete or sacrosanct that it is without fault is directly connected to *controlled folly*. *Controlled folly* is the only Point of View that is logical for the Shaman. While the brain is indeed a very, very large computer, it is not so large, nor is our ability to understand the mystery of the world so all-encompassing, that we can logically consider any worldview as anything more than *controlled folly*.

Because this is true, then the Shaman must *suspend disbelief* in order to accept the limits of his worldview. It is utter simplicity to live in a world where anything unknown can be disavowed by the act of not believing. This is not a safe practice by any means. Since the Shaman "bets his life" on what he says and disbelief may well hide danger, then the Shaman accepts the idea of *controlled folly* as safe practice. In place of disbelief, the Shaman accepts an unknown "as though it may be true", "as though it may be false", "as though it may not be true", "as though it may not be false" and eschews the seductively "true" and "false" dichotomies.

There are Shamans who claim to have dialog with inorganic beings. These beings reportedly react to the emotional set of their Shaman friends. They supposedly appear near bodies of water and live many more years than humans. A Shaman who does not have inorganic beings in his experience must live as though these beings actually exist and change how he *assembles* his world so that he can live in Harmony with even this unknown. This is the nature of the Harmony Function.

Points to Consider:

1. Changing Points of View releases energy which the Harmony Function governs.
2. The extent of the influence of Harmony Function in a Shaman's life can be measured by the breadth of ideas and concepts he can encompass.
3. Anyone can accomplish disharmony but it takes skill to attain Harmony.
4. The Shaman doesn't reject a Point of View because it is different from the one he has brought with him from childhood.
5. It is simply not impossible to understand how parochial a given worldview is until it is challenged through immersion in another culture.
6. A Shaman who desires to follow the darker side of knowledge limits his development.
7. *Suspending Disbelief* is a Harmony Function.

Story Chapter X

If this poor guy can remember anything I talked with him about, then he deserves all the attention I can give him. He had to be inundated with new information, but he stayed pretty calm. I think he may be growing up. I should knock on wood, I suppose.

He is having a lot of trouble with the idea of the soul and I suspect that the concepts of brain wave frequencies are just passing him by. I can't blame him. I'm not so sure that brain wave frequency is the best way to explain these events. I'm sure that in some ways talking about brain waves is understandable at first, but I wonder if it isn't a little misleading. It might even be very misleading. I still have time to get him to see this in other ways so he can have more than one description for his own personal use. That should help him understand it better.

If we weren't so all fired sure that the word is the actual thing I wouldn't have to worry about this, but Bob didn't catch that idea, I'm afraid. Maybe I can take a little bit and explain that concept to him before I go into the next concept. Maybe I'll open up a can of worms, too, but then that's what Harmony Function is all about.

"Before I start with the next set here, do you have any questions about what we already discussed?"

"Not really, but I don't think I understand the Beta, Delta, Alpha thing. I remember the last time you were talking I felt kind of funny, but then I got scared and I don't know why. Was it because of the brain wave thing?"

"Which question would you like me to answer? The one about your lack of understanding or the one about why you got scared? Or maybe I should address the funny feeling you had. What do you think?"

"About what?"

"That's what I thought. All right, what actually happened to you the last time we talked was that you had to assemble a world that was unfamiliar to you. When you start Doing, that can sometimes be scary. When I told you that you were within earshot of the soul, you realized that you were actually listening to something that would cause you to take the soul's existence into consideration. That was a new event for you, wasn't it?"

He didn't really assemble another world but he did get another description of the world that was so foreign to him that it might as well have been another world.

"I guess. I'm not sure that I still believe that stuff about the soul, but it is starting to make sense."

"If you stub your toe on a rock, the rock doesn't have to make sense either. It exists whether you pay attention to it or not."

"Is that supposed to be profound?"

"I don't know much about profound, but I am a little familiar with practical."

"Stubbing your toe on a rock is practical?"

"No, but paying attention to the existence of rocks is."

"I guess."

"If you stub your toe on a rock often enough because you don't believe they exist, you will change your Point of View about rocks. That's for sure."

"I believe rocks exist."

"I'm sure you do. Do you believe the soul exists?"

"I'm not sure about that."

"When your toe gets sore enough, you'll change your Point of View."

"Oh."

I'm going to slow this way, way down. I want to drive or pull him into the deepest levels I can with this subject matter. I need to leave the conscious Bob up in Beta. I'm sure that 'Beta-Bob' can entertain himself for an hour.

"Look, we live in a technical age. You, for example, are a technical person. You have your satellite phone, your blue-tooth, your iPad, your numerous apps and on and on. I need to use some sort of technical jargon to get you to pay attention to what is happening to you. So I use brain wave frequencies. I talk to you about Beta and Alpha and Theta and Delta and you sit there and nod. I don't really care if you use those names for the events surrounding you or not. What I really want you to do is to pay attention to the events sweeping you up. I want you to be aware that something is happening to you that you don't have words to describe. The best words I can come up with are the ones which can be applied to brain function. So I give you a model that you think you understand because it is familiar."

"So the brain wave thing isn't true?"

"Let me start over. Brain waves actually exist. There are four and maybe even more definable brain wave patterns. When someone begins to learn about, what I will call here, Shamanic activities, then it is convenient to describe the different stages of slower thinking patterns as connected to brain waves. That description may not be completely accurate. It could also be God's own truth. However, if describing the event as connected to brain waves is confusing to you then we could also say the event is connected to John, Paul, George and Ringo. If saying that the event was part of Beatles lore actually made sense to you, then that would work just as well. The sad thing is that the Beatles' analogy, unfortunately, doesn't make as much sense as the brain wave analogy does. Understand?"

"Kind of."

"Would it help if I told you how I see what happens?"

"Maybe."

"Okay. What I visualize is that I need to change how you look at the world. I call the event of changing how you look at the world, Changing Your Point of View, or Moving Your Assemblage Point. In order to accomplish that maneuver I slow my voice rhythm way down to a Delta beat as though I were hypnotizing you. The slower the beat or rhythm of my voice the stronger the Programming effect it has on those who listen. You are a very good subject."

"So what are you hypnotizing me to do?"

"You know if you could learn to ask the question about the actual event, you would learn so much more. I'm not hypnotizing you to do anything. I am trying to get you to look at the world differently. So far I've been a miserable failure."

"I don't think you've failed. I see things differently than I used to."

"But you don't say things any differently."

"What do you mean?"

"I give. Okay, I want to introduce you to the idea of the Harmony Function."

"You didn't answer my question."

"Really? How could I have missed that? Well, maybe the next time you remember it, okay? The Harmony Function is about how people get along with each other. It is connected to other things, too, but let's start with the idea of how folks get along. Okay?"

"I guess."

He followed the explanation about changing Points of View and actually used it to get himself in position to listen to this. Let's open this up with a little logic.

"Thanks. You may not have ever noticed this, but you can't sing harmony by yourself. While it is true that you have to Be One, it is also true that no man is an island. I think I read that somewhere. You have to be able to get along with other people. In order to have an advantage when it comes to getting along with others, you have to be able to adopt other Points of View. If you only hold your Point of View, you are not only boring, but you will end up in all manner of arguments. The art is to find the Harmony that is lurking in the other person. You understand this, right?"

"I think so."

Add a little real life experience…

"So when you interact with your dad, then you can adopt his Point of View, right?"

"That's easier said than done."

"So you're compartmentalized when you talk with your dad?"

"No."

"In reality you are. Here's the weird part of this. As long as you are compartmentalized, you can't sing harmony. Do you know why?"

"No."

Tie it in with what he already knows or at least what we have already talked about…

"Remember what the body is?"

"Ah... you told me this last time."

"The body is the instrument of Communication for the soul."

"Yeah, that's it."

"Thanks. So do you suppose that is true only for you or maybe it is true only for Shamans?"

"No, I guess it would be true for everyone."

"Right. It would be true for your dad, your mom, your kid sister, the guy down at the convenience store and anyone and everyone you will ever run into. So why aren't all those people communicating from the soul?"

"I don't know."

"Why don't you communicate from the soul?"

"Well, I must, then."

"No, you don't. It is very rare indeed that people communicate from the soul. The reason they don't is that they can't assemble a world where that event wouldn't be, let's say, normal. The world they assemble is a world filled with strife because they are compartmentalized, just the same as you. Harmony is difficult in that world. In that world, consciousness, or we could say Beta, rules. Please remember that using the word 'Beta' is a way of pointing at the event. It is not the event. The Shaman seeks to listen to the soul speaking or communicating through the other person's body. If he can assemble a world where that Communication can take place he can, perhaps, begin to open channels through which that rare Communication can take place."

"You just said that hardly anyone communicates from the soul and now you are saying everyone communicates from the soul. Doesn't one of those statements contradict the other? Just asking."

Explain it from a different angle or show him a Difference...

"Yes and no. Let's do something here. When I think about this event I don't call it the soul. I call it the Other. Maybe it would be easier for you to listen to this if I didn't use the word 'soul.' Using Other might be less offensive to you because that word doesn't have religious connotations. Is that all right?"

"Well, I don't like the word soul for that reason, that's for sure."

"Okay, let's say that the Other, underneath all the thought processes in everyone, wants to use its body to communicate. But let's say that we as human beings haven't evolved enough, as yet, to allow that Communication. If that were true then each person would be looking for a way to 'be at peace with himself' by finding a way for the Other to communicate through his body. The fly in the ointment is that consciousness, or ego, or self or whatever you want to call that, doesn't want to give up control. Maybe the conscious part of our thinking doesn't trust the Other. It doesn't matter the reason for the internal conflict, it exists. The conflict isn't right or wrong, it is just how things are at this historical moment. Are you with? I don't need you spacing off here."

Give him a space to catch up…

"I'm paying attention."

"Your eyes are pretty glazed."

"I'm paying attention, but I don't think I could repeat what you just said."

"Then it's up to you to get this clear."

"I didn't space out."

"Of course you didn't. It doesn't make any difference because it's in there anyway. That you're not conscious of it won't change the effect of the Programming. Anyway, back to the Harmony Function. So the Other is trying to say it's piece, as it were, and the consciousness is busy with survival things and everyone is looking for inner peace. Where does that leave the erstwhile Shaman? It leaves him trying his best to develop as much patience as possible. The reason for the patience is that the Shaman has to be above or perhaps beyond the conflict between consciousness and the Other. In this day and time, the Shaman can't very well hold forth about his vision of the Spirit of the Buffalo because that would fall on some really deaf ears. So what's a poor Shaman to do?"

"I think we need to go back to the time of the Spirit of the Buffalo. We need to live off the land and be more in tune with Nature. There's nothing wrong with that."

End the Programming cycle and start him back up to Beta before he dilutes the program…

"Of course you want to go back to the Spirit of the Buffalo. You have no idea what that is, so you could put off taking responsibility for what you know forever, right?"

"I take responsibility for what I know."

"You certainly do as long as what you know doesn't involve the Other."

"Well, you have to admit that's a pretty far-fetched idea."

He's back to the fear Programming…

"It is? Explain why it is far-fetched."

"Well, there's no proof that it exists. No one has ever seen the soul or the Other, as you say. How do you know it exists?"

Add some logic and "facts" to counterbalance the belief…

"Let's see, I seem to remember you talking about black holes in space, wasn't that you?"

"Yeah, I was explaining to you how black holes in space might mean that we could time travel if we could figure out how to utilize them."

"Have you or anyone else you know ever seen a black hole in space?"

"No, but there are mathematical calculations that indicate they exist."

"Someone has deduced their existence, then. Is that right?"

"Like I said, there are mathematical calculations that indicate their existence."

"Like I said, someone has deduced their existence."

"Okay, I suppose. But the calculations leave little room for doubt."

Weaken the defense as we go by…

"Let me get this straight. You can accept deduced black holes in space and the completely unknown Spirit of the Buffalo but you can't accept the existence of the Other. Is that about the size of it?"

"You know, you are hard to talk to."

"Especially when I'm saying something you don't want to hear. What do you think, that I'm going to look for Harmony in a non-Harmonic thought? Do I look crazy to you?"

"So why are you so pushy with this thing about the soul? You don't have proof of its existence."

Assert knowledge…

"I have proof of its existence. You are the one who doesn't have proof and even if you have it, you won't accept it because that would mean you'd have to change your Point of View or assemble a whole new world for yourself, and you're too lazy to do that."

"It's not that I'm lazy, it's that I don't believe that shit."

"Then how can you Be One?"

"I can Be One, as you say, without accepting the idea of the 'soul.'"

Tie the two concepts together with logic… Throw some crumbs to the Ego…

"Well, I'm sorry, but you can't. It is the idea of the Other and how the Other interacts with and through the body that is the essence of being a Shaman. You can't have one without the other. It is precisely the idea of the Other which Shamans use to heal, to see, to know directly and to do all the other things Shamans do. If you aspire to be a Shaman, then you aspire to utilize the Other in your day-to-day life."

"How can you use something that doesn't exist?"

"Now we're down to it. I want you to tell me how you know that the Other doesn't exist. People have been talking about the soul for millennia. But you know something that none of those people knew. The soul doesn't exist. How do you know that?"

"I can't prove it, but you can't prove it does exist either."

"The difference is that I know how to allow it. You will learn that too or you will never be able to affect people at all."

"I get along with people just fine."

"No, you're nice to people. I'm talking about affecting them. I'm talking about healing them in one way or another. Anyone can be nice. But only those who bring the Harmony Function from the Other actually heal people. Think about that."

"I'll think about it."

Harmonize...

"I know you will because you have to have this program working in order to advance as a Shaman."

"I'll say one thing for you. You don't take prisoners."

"I do unless the people I am talking to are important. You still don't know how special you are. You don't have many choices in any of this. It may take years to realize, but you are going to make a Difference in your world."

Harmony Function is sometimes strange. I have to push hard on ideas which are not harmonious to find a place where harmony can exist. I have to fight in order to have peace. Ain't life grand?

Points to Consider:

1. The teacher used two different concepts to illustrate the Harmony Function for Bob. One he was able to accept and one he couldn't accept.
2. Brain wave function was easy for Bob to accept and the teacher used it to establish that Bob could be in Harmony with a Point of View that he didn't bring with him from childhood.
3. The concept of the Other is something that Bob still needs to accept as an Harmonious Point of View.
4. The lesson was about Harmony Function, so the teacher introduced different Points of View so that Bob could observe the energy governing aspect on his own.
5. The teacher "buried" the Programming about Harmony Function by talking about other Points of View.
6. Harmony almost never comes without taking a stand and sometimes a hard stand.
7. The Shaman puts his life on the line to accomplish Harmony through changing Points of View.
8. The teacher didn't allow concepts from other times in Bob's life to interfere with the one being presented.
9. Bob must now consider being in Harmony with the Other, too.
10. The teacher allowed Bob the latitude to decide for himself how he will apply the Harmony Function.

Chapter 11: Do Function

Once a Shaman is at One with himself and his world and he is in Harmony with others, he again experiences a period of time where he has little focus. At the end of this period he begins to yearn for some method of putting what he knows to use. This is when the Do Function begins to become necessary to the Shaman.

The Do Function is the only one of the seven concepts which is directly related to action. The Be One Function has to do with thought and the Harmony Function has to do with the relationships. The Do Function brings Communication to reality. Communication is the tool used to learn the Do Function.

When Tribal Shaman brought his tribe together and when he brought two tribes together and when he started to teach Bubba Jr. how to become the Shaman, he actually had to use all three concepts. The Be One, the Harmony, and the Do Functions all form a single unit, in a way. Some people try to use only the Be One and Do Functions, to be sure, but whatever configuration is formed in this manner is weak at best, because it is impossible to communicate with yourself and without Harmony, it is impossible to communicate with others. The Do Function is the measure of the effectiveness of any Communication because Programming and changing Points of View allow Communication to Do real things.

Clarification:

Communication is not limited to speech. Communication includes all action. How the action is accomplished may tell more about a person's agenda and what he thinks than 1000 words. Any Communication is also an action. What a person speaks about and how he says what he says is as much a Communication as the subject he broaches. This is why the Do Function is learned though Communication. It is, after all, Communication which relates us to others of our kind. Every "real" accomplishment of the human race has been realized through Communication.

There are real things in the world that we cannot change. They exist without our involvement. Trees are a good example, as are mountains. Some real things need our involvement. Steel would be a good example, as would furniture or tools. In the realm of human endeavor, real things are made through the three functions of Be One, Harmony, and Do. Tribal Shaman used all three Functions to bring the two tribes together. That made a real alliance. He used all three Functions to teach Bubba Jr. how to become a Shaman, and he used all three Functions to make his extended family a tribe.

When the Do Function is active, something changes. A Difference is made. It is always something that people can see. Conversely, if no difference is made then nothing was Done. This is the most important concept of the Do Function. The Do Function makes things real, different, notable. This Difference is made real through Communication. Most of us consider Communication to be nothing more than talk. A Shaman Does things with Communication, and what he Does with Communication is make a notable Difference.

It is this function, which Shamans have employed for generations, that gives the idea of magic to Shamanic activities. Shamans think of the Do Function as a practical application of their knowledge, but it looks to be magic to someone on the outside looking in. There is no flash of light nor is anyone turned into a frog, but there is a different reality created. It may be nearly imperceptible, but something changes in the real world when the Do Function is applied through Communication and the Communication can be verbal or non-verbal.

Clarification:

Magic here is thought of as something that is accomplished, yet has no apparent "logical" explanation for its accomplishment. For instance, a Shaman who uses voice modulation to set his Communication in different brain wave frequencies may appear to be magical in his ability to transfer information and, therefore, Programming to another individual about seemingly impossible situations in that individual's life. To the Shaman, the Communication is simply the practical application of understanding of brain wave frequencies and what programs are held in which brain waves. To the individual receiving the Communication, the Shaman may seem to be simply holding a regular conversation. But the Shaman is applying the Do Function.

The real things that are made are almost always abstractions of one type or another. One notable exception to this is tools. Tools do not exist in a natural state, for instance. You won't find a wrench growing on a wrench tree anywhere. One of the best examples of a real thing which is an abstraction is law. You cannot measure law unless it is with the number of words used to write one. Law is real, yet it exists only in the minds of those who are governed by it. We talk about the law of gravity, for instance, but gravity exists without any human intervention at all. Laws governing traffic, however, exist only because of human Communication. They are real, too, just as real as the law of gravity. The difference is that the law of gravity isn't an abstraction and traffic laws are.

There are lots of "real" abstractions and there is something common about all abstractions which are "real." Someone believes in them. At times, a whole social group believes in a "real" abstraction, as with law. At times, only a part of a social group believes in a "real" abstraction, as with people who belong to a country club. The "club" is an abstraction. The clubhouse and golf course are "real." But the entire concept is an abstraction held in place by the members of the "club." Some "real" abstractions are intensely personal. An example might be claustrophobia. There is nothing life threatening inherent in close places, but to the person who suffers from claustrophobia, the threat can be "real."

In all of these examples, the people who believe in the reality of the abstraction treat the abstraction as though it actually exists and, therefore, it does exist. This is a very important concept for the Shaman. While the Shaman thinks of the soul or Other in the same way he thinks about gravity, he doesn't need to believe in gravity for it to function and he doesn't need to think or even believe about the Other for it to function. He thinks about different Assemblage Points or Points of View in the same way he thinks about other abstract realities. They exist because he believes they exist. To the Shaman, it is practical knowledge to consider a Point of View as nothing more than one of many possible abstractions. The Shaman's definition of the world does not depend on abstract thought. It depends on what he can Do through Communication.

Clarification:

The concept of abstract reality is one that we don't examine often. Consider that the word "abstract" can mean "…apart from any particular instances or material objects; not concrete." It can also mean, "…to separate by the operation of the mind; to think of (a quality) apart from any particular instance or material object that has it." This definition is taken from Webster's New Twentieth Century Dictionary.

In the case of the golf club example, the golf course and the clubhouse exist in terms of real or concrete objects. The membership to the club does not exist in real objects. The membership is abstract. The Shaman does not deal with the Other as though it is abstract. To the Shaman, the Other is a particular instance or even a material object. Therefore, to the Shaman, the idea that the body is an instrument of Communication is not an abstract idea. It is an idea which has substance.

A Point of View or the Assemblage Point, on the other hand, does not have substance for the Shaman. A Point of View is a quality apart from any particular instance or material object. For the Shaman, a Point of View can be compared to a kaleidoscope. Give it a turn and you see a whole new definition of reality. The new reality has no more connection to any particular instance or material object than the previous reality. No matter what is "seen", its interpretation is totally dependent on the Programming or "eyes" of the interpreter. Kind of gives *controlled folly* another spin.

For the Shaman, the Other exists, like gravity, without human intervention. He considers the body to be an instrument of Communication for the Other. The Other can choose any method of observing the world that is convenient for its purposes. Therefore, any given Point of View or Assemblage Point would be, theoretically, acceptable. Obviously some Assemblage Points would be more advantageous than others.

If the Other is to communicate through the body, it would need to adopt an Assemblage Point which allows that Communication to occur. A powerful consideration is that consciousness, or the body, exhibits a need for control. It is as though the consciousness or the body is at war with the Other and doesn't want to be an instrument of Communication. The war can cause glitches in the Programming. To the Shaman, these glitches are contrary to the natural flow of energy. He *sees* those glitches and through Communication tries to reprogram the glitch so that the Other can better communicate. This is the first application of the Do Function for many Shamans.

What actually happens in this reProgramming event is that the Shaman *sees* that a particular program is not following the natural order. For instance, in the example of someone who suffers from claustrophobia, there really is no actual threat. The Shaman may suggest that there is a different Point of View that may serve that individual better. The individual will accept the new Point of View or not. If he does, then he will have a new Assemblage Point from which to view the world. The new Assemblage Point will not contain the idea of close places being threatening and therefore the entire world will have changed for that individual. For that individual, there is now a new reality.

This is an example which may never actually occur, but many Shamans follow a script that is very similar. When a Shaman is talking with someone, it might sound as though he is having a normal conversation. However, there is a method in use. Hierarchies of ideas are being presented and those ideas have been carefully crafted in order to achieve a world description that is complete enough to support the new Point of View. This is how a Shaman employs the Do Function.

Clarification:

The concept here is related to the question of who operates the bio-computer. The Shaman acknowledges the Other as the computer operator. Most people don't. If the Other, as the computer operator, can be accepted as an operational set as opposed to an abstract idea, then internal or mental conflicts could theoretically be alleviated by simply offering thought pathways to an individual which clears the Programming of blockages to the Other, being the computer operator. For the Shaman to embrace such a practice, it would have to be active in his thinking machinery. In fact, the Shaman would necessarily force himself to employ the Do Function in Communication to prove to himself that the Other can and does communicate through the body.

In other words, the proof of the Other as the computer operator is realized through Communication. The act or Do Function of Communication would be directed at a particular mental blockage with the Intent of demonstrating a path of lesser resistance through the Programming of another individual. If that individual adopts the new thought process, then it stands to reason that the individual has a new program which works better than the old one. If we consider Programming in the bio-computer to be energy related, then we could say that each program which defines the Other as the computer operator should theoretically reduce internal conflicts both for other people and for the

Shaman. Of course, the only way to know is to suspend disbelief and adopt that Point of View.

The rules of knowing are very much in play to know and know how you know about the Other and the role it plays in the life of human beings.

Some Shamans use a different approach. This type of Shaman may Dream about an event or an action. The word Dream, as it is used here, is not the same as ordinary nighttime Dreams we are familiar with. This Dreaming is as deliberate as the conversation for changing the Assemblage Point. In this Dreaming, the Shaman may very well envelop the person he is talking to within the Dream. This type of Shaman has the ability to use Dreaming in such a way that the person he is "conversing" with actually *sees* the Dream along with the Shaman.

Both types of Shamans use the Do Function to accomplish notable changes in the "real" world. The difference in how they accomplish those changes is related to what their core Shamanic talents are. Without getting ahead of the story, suffice it to say that some Shamans Dream and some Shamans Stalk. Both types empower the Do Function with a type of concentration called Intent. This is not the, "I intended to go to the store, but forgot" type of intent, but the, "I *Intend* to breathe" Intent. In other words, both types of Shamans infuse the Do Function with the power of life itself.

This concept can be daunting to those who are new to the idea. It is important to realize that a Shaman does not enter into an action without putting his life on the line in the accomplishment of that action, even if the action is nothing more than a Communication. If the activity is not worthy of risking his life, then he most likely won't enter into the activity. For this reason, the *intense*-ity of Shamanic Communication is sometimes threatening to those who observe it. The very *intensity* of the Communication is what activates the Do Function and what makes the notable difference in the reality. It should be noted here that *intensity* is not necessarily boisterous. Intensity can be quiet. It is the action of Intending, which makes *intensity*.

It is important to consider that for Intent to be active, all three Functions must be present. For the Shaman, Doing without Being One and Being in Harmony would be without merit. If a Shaman creates a reality, he will always create a reality that benefits humanity, not a sole benefit for himself. This is the nature of the Be One, Harmony, and Do Functions.

Points to Consider:

1. Communication frees up the energy which is governed by the Do Function.
2. Communication changes things.
3. The Do Function incorporates the Be One Function and the Harmony Function to make things different.
4. Many Communications are non-verbal.

5. As the Do Function begins to govern the energies released by Communication which cause Differences, Communication takes on an aspect of physical activity.

6. Even when talking, the Shaman may Do one thing in order to Do something else altogether.

7. The Shaman uses Intent to "power" his Communication.

8. Intent may, therefore, provide the means to a "subliminal" Communication.

9. Since all Communication is by nature "abstract", it need not be verbal as in, "We are *talking* about this given subject".

10. The Shaman does not entertain himself with his Communications; he *Does* something with his Communications.

Story Chapter XI

Bob hasn't been by for a while. I think he's still having some trouble with the idea of the Other, but he's going to have to find a way to resolve himself with that one. There isn't really a reason to give him more information until that can be resolved. I am sure that it is more resolved than he thinks it is because he is beginning to respond from deeper and deeper levels of thought.

This is pretty normal. When these types of conversations begin to "take", they change how an individual thinks. I wouldn't go so far as to say that Bob has actually Moved the Assemblage Point as yet, although he has experienced events which are very similar a couple of times. I'm not sure that he noticed when it happened because I don't like to tell people that. It serves no particular purpose at this stage, anyway.

The next order of business for Bob is the introduction of the Do Function. This will be the first time that it will actually be fair to challenge him to act as a Shaman. Up until this point, he hasn't had enough information to make an informed decision. That doesn't mean that he's ever had a choice, it just means that he hasn't had enough information to make a conscious choice. Some people make that transition much easier than others and Bob is having more problems than some. It won't make any difference how much he kicks and screams because when it's all said and done, he will be what he was born to be, a Shaman.

The way the Do Function is taught is from mid-Alpha. It is the nature of Do Function to center between the subconscious and regular consciousness. This will become more meaningful to Bob later on.

"I'm bAAAaack."

"Why, yes you are, Bob. How have you been?"

"I've been good. How have you been?"

"Same as always. What brings you by?"

"I've been thinking about some of the things we've talked about and I have some questions."

"You do?"

"Yeah. I've been thinking about this thing with the Other. I read not long ago that the Greeks had a word for life that indicated the life of the spirit. Is that the same thing?"

Yes, it's the same thing. But with your fear of the word I'm going to walk around this a bit before I commit.

"I've known a couple of Greeks and I'm sorry, but I failed to ask them what their word meant. However, nearly every civilization and tribal group has, or has had, a word for the spirit or soul. The Greeks were a pretty smart bunch and I've heard tell that they thought about this subject at length, so I wouldn't be surprised that they had a word for spiritual life."

"Why do I have such a problem with the concept?"

"I really don't know. I suspect it is because you think anything having to do with organized religion is bunk. That's unfortunate because organized religion addresses many things that plague mankind and they address it in a sane fashion."

"Do you think that organized religion is okay?"

"Sure, for many people it is the only way they will ever have of looking at some of these concepts. Religionists tend to be a little less open-minded than I would like, but that doesn't mean that the ideas found in organized religion are false. It is also true that there are some Shamans who practice an immoral brand of Shamanism. That doesn't mean that everyone or everything connected with Shamanism is bad. In the same way that just because many religionists practice a religion of exclusion doesn't mean that all of organized religion is bad."

"Okay, but don't you think that Shamanism is basically bad?"

God won't get you if you think about Shamanism, Bob.

"No, I don't really see a great deal of difference between Shamanism and religionists. I think that when Jesus Christ died for our sins he included everyone and I think he gave humanity the ability to Move its collective Assemblage Point from 'an eye for an eye' to 'forgiveness.' Shamans have a long tradition that predates most religions and Shamans deal with aspects of the Other that most religions reserve only for their leaders. Of course, Shamans deal with aspects of the Other that are more or less reserved for their leaders, too. Perhaps some Shamans would refer to themselves as priests of some sort or another, but I, personally, would think that would be an error. What Shamans do is outside the realm of what priests do, I think."

"Okay, then you don't have a problem with the two ideas existing side by side."

No, Bob, they always have even it they haven't always seen eye-to-eye. But let's add a little fear to this mix to see if your fear is related to religion.

"That's how I think, but you should be aware that there are those inside organized religion who see Shamanism as a direct threat to their beliefs. Just as there are Shamans who see organized religion as a direct threat. I think some of that stems from the Inquisition, when the Catholic Church tried to wipe out all Shamanic thinking. It may have actually been a good thing for Shamanism because there was a good deal of speculation at that time about the power that Shamans actually held, particularly amongst Shamans. Those boys may have been just a little bit full of themselves."

"Don't you think that same thing is happening today?"

He doesn't seem to be afraid of religion so I wonder why he equates religion to soul?

He asked a straight question so let me give him a straight answer.

"It probably is, but the vast oral tradition has mostly been lost. There are, without doubt, people who have managed to salvage a good deal of that tradition and are actively passing it on to another generation. But in most of the 'civilized' world, that oral tradition no longer exists and it will take many generations to rebuild it. You are part of that rebuilding process."

"So how do you do that?"

"How do I do what?"

"How do you take a question I have and turn it around to set up what you want to tell me anyway?"

Good question, Bob. I wish I could take credit. I don't think you are going to like the answer, but…

"I have a good relationship with the Other."

"How does that work?"

I still need to tip toe around this because he's pretty touchy about the Other.

"I would like to say that it is because I am such a smart guy, but that would not be the truth. It's a lot like the relationship between a horse and rider. A good horse can anticipate what the rider is going to do and will already be setting up the moves so the rider can accomplish what he wants. In this case, the body is the horse, the consciousness is the mind of the horse and the Other is the rider. I think my consciousness has lost its fear of direction from the Other. I think my consciousness feels as though it has a good master."

"Is that the way it is for all Shamans?"

"I don't think so. I think there are some Shamans who have a, to me, weird relationship with the Other. Since I don't chat with those people, I don't know why they do what they do and it isn't any of my business. They have to express their relationship with the Other in the way they have to. As far as I know, all expressions of the Other are all right. Humanity learns from each expression."

"Do you think that some of these Shamans are bad?"

That's a strange question.

"I don't. I think that any individual has the right, if not the obligation, to express his relation with the Other in the manner appropriate to him or to the Other. It is not up to me to decide on those issues. Apart from that, when it comes to the Other, right and wrong as we define that dichotomy doesn't apply in the same way. Not only that, but if a Shaman expresses the Other in a way that is detrimental, then he will be the first to experience the detrimental effects of his labors. That is a pretty heavy cost for doing things designed to harm others."

"This is all part of what you want to tell me, isn't it?"
"Yes."
"So what is all this about?"

I thought you'd never ask. Check the rhythm of the voice and modulate it at ten and a half cycles per second. That will place him just about in dead center Alpha and that is precisely where this Communication needs to be placed in the thinking machinery.

"It all is connected to the Do Function. The Do Function is the third concept in a belief system which supports Shamanic activities."
"So how many concepts are there?"
"I think I've told you this already but there are seven. Each of the first three concepts build on the previous one. The last four stand pretty much on their own, although understanding each succeeding one depends on understanding the one previous. We are concerned now with the third concept which is the Do Function. There are many applications of this function and it is through the Do Function that the Shaman discovers who he is, and what he Does."
"So what do I do?"
"You work for the welfare department."
"I mean as a Shaman what do I do?"
"I don't know that you Do anything as a Shaman."
"Well, I haven't done much as a Shaman as yet, but I think I have to start somewhere."

Yes, you will. After this talk you will even have some idea about how to actually accomplish something, maybe.

"That's true. Here's the thing. The way you actually learn the Do Function is through Communication. But for the Shaman it is a particular Communication. It is focused between the Other and the consciousness. Another way of saying that is that the Shaman's Communication is directed somewhere between the conscious and subconscious mind. Some Shamans use a technique known as Stalking to accomplish this maneuver. Other Shamans use a technique known as Dreaming to accomplish the same maneuver."
"I was under the impression that some Shamans were healers and some were card readers or something."
"That may be true, but they all learn how to apply the Do Function through Communication."
"How do healers learn to heal through Communication?"
"It depends on whether the Shaman is a Dreamer or a Stalker. If he is a Dreamer, then he sorts through his Dreams to see which ones are pertinent to the subject who needs his help by communicating what he *sees* in his Dreams. If he is a Stalker, then he uses Communication to lead or even drive the person who needs his help to change how he looks at the world until that person gets

better through Moving his Assemblage Point. At least that is the quick and dirty explanation."

"There is a more complete explanation?"

Oh, yeah. But let's just keep to the basics for now.

"Of course. But it isn't time to get into that now. Now we need to discuss the Do Function. The Do Function must work in conjunction with the Be One and Harmony Functions. For that to occur, then the Other must direct the Doing. Something that you haven't considered is that Communication doesn't have to be verbal. For instance, one of my benefactors was a talking fool. He talked and talked, but he was a Dreamer. While he was talking, he would hold a picture in his mind that he wanted to communicate to you. That picture in his mind was his actual Communication. Most of the time you never noticed that he was 'sharing' that picture which was actually a real time Dream he shared with you. You felt as though you were generating the picture yourself due to his skill as a communicator. In reality, he projected his 'vision' to people through his Dreaming. He actually grabbed folks up into his Dream, and he could do this with a room full of people and all of them would *see* what he was Dreaming."

"Now, that's a skill."

"I suppose. But for him it was just what he did. Although he got very good at it through Communication."

"How does a Stalker communicate?"

"A Stalker acts. Again, you have to consider that not all Communication is verbal. A Stalker may talk and talk just like my benefactor, but he is constantly doing things. He will act sweet one minute and act angry the next. He lets you see what he wants you to see. You may know a Stalker for years and never see who he is. Every act is in concert with the Communication. He rejects you and accepts you in order to communicate about what he wants you to know. But it isn't the emotional show that constitutes the Communication. It is the emotional show connected to the body movements, the dress and even the personality he put on especially for you which make up the Communication. Another one of my benefactors would even incorporate other people into his Communication. Sometime they were willing participants and sometimes they weren't. He could use anything in his environment to communicate. Stalkers are not unlike hunters who use their environment to capture their prey."

"Is that what I am to you? Prey?"

"No. You are someone who needs to learn how the Do Function works through utilizing the act of Communication.

He did, at least, recognize that I have been using Stalking to communicate with him. That is a pretty astute observation. I don't think that he has a very good grip on the idea of Communication as a tool to learn the Do Function simply because he didn't ask about it. He talked around it, but didn't ask. It won't make any difference in the long run because he will have to understand that in order to put the Do Function to work.

Points to Consider:

1. The teacher was using Intent to communicate the program of Do Function to Bob.
2. Bob realized the Communication was occurring although there is no evidence that he understood how.
3. It is very likely that Bob's short-term memory of the event will say that the teacher answered some questions about a problem Bob had with integrating the Shaman's way with organized religion.
4. It is just as likely that Bob's long term memory will recall the stories about the teacher's benefactors and how they Communicated.
5. The teacher overtly demonstrated for Bob his own application of Be One Function and Harmony Function when answering Bob's questions about "right and wrong".
6. A successful Communication uses the Be One, Harmony and Do Functions working in concert.
7. At one level, the Communication made a Difference to Bob because he didn't defend his position or argue about the teacher's observations.
8. On another level the Communication still has to play out.
9. The Communication of the teacher was aimed at both Bob's conscious and subconscious thoughts at the same time.

There was a distinct Communication for both sets which did not necessarily carry the same message.

Chapter 12: Specific Function

As the Do Function begins to become active in the life of a Shaman, he has to spend a certain amount of time trying to fit his emerging knowledge into the world. Not all these efforts are fruitful. Because of his lack of experience, he is certainly going to try to accomplish things that he is not ready to do and he is going to try to accomplish things that his energy configuration will not support. It is on this background that Specific Function begins to make itself known to the Shaman.

It seems to be likely that the actual structural formation of the aura or energy body determines what will claim the Shaman. Specific Function works in this manner. It is an energy field which contains rules of engagement built into the landscape of the field. This is a pragmatic consideration for the Shaman. Why would he spend his limited personal energy trying to be something he is not?

The idea is applied to all aspects of the Shaman's life. For instance, it would be counter-productive for the Shaman to be self-involved because that would be contrary to the Harmony Function. The Shaman will necessarily put himself in Harmony with his Specific Function. His life would be in jeopardy if he were to expend energy in trying to counteract the rules of engagement found in his personal Specific Function and he would be energy bereft should he try to counteract the rules of engagement found in the general idea of Specific Function.

Our friend, Tribal Shaman, had all he could do to teach and understand the Be One, Harmony and Do Functions. It may have taken more than a generation or two for the successive Tribal Shamans to understand that there were other functions at work in their activities. As time progressed and the tribes became a people, they began to share certain beliefs about the world. The world certainly didn't change, but how the people perceived the world evolved and expanded.

With the evolution of world perception came the realization that a people needed to have certain members within the emerging society perform specific duties. There may have been someone who was gifted, for instance, at making flint tools. Perhaps someone else could make the best arrow shafts. As this specialization flourished, the concept of Specific Function began to make itself known to the Shamans.

At first, the Shamans led the people to define themselves as "The Mammoth Hunters" or "The People of the Plains" or some other such designation which separated them from the other peoples who inhabited their area of the world. Later, more specific designations were used, such as tribal names. Yet we are concerned with the idea of Specific Function and that idea began with the first separations.

Specific Function is more like a field of battle than an action. Be One is a kind of action although it is an action within. Harmony, too, is a kind of action, but an action of interaction. Do is all about action. Specific Function is more about the field where action can take place even though it is also a definition of a type of action.

"The Mammoth Hunters" defined themselves as such because of the things they did. The Mammoth Society had to be geared to harvesting mammoths. The guy who worked flint had to have special or Specific knowledge which pertained to mammoths in order to make the tools which would kill them. The arrow guy had to have Specific skills which pertained to how the tools were delivered. Everyone in the society had to develop Specific skills pertinent to mammoth harvesting whether they actually killed mammoth or not. Hunting mammoth required an entire life style, no doubt. So the Shaman who led his people out of opportunistic hunting and gathering into being "The Mammoth Hunters" understood that Specific Function defined the field of endeavor as well as the life style.

There were once, long ago, discussions between the different types of Shamans as to why some Shamans *saw* certain functions in one way and other types of Shamans *saw* them in another way. Each type had to then "walk a mile in the other man's shoes" in order to *see* how it was possible to experience the functions in different manners. This is why Seeing Differences or Moving the Assemblage Point is necessary to understanding Specific Function. Let's take as an example one of the major divisions in types of Shamans. One type of Shaman falls into the category of Dreamer and another type of Shaman falls into the category of Stalker. These two categories define, in general terms, all classes of Shamans. Dreamers are not the opposite of Stalkers, but the two types have different Specific Functions and apply Specific Function in different manners.

Clarification:

The terms "Dreamer" and "Stalker" are from another era. Both words accurately describe or are accurate names for the two types of Shaman. The word Dreamer, as it relates to Shamanic activities denotes one who uses a type of Dream which extends into the waking world. The Dreamer does not wander around the world as though in a Dream but he Dreams the world as it is at this moment and interacts with and in it while in his Dream. This type of Shaman has exacting control over his Dreams. By way of example, this type of Shaman could see a particular landscape or even a nook in a garden, then commit even the minutest details of the garden to memory. With practice, he could "visit" the garden in his Dream. With repeated "visits", it is possible for this type of Shaman to "materialize" in the garden while Dreaming. This takes an extraordinary control and attention while Dreaming. It is not something that an individual can accomplish without dedicating a large portion of his life to the realization of Dreaming.

The word Stalker has a negative connotation in modern English. At one time, the word referred to an individual who captured game animals through stealth and accomplished the capture as an individual, not as a part of a group. It is in this vein that the word Stalker is used to define another type of Shaman. The hunter type of Stalker used his knowledge of the habits of the game animals to capture them. The animals had their natural survival instincts to protect them, but the hunter used their very survival instincts against them. The Stalker Shaman does something similar. He uses the survival instincts of consciousness against itself in order to rewrite the Programming in the bio-computer so that the Other can use the body as an instrument of Communication.

Let's take the Dreamer Shaman first. The Specific Function of a Dreamer is to Dream Dreams. Dreamers don't think of Dreams exclusively as nocturnal events. They think of Dreams as being part of the everyday world, but at the same time as non-ordinary events that are concurrent with the waking world. To the Dreamer Shaman, the Dream world and the waking world Are One and in Harmony. In the Dream world, the Dreamer Shaman can affect what he Dreams so that what he Dreams bends to his will or his Intent. If a Dreamer Shaman Dreams a Dream where he doesn't care for the outcome of events, he simply returns to the Dream and Dreams it again until events are in Harmony with his desires. If the Dream is about activities in the waking world, he *sees* the outcome of those events and molds them to his desires. The Dreamer Shaman may also visit worlds which do not, apparently, coincide with the waking world in any way, but the Shaman may find meaning or Harmony in his Dreams which allow him to make sense of the world he *sees* while "awake". The Dreamer Shaman may also have bits and pieces of Dream while he is awake which address events he is experiencing in real time. To the Dreamer Shaman Dreams are the Specific Function of what he Does. His Specific Function is Dreamer, however, and that colors all that he knows and applies to the Be One, Harmony, and Do Functions.

The Specific Function of a Stalker is to treat each encounter with those who inhabit his world as though he was entering into battle. Stalkers don't think of chance encounters or coincidences. They think of each encounter as a battle for energy and they think of those "random" encounters as a Being One event. During an encounter with others, the Stalker Shaman utilizes a number of thinking tools that one would expect to find only in a warrior. Principle among those thoughts is, "Any battle is a battle for your life." Therefore, a Stalker Shaman does not even engage in conversation if there is a doubt about the outcome. If the outcome of the encounter is not in Harmony with the Stalker Shaman's desires, he returns to the encounter and Stalks it again until the energy outcome is what he has *seen*. The Stalker Shaman may employ an illogical, to others, set of ploys to affect the battle because he is following the dictates of the Other or soul and what he "wins" in the battle may not even be noticeable to those he wins it from. The Stalker Shaman enters into each battle as though his life is at stake because gaining or losing energy is the Function of what he Does. His Specific Function, however, is Stalker and that colors all that he knows and applies to the Be One, Harmony and Do Functions.

Dreamers learn to Stalk and Stalkers learn to Dream. The Dreamer learns to Stalk so that he can see how Specific Function operates for a Stalker. The Stalker does the same thing for the same reason. It should be obvious that neither the Shaman who Stalks nor the Shaman who Dreams take on the Assemblage Point of the other personage so that they can be better or find worldly comfort. To deliberately move the Assemblage Point from one type of Shamanic Function to another is difficult and both types of Shaman use the movement to better understand their own Specific Functions.

A Dreamer necessarily has a different set of information pertaining to the Be One, Harmony and Do Functions than does a Stalker. Both sets of information could be true at the same time, but appear to be widely dissimilar in certain aspects. Specific Function solves both sets of equations and unifies them. The method of Communication of the Do Function of a Dreamer is different than the method of Communication of the Do Function of the Stalker. As a consequence, the Specific Function of both appears to be different as well. The energy governed by Specific Function is the same in both cases, but the expression of that energy is different in each case.

Clarification:

Specific Function can be considered as a field of endeavor. In some ways, it could be thought of as though a battlefield. Where a battle is fought has historically had as much to do with who the eventual winner of the battle would be as the advantage in weaponry or the will of the combatants. The battlefield General who understands the terrain has an enormous advantage over an opponent who does not understand the terrain. Likewise, a Shaman who understands the Specific Function of the Other has an enormous advantage over anyone who does not.

Therefore, the Dreamer Shaman would use his knowledge of the Specific Function of the Other in Dreaming and the Stalker Shaman would use his knowledge of the Specific Function of the Other in Stalking. The two different types of Shamans are not at war with one another, however. They are at war to free the Other to express. The battlefield is the thinking machinery in the bio-computer.

Energy can have different configurations and it is an energy configuration that determines which expression a given Shaman will have. It seems that Specific Function governs the type of energy which a given individual expresses. For instance, the Stalker Shaman has energy that allows him to interact with non-shamans in what appears to be a teaching function, although the Stalker Shaman is always capturing excess energy through his Communication. The Dreamer Shaman captures energy through Dreaming and doesn't seem to have much energy to deal with others at all. Both Shamans learn Specific Function through Moving the Assemblage Point. It is because Moving the Assemblage Point requires energy that Shamans are forced to become proficient at what they Do. When a Dreamer Shaman attempts to Move his Assemblage Point to that of Stalker, he expends energy because he is working against what his natural Specific Function dictates. So because of that movement, he can see what his Specific Function is actually dictating. The same is true for the Stalking Shaman.

Points to Consider:

1. Observing Differences frees up the energy governed by Specific Function.
2. Making Differences defines Specific Function.
3. Living in the desert or the tropics defines much of a resident's life style and may even define a specific thing the resident does. In the same way Specific Function is at once a field of endeavor and a definition of action.
4. Specific Function, as it is expressed by any given individual, may be controlled by the energy configuration of the "aura" of that individual.
5. In order to better understand the Specific Function in oneself, it is always useful to act with the Specific Function of another from time to time.
6. Some male Shamans even go to great lengths to adopt the Specific Function of women.
7. Identifying one's particular Specific Function is an energy saving endeavor.

Story Chapter XII

Bob had to think about the Do Function for several weeks. Still, because he still hasn't come to grips with the idea of the Other, he is not being as effective as I would like. It is his process and I can't do much about that even if I wanted to. Each individual has to go through their Programming in a manner appropriate to that individual. Bob is no exception.

Even so, I will have to begin to exert pressure on what appears to be immaturity. Since this pressure is disciplinary by nature, he will not enjoy it. Some people get pouty and sulk around for days whenever pressure is exerted on their favorite defenses. Bob has never demonstrated this type of silliness. He resists the pressure, but when he has run through all his defenses, he seems to capitulate and cleanly go on with the new idea. The one exception to this has been his continued resistance to the Other. This is strange because there are levels of his thinking that appear to be unaffected by this resistance.

Over the next few sessions, I'm going to resist right back and resist hard enough that he will have to commit one way or another. In some ways I have to be the tyrant that he doesn't have in the world where he lives. I have to insist that he defend his positions with honesty. This will not be a pleasant passage for my friend Bob.

"Hey Bob. How you doing?"

"I'm all right, I guess."

"That well, eh?"

"Actually, I'm good."

I might as well set the tone for this conversation right up front.

"Then say that."

"Okay, okay."

He has been introduced to the idea of the Do Function and Communication as a means to accomplish things so I'll just hold his feet in that fire. I'll start slowing down the rhythm of my voice to see where he gets past all this stuff. I need to get him below his resistance before starting to set this program.

"Don't 'okay, okay' me. Say what you mean and mean what you say. If you're going to begin a conversation with inaccuracies, then everything you say consequent to that will be just as tainted. It's time for you to start being careful with your own Programming."

"Yes, sir."

"Do you wear your seat belt when you drive?"

"Yes…why?"

"If you're that careful when you're driving, you need to be 10 times as careful when you're Programming yourself and I don't want to have this conversation

again. You're a grown man. Act like one."
"We're a little testy today, are we?"

Here we go with the defense series.

"No, we're not. We do have some rather important ground to cover and I don't want you screwing it up with silliness."
"Okay, I'll pay attention."

"Gee, that wasn't painful now was it?"
"No."

I dislike these necessary exchanges. I always have to remember that folks can find it hard to simply let go of being in charge. It is scary, I suppose. Even if I can't suppose, I must honor how they see their world.

"So how are you coming with your Communication?"
"I've been talking to people but I don't think I know any more now than I did the last time we talked."
"Why is that?"
"Well, what am I suppose to be learning?"

Slow it down even further.

"When you talk to people, what do you talk about?"
"I talk about work or the news or something like that."
"No wonder you're not learning anything. Do you ever talk about something that will make a difference in someone's life?"
"Like what?"
"Boy, what am I going to do with you?"
"What do you mean?"
"Have you learned anything that has changed your life?"
"I think I have."

There's a fear here. I need to be more intense than the fear.

"I think you have, too. Why aren't you explaining those things to other people?"
"I'm not sure they really want to hear those kinds of things."
"One of two things is true then. One is that you need to talk to a different class of people. The other is that you aren't paying attention to how people show up to talk to you."
"There's nothing wrong with the class of people I talk to."
"Right. Then you aren't paying attention to how they arrive."
"What does that mean, 'how they arrive'?"
"It means that the spirit is bringing people to you for you to talk to and you

aren't paying attention to when that happens."

"So how does it happen?"

"If you're going to learn about this, you are going to have to Move your Assemblage Point. You can't go on thinking about yourself and others in the same old numb way. What do you say to that?"

"What am I supposed to say?"

"You should say whatever it is that you feel like saying. That's part of your problem. You're always looking for someone to validate your life. You are the only person who can validate that. If you don't have the chutzpah to care enough about other people to make a difference in their lives, then you need to stick your head in the sand and ignore everything I've ever told you."

He recognizes the truth, but I'll bet he'll defend his position again in a couple of minutes. But why does he need validation? What is it that is blocking his development? I guess I need to slow this down as far as I can so that he can get past this scary.

"Has the cat got your tongue? I'm going to let you up a little. I don't think for a minute that you don't know what I'm talking to you about so I'm going to pretend that I didn't hear any of the stuff you were trying to get me to buy into. Here's the thing. You know when someone needs your help. Not only that, you know how to say things to them that will make a difference. I know you know because you've told me how you do that very thing at your work. The difference is that at your work you can justify your actions because it is your 'job.' Well, it's your 'job' to help anyone the spirit brings your way, too. The sooner you accept that fact, the easier it will be for you."

"At work I have to do the best I can and I do what I can to help those people."

Here it comes.

"That's what I'm saying. I'm also saying that you can help other people too. But to do that, you have to do it for the hell of it, not because you are getting paid."

"How do I know if I'm doing the right thing?"

"You won't until after you do it. Don't expect that anyone is going to say, 'Thanks, Mr. Shaman, you've made a huge difference in my life and I won't ever forget it. In fact, our next child will be named Bob.' That just isn't going to happen. Most of what you will have to say to folks is not going to be well received. It might take years for them to incorporate what you say into their lives."

"You know, that is not very encouraging."

"Oh, but it is. You have to be able to say those things in such a way that they never know what you have actually done. The worst thing that could happen to you would be to develop into a guru. You have to understand that while you have obligations to help others, you are not responsible for them or for their lives."

"I don't think I understood that."

"You are obligated by the Other to offer help to those that are placed in front of you, but at the same time you are not able to go to the bathroom for them."

"Huh?"

I figured that would throw him.

"Going to the bathroom is a response. Breathing is a response. Think about that. I can't breathe for you, nor can I be responsive or responsible for other aspects of your life that pertain solely to you. Even so, I do have an obligation to talk to you. Neither you nor I chose that obligation, it simply is. Go figure, one day there you were, talking about I don't know what, but full of energy that needed to be directed. I couldn't direct it; I could only tell you things that would allow you to direct it."

"Okay, so if someone shows up around me, then I have an obligation to talk to them about these things?"

At least he's listening.

"Sort of. It depends on how they arrive at your doorstep, as it were. Take you again. You kept coming around and talking to me. I was grouchy and did my best to let you know that you were a blooming idiot. Did you take the hint? Noooo. You came back for more. So I began to check. I trotted Programming out and you stood up and saluted. Then you came back for more. I then had an obligation to talk to you. I am not responsible for what you do with the subject matter. If you use it, fine. If you don't use it, fine. But you used it. That meant that I had further obligation to talk to you. And so on."

"Okay, but what do I learn from talking to people? Isn't that where this started?"

"Yes, it did. You learn how you do things. You learn whether you are a Stalker or a Dreamer. It depends on what method you use to present ideas to people. Do you act? Do you show them a personage that you make up so they are busy talking to the personage while you sit back and listen?

"Do you hold a picture in your mind while you're talking? While you're holding the picture in your mind, do you keep on talking until *they* start talking about the picture you're holding? What do you do?"

"You know, I think I hold a picture in my mind."

That's a step in the right direction.

"Great! Now learn to show them a personage so you can figure out how to project the picture better."

"But that would mean that I have to do something that is not natural to me."

"You know, for a white boy, you're pretty quick. Of course, that's what it means. This is what Specific Function is all about."

"You've been talking about Specific Function all along, haven't you?"

Yes, Bob, I have.

"You got it, pale face."

"I thought you learned Specific Function by Moving the Assemblage Point."

"What do you think you've been doing here?"

"I've been listening, I think."

"Yes, you have. But what have you been listening to? Have you listened to your own responses?"

"I think so."

"I don't, but let's check. When did your attitude change?"

"My attitude hasn't changed."

"Why, it most certainly did. It changed at the time I asked you if the cat had your tongue."

"Oh, yeah. I was acting a little rebellious up until then because I thought you wanted me to tell people things they wouldn't want to know."

"Then after that, you began to allow room for the idea of actually helping people that came to you for help. What caused the change?"

"You did. But I started to see things from another perspective."

I'm not responsible for you. You have to do that on your own. I can only point the way.

"You moved your Assemblage Point, or another way of saying it would be that you began to see things from a different Point of View."

"But you helped me. How did you do that?"

"Part of my Specific Function is Stalker and you don't have a clue to whom you're talking."

The thing about Bob is that he responds well once he gets past all his defenses. It seems as though he begins to respond once I reach lower Theta or upper Delta with my voice modulation. That would indicate that there may be some blockage in lower to mid Theta that he can't afford to look at. Hmmm.

Points to Consider:

1. The teacher used some "tough love" to more or less force Bob to pay attention so he could see a Difference.
2. It is necessary for Bob to be very careful with his Communication.
3. The teacher used his Stalking skills to put Bob off balance so that he would not ask for the teacher's validation.
4. The teacher was consistent by actually demonstrating to Bob what he was talking about.

5. The teacher used the term "make a Difference" instead of telling Bob to observe a difference. The key word was Difference even though we can't tell how the teacher was Seeing or Dreaming or even Stalking the lesson.

6. Bob didn't realize that he was assembling a new worldview through the simple idea of changing why he does something; from only doing it if he is paid, to doing something "for the hell of it."

7. The teacher "unloaded" the Programming Bob had by telling him that he wasn't "responsible" or "couldn't respond" for certain aspects of other people's lives.

8. The teacher then challenged Bob to Move his Assemblage Point to a place that isn't "Natural" to him.

9. Again, the program for Specific Function was buried in other conversation, but this time Bob was ready and caught the teacher at his game.

Chapter 13: Natural Mind Function

Moving the Assemblage Point is an accomplishment in a Shaman's life. It isn't a crowning moment, but it is an important step. It begins with being able to simply accept other Points of View as easily as changing clothes. It progresses to being able to *see* whole other worlds. Even so, the major work a Shaman realizes is in the area of belief. The Shaman learns to believe on purpose. To deliberately believe and thereby change the world is as great an accomplishment as anyone can achieve. It is the definition of Shamanic activities.

Natural Mind Function, like Specific Function, is more of a field of endeavor than an action, although action is necessary to utilize it. Specific Function is related more to the body and Natural Mind Function is connected to the spirit. Body and spirit are the closest connections we can make at this point, although we could say that Specific Function is objective and Natural Mind is subjective. This wouldn't be entirely true either, but we need to have some beginning point.

As society began to form within the tribes and the people were more defined by tribal names, a phenomenon began to present itself. Some individuals seemed to move into the Shamanic knowledge with little or no effort, while others struggled. The Shamans were perplexed about this turn of events and began to look for reasons. They employed the art of Not Doing to allow the answer to present itself. What they discovered was the Natural Mind Function.

When Be One, Harmony, and Do Functions are applied in the consciousness or to the body, they have certain characteristics. When the same Functions are applied to the spirit or soul, they have different characteristics. A lot of the change in characteristics has to do with the direction of thought. If thought is directed inward from consciousness toward the subconscious, then one set of characteristics applies. This could be called logic. If thought is directed from deep subconsciousness toward consciousness, then a different set of characteristics applies. This could be called belief. In order to make this easier to understand, we will use Beta to signify consciousness and Delta to signify deep subconsciousness. Those early Shamans didn't have either designation to use so they decided to call the duality "body and spirit." Even today, it is sometimes still a useful designation.

What the early Shamans *saw* was that some individuals made the move to thinking from Delta to Beta with no problem and some individuals could only think from Beta to Delta. They also noticed that those who could think from Delta to Beta also moved their Assemblage Point around almost at will. Those individuals who thought from Beta to Delta could not move their Assemblage Point at all. As a result of their Seeing, the early Shamans decided to use Not

Doing as a method of teaching the Natural Mind Function.

The idea of the Natural Mind Function is that there is a natural order to all things. The mind or the thinking machinery is included in this set. When the thinking machinery is functioning properly in either direction, there are certain things that are important to an individual and there are things that lose their importance. In order to teach the natural order of the Beta to Delta thinking processes, the early Shamans devised a code of conduct which they, for lack of a better term, called the "Warrior's Way." There were many, many things that a young man had to learn in order to become a warrior. He had to think of his people before he thought of himself. He had to keep his body in good working condition. He had to be proficient in procuring food for himself and for his people. He had to master the arts necessary to defend his people. He had to be a good father and husband. The list goes on and on. All these things pertained to the body. They had to do with the natural order of how to think as an individual aspiring to be a warrior.

One of the most significant things a young man learned was that as a warrior, he had to consider himself as already dead. This is something that warriors of today also have to absorb, otherwise they will not have the necessary edge in battle. If a warrior has nothing to lose, then he can throw himself into the battle without holding back to protect his hopes, his fears or his loves. When a warrior arrived at this juncture, he was ready to accept the challenge of moving his Assemblage Point. In other words, he was ready to give up control.

Giving up control is a serious matter. It is fraught with all manner of frightening possibilities. The most frightening of all is the thought that something or someone may not have the best interests of an individual in mind. Still, this is a thought that pertains to Beta to Delta thinking. It is not a thought that pertains to Delta to Beta thinking because the actual master of the body is in control in this direction. The early Shamans called this master the spirit. We call it the soul, but we could simply call it the Other.

The warrior who had realized that he needed to consider himself as already dead was motivated to allow the Other to control him. He may have already had many, many experiences where the Other had shown that it was a better protector of the body than consciousness. The problem with learning about the Other through battle was that battles are dangerous. Another method was needed and that method was Not Doing.

Not Doing allowed the warrior cum Shaman to observe the natural order of the Other in his life. He came to trust that still small voice that suggests, once, to follow a given path or to broach a certain subject. With experience, that voice replaces the internal dialog of consciousness to the point that every action is directed from that place. As action is more and more so directed, new Assemblage Points are utilized to construct the world we see from an increasing number of perspectives. This is not painful, but it is instructive.

Another thing those early Shamans discovered was that the Other is just as capricious as consciousness. It guards secrets, it explores areas which are best left unexplored, it can use its power in cruel ways, yet it can help heal or care for the body in many ways. It was fortunate that the early Shamans employed the Warriors Way to teach their craft because it is this discipline which keeps the Shaman from getting lost in the myriad intricacies of the Other.

The Warriors Way had another advantage. As the Other took control of the Shaman, he came to realize the true nature of belief. To the Shaman, belief is directed by the Other and it is not an arbitrary action. The Other expresses itself by belief which courses through the Delta to Beta thinking and therefore a description of reality exists for the Shaman. The Natural Mind Function governs the energy that the thinking mechanism uses to perceive reality. This event requires discipline in the thinking mechanism which the Warrior's Way provided.

Clarification:

Believing from Delta to Beta has a different set of characteristics than believing from Beta to Delta. This fact is pivotal for the Shaman. Consider that as we grow, we learn the component parts of thought. As very small children, we learn the difference between real and pretend. As we grow a bit older, we learn the emotional sets we may very well use for the rest of our life. As we grow even older, those emotional sets break apart to form the Programming of feelings. Then as we finally mature, we fine tune logic. This means that our logic is rooted in our beliefs about the difference between real and pretend. There is a possibility that an individual who has less than three years of age could make mistakes here.

As a point to consider, mistakes in Programming could very well happen during the entire maturing process and even after an individual is grown. Once maturity is achieved, for most people, the only way back to belief is through that nebulous commodity called faith. This is why faith is programmed from an early age. However, the Shaman endeavors to move his awareness to the site of those early beliefs. Faith in what he believes takes on a different perspective due to the direction of his thought process.

The Shaman is aware that if he changes a Point of View held in Delta belief Programming, then the very world he *sees* changes. If he changes his beliefs to include a more peaceful or profitable world, then the world he *sees* is, in fact, peaceful or profitable. The individual whose awareness is centered in Beta may be able to believe in a peaceful or profitable world and realize the Programming to change his world through faith, and he may not. For the Shaman, such a change is a deliberate act. For non-shamans it is a hopeful act.

When a new belief is introduced in the Delta region of thought, it could take several years to work its way up through the thinking machinery until it reaches the Beta region of thought. Through the deliberate use of *recapitulation,* a Shaman can free up enough room in the thinking and Programming mechanisms to accomplish the same feat in a matter of days. Through disciplined use of *recapitulation,* a skilled Shaman can accomplish the feat in nanoseconds. The mechanism for such disciplined *recapitulations* is engaging the Beta to Delta thinking machinery in Not Doing while the Delta to Beta thinking machinery is engaged in changing *perceptions* of reality.

Clarification:

> *Recapitulation* is a tool for sorting through the life events, and therefore Programming, of an individual as they return awareness to Delta. *Recapitulation* could be defined as an event-by-event reliving of the life of an individual. The reason for *recapitulation* is to find and correct the Programming errors of youth. For the experienced Shaman, correcting Programming can also include redefining possible realities or beliefs so that the Shaman can virtually *see* any defined world he can imagine.

Points to Consider:

1. Specific Function is, or can be considered as, an objective or consciousness-related function, while Natural Mind Function is, or can be considered as, a subjective or subconscious function.
2. Thought can flow in two directions. It is not limited to consciousness.
3. It is illogical to think that logic is the only type of thought a human being can utilize.
4. Belief can and does shape perceived reality as much, if not more, than logic.
5. It is logical that every Doing has a corresponding Not Doing.
6. Natural Mind Function governs the energy released by Not Doing.
7. The thought path from Delta to Beta requires discipline.
8. The Not Doing of the internal dialog is Not Doing.
9. Belief is an action. As such, it determines what reality or part of reality we watch.
10. To the Shaman, belief is a deliberate act of the Natural Mind Function.
11. Recapitulation could be thought of as the Not Doing of memory.
12. Recapitulation could also be thought of as allowing the Natural Mind to Function.

Story Chapter XIII

The thing about Bob is that he is not too bright and not too dull. In the words of Goldilocks, he is just right. This has been a plateful for the poor guy and he hasn't really been too bad about it. He has progressed steadily and not at all too fast. I would be worried if he was progressing too rapidly.

Even though he still isn't asking the right questions or even asking questions at the right time, he is opening doors so I can walk through. I'm sure if you were to ask him about that, he might have a different take on it. Anyway, when he asks his questions he tells me more about himself than he suspects. The next session we have is going to be tough on his worldview. It is fairly common for folks to defend their worldview with every trick in the book, but the most common trick is to act like they don't understand. In some ways it's true that they don't. In other ways, they do understand and are terribly threatened by the mere possibility that another worldview can even be possible.

The neat thing is to watch someone discover that multiple worldviews are an advantage. It's kind of like showing someone a new advance in technology and watching them play with it for a few minutes, then adapt to it like it was the most natural thing in the world. I think Bob really did enjoy seeing the world from another perspective, as he called it, the last time we talked. My bet is that he has been trying on other 'perspectives' ever since.

I don't think he is comfortable with the idea of being a Dreamer, though. I can understand because he doesn't have, as yet, a method for putting what he does to use. One reason is that he has yet to accumulate enough energy. Unfortunately, he has a tendency to waste his energy. Part of the reason for the waste is that he is having trouble believing that energy exists, at least in the way Shamans think about energy.

"It's Bob the Dude."

"It is. It is. What's new?"

"Nothing."

"Nothing? I figured you would be just full of great gossip from the world of the spirit."

"Sorry, there hasn't been much news from that front for longer than anybody can remember."

"Is that so?"

"Yes it is. So tell me, how are you coming with communicating with the folks?"

"Okay, I guess. I've had some interesting conversations with some people."

"I seem to remember that you were talking to some guy over at the beach a while back about some things. You been back over there?"

"No. Actually, I've been talking to some people I met at the coffee shop. It wasn't as scary as I thought it would be."

"I'm shocked. You've actually been talking to people at the coffee shop? Will wonders never cease?"

"I thought it would be some kind of fight or something and it wasn't. They were pretty cool."

"So did you Dream or Stalk?"

"I still don't know for sure but I know I had a picture in my mind about what I wanted them to see. But then I always have a picture in my mind when I'm talking to someone."

"Who knew?"

"You probably did."

"No, I don't know anything about that. The only person that any of this is important to is you."

"So... why don't I know who I'm talking to?"

"You've been coming by here for what? Three, four years? And you don't know me yet?"

"You said I don't know who I'm talking to."

Oh! So that's why he's got the butter out. I still won't validate him because he has to verify his own observations. Let's just get to the matter at hand.

"You don't. But I don't have time to get into that now. Now we need to talk about Natural Mind Function. Do you know how you learn the information needed to understand Natural Mind Function?"

"No."

This is probably going to throw him for a little.

"By Not Doing."

"Say what?"

"Ever since the last time you were here, I'll bet you've been running around looking for people to talk to, haven't you?"

"You told me to communicate so I could learn what I do."

"I certainly did. Well, now I'm telling you to Not Do so those people can find you."

"I can feel the hot air as this rushes by my head. I'm not getting this at all."

I'm sure it's going by too fast for him to grasp it.

"Your life is filled with doing stuff. You probably think that you need to stay busy in order to accomplish something. There's nothing wrong with staying busy, but that doesn't mean you can't Not Do while you're busy accomplishing."

"If that was an explanation, it didn't explain much to me."

"Not Doing is a method of allowing the Other to show you stuff. For instance, if you're at the coffee shop, instead of starting a conversation, wait until the other people start it. Then wait to see what they want to talk about. If they start to make overtures in the direction of the things you've been learning, then speak up. If they don't, then wait until the person who wants to talk about those things shows up. That is an example of Not Doing. There are lots of Not Doings. If you forget your very important papers in the morning, instead of going back for them, continue on and see what the Other is trying to tell you. Who knows, you may find that leaving them behind was the best thing that could have happened."

"I can kind of see the thing about waiting for the people to talk, but deliberately leaving important papers? That would be irresponsible."

"Maybe. But you would have to try it before you decided, wouldn't you?"

"You said there were lots of Not Doings. Can't you give me better examples?"

"Okay. Instead of attacking events like you have to do something about everything or try to control everything, start to practice Not Doing. Look for the appropriate Not Doing in a few things to start. Then expand the idea into as much as you can."

"Okay. But what is the Natural Mind Function, anyway?"

"To start with, you need to understand that both Specific Function and Natural Mind Function are, let's say, male expressions. Later we'll talk about female expressions, but male and female are misleading words."

"Male and female? Why not use yin and yang?"

"I want you to learn about this as cleanly as possible."

"If you say so."

"Specific Function has to do with anything having to do with the consciousness including the body. Natural Mind Function has to do with anything pertaining to the subconscious including the Other."

"And that means…?"

"Specific Function is connected to the way the conscious mind and body act and interact, in a way. Natural Mind Function is connected to the way the subconscious mind acts and interacts with the Other and with other people."

"Well now, that just cleared this all up. Why didn't you say so before?"

"Fair enough. Look, if the body and mind are functioning well, then we say that the consciousness is in good shape. If the Other is functioning through the body, we refer to that as the subconsciousness working properly. The last time, we talked about Specific Function, which is all about consciousness. This time we are talking about the subconsciousness. Both Specific Function and Natural Mind Function have masculine aspects. We are going to refer to those aspects as more nearly masculine characteristics. I don't want you to think of this as only masculine because you have always used the word 'masculine' as being the opposite of 'feminine.' To think about this in that way is only confusing."

"Okay, why didn't you say that to begin with?"

"I thought I did."

"You might have, but if you did I sure didn't understand it."

"Do you understand it now?"

"No, but it is clearer."

"Okay. Specific Function is a field which allows for thinking from the consciousness down toward the subconscious. Natural Mind Function is a field for thinking from the subconscious up through the conscious. Both directions have a natural order."

"And that is?"

"When we think from consciousness down towards the subconscious, then logic is in control. That is how it should be. Logic has a Specific Function of ordering thought. Logic tells us that we have talents and that we do the things we are talented at best. Specific Function allows us to fit into our society and make valuable contributions. Natural Mind Function does much the same, but in the other direction."

"So Specific Function lets us use Beta to look at Alpha and so on, right?"

"Exactly."

"Then Natural Mind Function would let us use... what? Delta to look at Theta and so on?"

"Yep. But remember here that Delta is the home of belief. So what would that indicate?"

"I don't know. That we would believe that emotions exist?"

"You may be closer than you think. Consider this thought for a minute. Modern mind/brain theory sometimes uses the word 'ego' to define the computer operator. I think that word has a special definition when it is used in that context and I don't think it means the same as it does in common usage. When we, as Shamans, talk about thinking from Delta to Beta, we consider the Other to be the computer operator. This would mean that the Other chooses the belief we use as the 'machine language' of the day. Now what if the world we perceive is dependent on the belief of the day? Wouldn't that be a kick?"

"Wait a minute here. What are you saying?"

"That got your attention, now didn't it? What I am saying is that the Natural Mind Function of Delta to Beta thinking is controlled by the Other. Further, I am saying that the point of control is Delta, which is where belief about reality is formed. If the Other has the liberty of Moving the Assemblage Point wouldn't the Other be able to 'adjust' beliefs in reality?"

"Are you saying that you can see reality any way you want?"

"No, I'm saying that the Other can see any reality it wants."

"I don't believe that. There are physical laws that we have to deal with. We live on a planet governed by those laws. How can the 'Other' adjust that?"

"You're assigning 'reality' a value that it just doesn't have. You don't deal with that 'reality' anyway. Where do you obtain your groceries? At the Serengeti Super? I don't think so. If you want to go to L.A., you just hop on a plane and in a few hours, you're there. I don't think you wander around in the woods gathering berries for the winter, I don't think you have to have your horse shoed too often, I don't think you worry about staying warm when it's cold, and I think your biggest problem is how to dispose of all the waste you generate. I assure you the Other has the ability to adjust that perceived reality."

"I don't think that is reality. That is simply the technology of our age."

"I'll tell you what. Why don't you go out to the landfill and tell me how that isn't real."

"The landfill is real."

"You bet it is. Now tell me that if we as a society believed differently, we couldn't change that."

"You have a point."

"Now, if we could change that by believing differently, I wonder what we could do with racism or child molestation. I'm sure that with enough practice we could actually see the sun as a different color, but why not deal with things that are at hand?"

"I don't think about reality like that."

"How do you think about reality, then?"

"Well, not like that."

Here come the defenses.

"Then how?"

"I don't know! I guess if the sun were a different color or if I actually saw spirits, then that would be a different reality."

"Well, change your glasses and the sun will be a different color. Then with your regular glasses, look around. You will be looking at a world of spirits. All humans are souls, after all."

"I don't mean like that."

Here's that fear again. It's time to start putting pressure on that fear alone.

"No, you want to see some fictional world. You want to see auras or luminous eggs and inorganic beings. If you were to see a ghost or some other inorganic being, you would crap your pants. Hell, if you can't deal with the spiritual you can already see, then how are you going to deal with things you can't even conceptualize?"

"So are you saying that inorganic beings don't exist?"

Changing the subject won't stop this onslaught. I've got to keep the pressure up on this.

"No! They do exist, but you have to crawl before you walk and walk before you run. If you were fortunate enough to live in a society of Shamans, then perhaps you would be able to simply follow the emotions they would emanate and see whatever they would see. But, you don't. You live in a world where that kind of knowledge needs to be rebuilt and you are part of that rebuilding process. So deal with the world you can deal with and search for the unknown."

"How can I do that?"

Damn if he didn't back it off again.

"You start by Not Doing. That will allow you to become attuned to the instructions of the Other. As you learn to pay attention to the Other, whole worlds will be revealed to you. But for now you have to start where you are. As you grow, you will learn that you can deliberately believe different realities and go into them and live, if you choose. Until then, do what you can do. But to accomplish that, you need to be a lot more honest than you are."

"I'm honest."

Maybe if I program honesty for a while I can use it in the next session.

"No, you're not. You kid yourself about a lot of stuff. Like this argument you've been waging for all this time about the existence of the soul. You know perfectly well that the soul exists, but you lie to yourself about that and then hide the lie behind 'not understanding how it can exist.' What a crock. Here's another one of your 'pet theories': You say that you don't want to really get involved with Shamanic activities, yet here you are time and time again at my place where you know you're going to get more information about Shamanic activities. Who are you trying to fool? Yourself?"

"I'm not trying to fool anyone."

"May I be brutally honest here?"

"You don't need my permission."

"No, I don't, but I'm asking if you would mind?"

"I can take anything you can dish out."

Let's just see, then.

"Okay, I'll take that as permission granted. Here comes. You know any damned fool can pretend to be something, but only those with actual talent can really do some things. Take a musician for instance. You or I could sit down at a piano, or pick up a guitar and make musical sounds, but only people born to music can take those instruments and make music. The same is true for you. Here you are born to the Office of Shaman. The reason I can say that is that I recognize myself in you. But you… *you* have to argue about that. You have to tell this elaborate lie to yourself about how you aren't what you actually are and then you go around learning all you can about the subject, all the while looking desperately for someone to give you permission to act the fool. You're a clever lad, you are."

"It's not that I'm lying to myself, it's that I'm not sure, is all."

Robert! I have to slow this down even more and increase the intensity. Let's see if

I lower the rhythm a few more cycles per second if he won't be below where this fear or program is.

"Peddle that BS somewhere else. I don't buy it. You know full well that you're lying through your teeth. If you're not sure, then why are you here? I'll tell you why. You're here to learn all you can. The problem is that you want to stick your toe in the water and say that you're swimming. That isn't very honest, in my book."

"But I really don't know if this is a life I want or not."

"You know, the only reason I don't throw you out of here on your ear is because I don't have patience for volunteers. What damn difference does it make if you want this life or not? You are this life. The only thing you can possibly accomplish by pussyfooting around is to make a fool of yourself."

"I'm not making a fool of myself."

"Oh, no. You're just pretending to be something that you're not, right? I hope you're not trying to fool me with this crap. It's bad enough that you are trying to fool yourself."

"I'm not trying to fool anyone."

"Of course you're not. But even though you're not trying to fool anyone, let's get this absolutely straight. If you're not willing to be Brutally Honest with yourself, then we really haven't any more to talk about. You have to come to the place that your self-importance no longer matters. As long as you are locked into your self-importance, you cannot think from Delta to Beta or whatever name you want to give the event. You will stagnate here at present level."

"So what are you saying? That because I want to discover whether this is right for me or not that I'm lying?"

"No! I'm saying that you already know that you haven't a choice. Furthermore, I'm saying that what you are lying about is that it is only self-importance that keeps you from doing good things for others. Nothing more or less. If you want to throw away what you are simply because you are too lazy to think about the folly of self-importance, that's your right. It is also your right to make something of yourself. It all depends on how important you want to be. If you want to be a person of substance, then you will exchange your self-importance for sobriety. If you want to be a hollow shell, then you will continue as you are. It's of no importance to me."

"It's important to me."

"Then make your decision."

"I don't want to be a hollow shell."

"Then, my friend, you need to put your money where your mouth is."

"Well, I can't do that overnight."

"If you can't, then I don't have the time or patience to put up with you."

"You don't cut any slack, do you?"

"No, I'm honest with myself and with you. Why should I baby you? So you can continue to play games with everyone around you? No, I don't think so. If you aren't going to jump into the deep end of the pool, then you need to stay away from the water. It's too dangerous."

"What will happen if I 'jump in the deep end'?"

"You'll sink or swim. Which one do you want to do?"

"I want to swim."

"In other words, you want to live?"

"Yes, I do."

"Then live because you want to. I can't give permission for one way or the other. It's up to you."

The boy actually did pretty well with this subject. He did try to squirm out from under some important points but everyone gets at least one check. The next subject on the agenda is Empathy Function. This is a feminine function and talking about it will bring all his feminine Programming to the surface. I wonder if that is where the fear about the Other is hiding?

Points to Consider:

1. This lesson was about Natural Mind Function, even though it was mentioned very few times.
2. The teacher chose instead to demonstrate Natural Mind Function.
3. Honesty which emanates from the Other is, at times, cuttingly direct and allows very little room for excuses which deny it's right to exist.
4. Handling the Honesty emanating from the Other requires discipline and understanding in a Shaman, therefore.
5. Sometimes the only way to protect others is to Not Do by simply picturing the idea to be communicated.
6. Since Natural Mind Function is a "male" concept it can be hard on those it visits.
7. It is not possible to activate the Natural Mind Function without allowing the Other full reign in a life.
8. Bob Agreed to choose life.

Chapter 14: Empathy Function

Empathy is generally thought to be the ability of one to feel the physical sensations of another. But Empathy Function controls a set of energies which govern the ability to feel all the sensations of everything, as it were. It, like the Specific Function and the Natural Mind Function, is more of a field of endeavor than an action, but action is part of the field. Empathy Function is related to the subconscious as opposed to the conscious. It is thought of as feminine, whereas Specific Function and Natural Mind Function are thought of as masculine. To say masculine and feminine does not mean that they are functions relating to men and women, but are more like Yin and Yang.

Clarification:

> Masculine and feminine can be confusing concepts. While it *could* be true that women are more likely to develop or understand the Empathy Function and men are more likely to develop and understand the Natural Mind Function, it is necessary for the Shaman to develop both the masculine and feminine aspects of his knowledge. It is better, therefore, to consider masculine and feminine concepts with other measurements at the same time as the masculine and feminine measures. For instance, Specific Function could be thought of as "harder" and Empathy Function could be thought of as "softer". Another set of measurements could be a comparison of subtle, as in more subtle and less subtle.

Empathy Function was discovered when named tribes started to become small nations. Tribes united and regional rulers began to emerge. These rulers may have been chiefs or perhaps warlords of some type, but they united other leaders under them and this was a new idea. Up until this time, tribes had leaders and the tribes could come together as a people, but each local group had its own leadership. This time was marked by a stronger type of leader, one who could unite the strong wills of all the tribal leaders of his people.

This new type of leader was a strange creature. He had the characteristics of a warrior, to be sure, and he was possessed of a kind of spiritual vision which he used to sway others. He could use the spiritual side of his personage to urge his people to organize, form political and social pacts and even pay a tribute to him and his leadership group for the work they did on behalf of the people. Still, he needed the Agreement of the Shamans to stay in power.

The problem the Shamans faced with this fellow was how to know what was in his heart. Was he really thinking of the people or was he more interested in the power his Office could wield? Were his projects going to bring a better life or plunge the people into war? How could anyone know the future? The Shamans could not afford the time to Not Do and let the answer come to them. They had to know what the man was capable of and what he could be trusted to do.

Some Shamans always seemed to have those answers. How they knew was a burning question. Then it was discovered that the Shamans who knew were also Shamans who were honest with themselves and others. In fact, their honesty was without compassion. Not only were these Shamans honest, they were brutally honest. This meant that those Shamans were completely without pity in their honesty. In some ways, they did not exhibit humanness in their honesty.

This, too, posed a problem. There were some who thought that this inhumanness in a Shaman indicated great Power. Some thought it indicated some type of ongoing spirit possession. Yet the brutally honest Shamans themselves thought it was nothing more than the expression of the Other. There was one other characteristic these brutally honest Shamans possessed. They thought from Delta to Beta. Because they could think from Delta to Beta, they could move their Assemblage Points so they could see the process of perception. In other words, these Shamans could see several Assemblage Points at one time. This position was, of course, yet another Assemblage Point, but it afforded those Shamans the ability to see exactly how that new type of leader would behave.

The main body of Shamans wanted to know how those few Shamans could accomplish this feat. It was through Empathy Function that this type of perception was possible. Adapting to the landscape of Empathy Function allowed the Shaman to not only see into a given individual, but also to plot the course of his most likely activities. In some manner, those Shamans actually could become that person, or perhaps it is better stated that they could take on complete aspects and characteristics of that person for a period of time and see the world through that person's eyes.

Clarification:

Adapting to the landscape of Empathy Function indicates that the Shaman would take note of the features of Empathy. That would mean that he would adopt a selfless attitude, think of other people with kindness, accept other Points of View in a non-judgmental way, and generally adapt to a calm and collected stance. Still, the Shaman is a warrior as well. That would indicate that he would look at the landscape of Empathy Function as a field of battle.

An unknown Eskimo Shaman once said, "Life's greatest danger lies in the fact that people's food consists entirely of souls." We generally think of the Empath as a benevolent, but tortured individual who only wants to help his fellow man but suffers greatly because of the pain he feels. This is only a half truth. The other half of the truth is that the Shaman uses the Empathy Function to recognize and defeat those who would devour his very soul. He uses the landscape of Empathy Function as a field of battle while holding the gentle Agreement inherent in the concept.

The Shamans who could direct thought from Delta to Beta made a strange claim. They claimed that if they could but identify a belief of a given individual, including that of a leader, and adopt that belief as their own, they could construct a set of emotions, feelings and even logic that would be nearly identical to that of the other person. Armed with such information, they could predict a probable course of action for any individual.

Such an individual would have evoked a certain respect in his community. It is not likely that the respect generated by these Shamans would have been all warm and fuzzy. It is more likely that it would have been the respect generated through abject fear. It was much easier for the Shamans who directed thought from Beta to Delta to claim that the Shamans who wielded the Empathy Function had powerful totems, had spirit helpers, or some other such, than it was to pay the price of moving awareness to Delta. It could certainly have been considered dangerous for the Shamans who were still attempting to move awareness to Delta to allow the Shamans wielding the Empathy Function to even get a glimpse of their beliefs. However, a Shaman who wields the Empathy Function does not listen to the stated beliefs of anyone. They, instead, observe the action of Communication to determine what an individual regards or believes is real.

Clarification:

To observe the action of Communication to determine the belief of an individual requires a grasp of the idea of Communication as a Do Function. It is common to use words for misdirection and even for outright deception. However, it is difficult to do the same with actions. It may be impossible to hide the true nature of an action. The problem is to determine the action of a Communication. In other words, when someone says something, the question to be asked is: "What are they Doing?", not "What are they saying?"

Discernment of this nature requires that the listener exercise more than average honesty and an extraordinary kindness. The honesty must supersede the message of words and focus on the action or the Doing of the Communication. The kindness is necessary to allow the listener to accept the action of the Communication for what it is, not what it says. Empathy is defined as the intellectual identification of oneself with another. In other words, self must be subject to the other person's belief. That indicates that self cannot be more important than the other individual. This requires both honesty and kindness. It is nearly impossible for kindness to exist in the presence of self-aggrandizement. To bring self into submission requires non-pitying honesty. Brutal Honesty, if you will.

To the Shaman wielding or acting on the field of Empathy Function, a set of beliefs define a Point of View, or Assemblage Point. If that Shaman were to move his Assemblage Point to encompass a set of beliefs, he would see the world as defined by that set of beliefs. This ability to adopt the Assemblage

Point of other people gave rise to the ability to move the Assemblage Point to any position which suited the Shaman. Access to Empathy Function begins with accepting the proposition that Brutal Honesty is not brutal, but is possible. To master Empathy Function, suspending disbelief and controlling folly are prerequisite.

Clarification:

Moving the Assemblage Point to encompass a set of beliefs indicates that the moved Assemblage Point sees the world through the beliefs, emotions, feelings and logic of another. This means that the world is seen through the Programming of the other individual; it is seen through his eyes, as it were. With a bit of practice, it is possible to construct a belief system which is outside the norm. The other than normal belief system comes complete with emotions, feelings and logic. The emotions, feelings and logic may need some degree of tweaking, but they are there and come with the system of belief.

A word of caution here: Constructing a belief system which is other than normal does not represent power. It does not represent totem interference or aid in one's life. It does not represent the closeness of a spirit helper. It represents nothing more or less than a practical application of the hardware in the biocomputer.

Not every application of the Empathy Function is wholesome. Some Shamans use the Empathy Function to "become" animals. The shift to "below," as it is called, is the easiest of Assemblage Point shifts to make because it requires very little effort. The Shaman who gets trapped in this shift of Assemblage Point is a decadent individual. There are shifts available that are more of a challenge, but are not so morally base. For some individual Shamans, the attraction of base instincts has a very strong pull. To a certain extent, every Shaman has to have certain friendliness with the base part of himself, but that thought leads to a dead end. To allow the errors of conscious thought free reign in the Other or in the subconscious is counter-productive, to say the least. To be sure, there are Shamans who will not or cannot progress beyond the point of that shift to "below." There are also Shamans who wish to progress beyond that point and do. It is well to remember that morality, like speed in an athlete, cannot be coached. Those who have morality, have it. Those who don't have morality don't have it. It is the right of each individual to do all he can with what talents he has.

Shamans can also use the ability to move the Assemblage Point in order to see more than one other Assemblage Point at a time while Dreaming. But these are not ordinary Dreams. These are Dreams that are real enough to live in. This type of Dream is built one element at time until the location is complete. This type of Dreamer will start with a stone, for example, and study the stone until he can Dream it exactly as it is. Imagine a Dream with dogs barking and people walking and lights that flicker in the dark. A Dream with shadows which move as the wind blows and clouds hiding stars and children laughing somewhere off in the dark. Imagine the Intent to build such a place in a Dream. Imagine the Intent to build such a place in the physical world by Dreaming it so.

Clarification:

Consider that constructing a belief system comes with programs all ready for use. If a Shaman were to construct a belief system that could define Dreams as overlapping reality, then he could tweak the programs so that the Dream could reflect reality and reality could reflect the Dream. For the Shaman, the reality of television, computers, GPS, cell phones and commuting is held in place through the humans who subscribe to that belief system. In other words, those people share a common general area for their Assemblage Point. That there are other Assemblage Points available that would open windows on other worlds is, to the Shaman, quite logical. Within that thought or concept then, it would be just as logical to view Dreams as nothing more than another way to move the Assemblage Point or, in other words, to view other worlds whether those worlds exist or are created by the new system of belief.

The wisdom of the early Shamans to teach the Warrior's Way becomes more and more apparent as the Shaman progresses into the complexities of his life. He cannot deny his experiences and he is driven to progress, but without a sound base he can become trapped by his seeming power. Unless the Shaman can affect the world we live in, his abilities are of no consequence. This is the great test of the Empathy Function.

The Shaman uses the landscape of Empathy Function through Brutal Honesty to stay aware of the natural order evident or lacking in the real-time world in which he lives. He thereby has an inventory of actions which can be performed in order to bring natural order closer to fruition. Since the list of possible actions is extensive, he knows that he can only achieve, perhaps, a few of the actions necessary or possible with his knowledge in his lifetime. The rest of the list will be passed on to future generations of his line of thinking.

Points to Consider:

1. Empathy Function harnesses the energies generated through Honesty.
2. Empathy Function governs a wide range of the Other's activities.
3. The Shaman who aspires to Empathy Function must already have a moral code or is likely to be trapped by the baser side of his craft.
4. Part of the art of employing the Empathy Function is to employ the Brutal Honesty to the Shaman which allows him the ability to acknowledge the Points of View he sees in other people as a statement of fact. The operative idea here is Brutal Honesty.
5. Empathy Function is not safe for novices but an understanding of it is necessary to progress on the path of knowledge.

Story Chapter XIV

I hate to say this out loud for fear of jinxing him, but Bob is starting to show some signs of maturity. It probably isn't as much maturity as it is that he is becoming more and more sure of himself. This is a natural effect of thinking about Be One, Harmony, and Do. Even though he still doesn't have all the information in this set, he does have the tools to learn the set. There are many Shamans who do stupendous things who never learn the belief structure per se. Yet those Shamans have one thing in common. They use all the tools.

It may not have been fair to Bob, but I've never told him that the tools are teaching tools. I didn't want him to gain too much confidence too soon. That would have truly been unfair. Had he thought he knew things he really didn't know, he may very well have missed the process or the time for maturation. The Shaman game is for older folks and not really for young people. It takes an exceptional young person to act as Shaman.

I know he will have some issues with being Brutally Honest with himself. I suspect that he will have less trouble with being that honest with other people, but then it is sometimes harder to be honest with yourself. That won't excuse him, but I can understand. If he doesn't resolve his problems with honesty, he won't be able to resolve his problems about the Other. If he can't resolve those problems, I'll have no choice but to let him go to fend for himself.

"How's it going there, Roberto?"
"Okay, I guess."

I might as well wade right off into this even before I can begin lowering frequencies.

"That's good. So let me ask you a question."
"Okay."
"Why are you here?"
"Oh, you know, I thought I'd come by and shoot the shit for a while."

That wasn't as considered as it might have been.

"If that's all you want then you need to go somewhere else. Go down to the coffee shop. They don't mind how much dead shit piles up down there."
"Okay, I'm not being entirely honest."
"You're wasting my time, Bob."
"All right. Look, I really do want to know more about what you've been telling me."

Since he has always responded to being pushed away, I'll opt for that ploy.

"So? It doesn't make any difference what you want to know. If you can't be honest with yourself then you've come as far as you can. I can't change that. It is not in my power. It won't make any difference how much more you 'learn' if you can't apply that learning because of your self-importance."

"Okay, you probably have a point, but I don't see what my honesty has to do with what I can learn."

Slow this down little by little. There is something different in his responses tonight. I'll try lowering the rhythm of my voice by a cycle per second every statement or two to see if I can entice this out.

"Okay, Bob, let me explain it to you. Do you have any interest whatsoever in propagating plants?"

"No, why?"

"If I explained how to make soft wood and hard wood cuttings would you have any idea what I was talking about?"

"Not really. But what does that have to do with learning more from you?"

It doesn't have anything to do with anything. It is a move that Stalkers make. If you are stumped by something, change the subject or look at something/anything else.

"Here comes. Do you have an idea about the meaning of hardwood and softwood cuttings or not?"

"No, I don't have a clue about hardwood and softwood cuttings or even what that means."

"Very good. That is precisely my point. It would be a waste of your time and mine for me to explain the intricacies of plant propagation by means of either hardwood or softwood cuttings simply because I would be a bore to explain it and you have no use for the information. Isn't that true?"

"Well, I don't have a use for information about cuttings, but we have never talked about that subject."

Now, come back to the subject.

"No, we haven't. We have talked about lots of other things including Brutal Honesty. But what I am saying is falling on deaf ears.

Why should I continue to bore you with information that you can't use?"

"I can use the information about Brutal Honesty. I just don't know how to be that honest with myself."

Don't show weakness to your adversaries.

"Then you agree that I'm wasting my time."

"No, I don't agree."

Agreeing stores energy. Disagreeing looses energy.

"Bob, I've been talking with you for ten minutes. You haven't one time told the truth about anything unless I pushed you. You call that a good use of time? Why would I even consider talking more to you? Without a brand of honesty that you apparently don't possess, you can't employ the last concept we talked about. You want to have your cake and eat it too. You want to impress your friends about all the spiritual stuff you know, but you don't want to actually put any of what you know to use."

"I want to put it to use. That's why I'm here."

I know, but I have to win this battle this time.

"No, you're here to con me into giving you more information so you can continue to impress your friends."

"You've got that wrong. I want to learn."

"Okay, let's see. How do you think you can learn Empathy Function if you can't think from the Other out towards consciousness? It takes painstaking honesty to accomplish that feat. That's why they call it Natural Mind Function because it allows the 'natural' mind of the Other to function in place of the self-important mind."

"I don't understand what one has to do with the other."

"Come again?"

"Let's say that I can't accomplish the Natural Mind Function. Why does that prevent me from learning the Empathy Function?"

It sounds like an innocent question, but it's really a dead end and he knows it. Keep it slow, there is a different tone in his voice.

"Do you remember that I told you that these last concepts were like fields of endeavor?"

"Yeah, kind of."

"Okay. If you can't endeavor on the field of Natural Mind you have no chance at all of endeavoring on the field of Empathy. If the Natural Mind Function isn't present, then the Empathy Function can't even be accessed."

"Why is that?"

"Didn't I explain that Natural Mind Function belonged to the subconscious? Did you think I was joking? Do you think you can fake that?"

"No, I didn't think you were joking and I don't want to fake anything."

"Of course. So you're telling me that the Other, which you're not sure you believe in, is in control of your being?"

"No. I can't say that."

"Exactly. Then let me explain this one more time. Natural Mind Function is achieved through Not Doing and Empathy Function is achieved through Brutal Honesty with yourself about your actual nature. Empathy Function utilizes that honesty to sort through what you know and what you don't know so that you can access the Direct Knowing of the Other. How do you hope to access Direct Knowing if the Other isn't in control of your being?"

"Oh."

"That's the best you can do? 'Oh'?"

"This all makes so much sense when you explain it. But when I leave here I can't remember half of what you tell me."

Keep it very slow. He's on the verge of something here.

"At least you're being honest. That's a start."

"So how do I get the Other to be in control of my being?"

"Oh, I don't know. Maybe by inflating your self-importance. Perhaps by lying to yourself about anything that might deflate that self-importance. What do you think?"

"No, I don't think that will work."

I had to check.

"Neither do I. That's why I'm telling you that until you can be honest with yourself I really may not tell you anything more. You can only damage yourself by pretending to know directly when you are actually using that statement to build yourself into something you're not."

"Why would I try to make myself something I'm not?"

"I don't know! You tell me."

"I'm not."

"Methinks the Roberto protesteth too much."

"You think that I really try to impress my friends with what I know instead of learning?"

This is a series of firsts. He's broken through something.

"I know you do."

"How do you know?"

"Do you read poetry?"

"Once in a while, but what does that have to do with this?"

"There are poets who, as they say, bare their soul. And there are other people who write in rhyme. One has and demonstrates depth and the other tries to replace emotional, soulful honesty with technical skill. If you wrote poetry, which category would you represent?"

"Technical skill."

He may be ready to face his fear of the Other, by Gollies.

"Thank you. Technical skill represents logic. There is nothing wrong with logic except when it tries to replace the brutal, gut wrenching honesty which emanates from the Other. That type of honesty is like speed. You can't coach speed."

"You're a hard man."

"Poor baby. If you can't stand the heat, get out of the kitchen."

"I can stand the heat."

Well, let's just go for this.

"Let's see, then. So tell me when you decided that the whole idea of the soul was bunk."

"I don't know. I don't remember."

Keep the pressure and intensity up but proceed with caution.

"Goodbye, Bob."

"Give me a break, will ya?"

"I am giving you a break."

"You know what I mean."

"No, I don't have the slightest idea of what you mean."

"You're pressuring me. You know that you are."

Isn't that what you came by for?

"Bob, I'm letting you go pretend to be anything you want. That isn't pressure."

"But I don't want to go pretend something."

"Then tell me when you decided that the whole idea of the soul was bunk."

"DAMN! Let me collect my thoughts."

Whoa, he wants to fight about this so he's really, really close.

"Sure. Collect away – somewhere else."

"LET ME THINK!"

Wow, this thing was programmed really, really hard and there is a ton of emotion surrounding it. Intensity, but slow intensity, is needed here.

"Ooo, fighting emotions. We must be getting close. I suppose the next thing that'll happen is if you don't get your way you'll pick up your ball and bat and go home. Fight or Flee, Fight or Flee."

"I'm not going anywhere until I figure this out."

He's always run way before this, so he is ready to get this out of his system. I don't want to push him away so maybe if I mark where I've seen this before it will help him find it.

"Well, you have that right. Okay, I'll give you what may be a help. I suspect that there was an event when you were a small child. The reason I think that is because you don't seem to have problems with most of your Theta thinking.

I would guess that this would be back about the time you were four or five at the latest. It could be as much as a year earlier, but I doubt that you would have developed enough speech at that age."

"The only thing I remember that happened at about that age is my Grandmother died. I must have been maybe five at the time because I hadn't started school yet. At least I don't think I had. My Grammy lived with us and we used to do all kinds of things together. She was the best playmate I ever had. She used to take me swimming and would stand on the edge of the pool and tell me what to do. Believe it or not, she taught me to swim without ever getting in the water."

Don't interrupt. This is it. It was about his grandmother. This is important for this guy.

"She could be tough, though. You kind of remind me of her in a way. One time I did something I shouldn't have done and my mom was pissed. I think my mom actually whacked my butt about it, which tells me how bad it was. I can't remember exactly what it was, but it had something to do with the car. I think I had gotten in the car and put it in neutral and the car backed down the drive and into the street. Man, was she mad. My Grammy didn't say anything about it that I remember, but I do remember that she was mad too.

"I remember that she asked me if I was ever going to do it again and I said that I wouldn't. Then she put on her glasses. I think she had been crying, but she put those glasses on and didn't talk to me for *awhile*. Man, that was worse than the whack I got from my mom.

"I think she died later that year because I wasn't in school yet. You know, I still miss her. She was the greatest."

Uh oh. She died. No wonder this is so strong.

"That's the whole story?"

"No, after she died I really went bonkers for a while. But I remember one time my mom was talking to me and told me that my Grammy was gone, but that her soul was still with us."

Oh Bob, your mom was doing the best she could.

"That made you mad?"

"Yeah, I guess it did. I wanted my Grammy, the one who played with me and took me swimming. I didn't see any 'soul,' I just missed her. I still miss her."

"She's gone, my friend, and your mom explained it the best she could to a five year old, don't you think?"

At this point, what remained of Bob's resistance crumbled. In a similar way, Bob made it over to a nearby chair, fell into it and broke down completely. He cried for a long time. He had to rid himself of a demon that had lived in his mind for many, many years. I couldn't bring myself to interrupt, even though tears are always shed for oneself. In this case, I think it was simply mourning which has been put off for too many years. There is no doubt in my mind that Bob will find that this one event will free up his thinking machinery and the emotional intensity of this liberated memory will be applied to his emerging life as a Shaman.

"So that was the Other?"

"That was the Other speaking to you. It will be a while yet before you can understand what just happened. I will tell you that what you just learned was not about your Grams or about your mom. After you get reacquainted with the Other, you will be able to use what you learned as power. But until you can claim that knowledge as power, you will continue pretty much as you are. I suspect it won't take all that long. The Other has been Stalking you for a long time."

Points to Consider:

1. This lesson was about the Empathy Function so the teacher had to use Brutal Honesty with Bob to release the energy that Empathy Function governs.
2. The Brutal part of Honesty is rarely pretty.
3. The teacher showed Bob an enormous kindness.
4. Both the teacher and Bob had to confront and utilize their own Honesty.
5. Both the teacher and Bob exhibited great courage.
6. Bob had to come to a crossroad. He either could understand that thinking was possible from Delta to Beta or he may not have continued with the teacher. This was not an arbitrary decision on the teacher's part.
7. Bob will never again be able to accept emotional defenses as a valid excuse for someone's actions including his own.
8. The teacher applied Empathy Function to allow Bob his grief.

Chapter 15: Intuition Function

In the movement towards knowledge, the Shaman who can achieve the Intuition Function has arrived at adulthood, as it were. The Intuition Function is, like Specific Function, Natural Mind Function and Empathy Function, more of a field of action than an action proper. It is thought to be feminine in nature and relates to objective thought or consciousness. It is the Function which unites the six previous Functions.

The tool for learning about the Intuition Function is Direct Knowing. It would seem, then, that the function is all about being intuitive or aware at a distance. In a way it is, but that awareness at a distance is a statement which is misleading as a reference to Intuition Function. The Function actually concerns the issue of the Other expressing itself in the life of the Shaman. The Be One Function opens the idea of being "an instrument of Communication." The Intuition Function is the completeness of the idea of that Communication. It is the Other at work in the body and mind of the Shaman.

When tribes coalesced into a people and the people became a small nation, the first Kings or absolute rulers came into being. The Kings did not need the Agreement of the Shamans to be King. They bypassed the Shaman by claiming that they were descended from gods. If you are a King and a god, you don't really want a Shaman to *see* who you are. You may even be a bit unhappy if some upstart Shaman were to come along and *see* who you really are and start running his mouth about what you mean to do. There is no doubt that when the first Kings started to claim god-like bloodlines there were a few Shamans who trotted down to the King's headquarters and went back home to let the folks know what a farce he was. Whenever a divinely blooded King heard about a Shaman who was bad-mouthing his royal highness, that Shaman was invited to the kingly residence and promptly shown the power of the throne. Not many Shamans survived that invitation.

Some kings felt as though having any Shamans in the kingdom was bad form and did their kingly best to exterminate the entire Shamanic culture. They were relatively successful. Then the Church came along and took up where the Kings left off. The Church saw Shamanism as a direct competitor to a niche it wanted for itself. Becoming a Shaman at that time was a dire career decision.

It was at this point that the Shamans had to reassess the nature of their power. Shamans had considered the rituals, rattles, incantations and other relics of their office to be the symbols in which their power resided. When they began to die at the hands of tyrants, they began to reconsider. It is the nature of human beings to defend our world mythology nearly to the death, but once we are faced with our mortality, we drop the unnecessary. Shamans are no different. The Shaman has the same capacity for self-delusion that anyone else has. Yet when the Shamans of times past were threatened by the tyrants of those times, they began to *see* that the Other was the active force in their lives. It came as a surprise to them that the Other did not protect them from death at the hands of the tyrants.

The Other would instruct them about how to use knowledge to defeat the tyrant. The Other would teach them to *see* the resolution of the struggle. The Other would guide them through the battle, but the Other would not or perhaps could not interfere in the life and death of the body. The Shamans had to intuit the dictates of the Other and so the name of this field of energy was known as the Intuition Function.

Clarification:

That the Other will not or cannot interfere in the life and death of the body is a concept which bears careful examination. It may need to be considered and reconsidered. To cultivate a relationship with the Other is to cultivate a relationship with an entity which has a much different regard for death than does the body. While the Other protects the body it can also allow the body to die. The Other is highly indifferent and teaches its lessons whether we like them or don't like them.

In some ways, it is during times of life threatening stress that Shamans accept the true nature of their Office. The human organism behaves differently when it perceives itself to be in a life threatening situation. During the 1970's there was a gas that could be obtained for therapeutic reasons. The gas consisted of something like 35% carbon dioxide and 65% oxygen. The carbon dioxide level was approximately double the normal carbon dioxide levels in air. This gas was inhaled through a mask as is used to administer anesthesia. For a novice, it was not possible to take more than three breaths before the mask would be clawed off the face. Even for people with experience, 20 breaths was a benchmark never achieved.

The reason the mixture provoked such a reaction was that the body perceived the carbon dioxide level to be dangerously high, so high as to be life threatening. This was not the case because the oxygen level was much higher than normal. No matter how logically the mixture was explained, the body always perceived just a few whiffs of the mixture to be life threatening.

The therapy consisted of two parts. The first part was to identify a symptom in an individual undergoing therapy, then try to present reasons to that individual as to why the symptom was not real. If no progress was made, then the individual was asked to partake of the mixture. As the mask was being clawed off the face, the facilitator asked a pertinent question about the symptom. The individual always answered and the answer was always completely void of deception. It was as though the Other answered.

The Shamans couldn't understand why Kings, and later the Church, were so threatened by their existence. It was simple. Shamans were instruments of Communication for the Other. Kings weren't really divine and so they didn't want Shamans communicating about that particular thought. The Church was supposed to be saving men's souls and if the Shamans were instruments of Communication for the Other, then what could the Church offer that Shamans didn't already have? The answer for both Kings and Church was to eliminate the Shamans. This turn of events made the Shamans aware that the Other was the very essence of their power and so they had to discover how the Other functioned.

The Shamans realized that for them to exist in the world of Kings and Church, they had to practice their art without being the center of attention. The idea of being in the world but not of the world took on meaning. The problem the Shamans had created for themselves was that they had become enamored with power. They had power, to be sure, but it was a strange power. If the Shaman puffed himself up with thoughts of his accomplishments, the power failed. The energy flow became an energy trickle. It was only the Shaman who could wield his power in humility who continued to grow.

Clarification:

> Power needs to be considered several times here. The only power a Shaman or anyone else has is the power to Communicate. A Communication emanating from Beta is rather common and therefore relatively powerless. A Communication emanating from the Other is very rare and carries a great deal of power.
>
> To Intuit the subject matter and craft a Communication which alters the course of another life would represent a great power, indeed. So what would be the motivation or even the characteristics of such a Communication? One characteristic would, obviously, be that the Communication would have to make a Difference or change something in the listener. To alter the course of another life the Communication would have to consist of the type of Brutal Honesty one would experience in a life or death situation. The motivation for the Communication would have to be consistent with the characteristics. In other words, the Communication would have to be so honest and to the point that the communicator would "bet his life" on its veracity and accuracy.

Because of the tendency of humans to see themselves as important, it is easy for a Shaman to be trapped in the fantasy of his power. If a Shaman can heal, for instance, he attracts a following of people who desire his services. He can be seduced by the clamor of his "fans." Even though he can continue to heal, he is not likely to be able to wield that same power on his own behalf if he is threatened by a tyrant unless he remains subservient to the Other. The Other shares its presence with the Shaman through a quiet voice and that voice feels very much like Intuition.

As a consequence of the pressure from King and Church, the Shamans adopted the thought that they needed to live their life as warriors. They were men of knowledge only when that was needed, then they reverted to warrior again. They discovered that the Other has a different set of requirements than the body. It does not usually insist on the body being aware of its existence. In order for the Shaman to utilize the energy and direction of the Other, he must emulate its action. The Other does not seem to be aware of time in the same way that the body is aware of time. The Other has the feeling of ancient age in comparison to the body. The Other exhibits patience with learning which seems to indicate that what is not learned this time will be learned the next. Shamans adopted all these characteristics and more in order to find a peace with King and Church.

Today's Shaman does not often face the threat of tyrants. One reason may be that in today's world, Shamanic knowledge is at a very low ebb. Those born to the Office have a limited body of knowledge from which to draw. This is a time of rebuilding. Perhaps it would be well to remember that those who do not learn from History are doomed to repeat it.

Clarification:

The Other seems more interested in "getting it right" than it does with speed. For instance, if an individual makes several steps in the direction of the Other in a lifetime, the Other will accept those few small steps just as easily as it will accept the complete journey. Therefore, the Shaman must emanate the Other and accept what is possible for a given individual. However, the depth and breadth of the Shaman's personal understanding is another issue.

Because the Shaman is "betting his life" on the veracity of his Communication, then it behooves him to align his Communication with contemporary and historical accuracy. In the course of his interaction with other people, it is conceivable that he will encounter a wide variety of educational and economic backgrounds. It would be hard to conceive of Shamanic effectiveness in our modern world without the ability to fit any Communication seamlessly into such diversity. The possessor of multiple Points of View would have a considerable advantage in such an environment. An even greater advantage would be to have the Brutal Honesty wrought from the personal understanding of the thin line separating life and death.

The knowledge of what the Other does results in the Shaman exhibiting certain characteristics and energy levels that set him apart from the ordinary. Still, it was difficult for the Shaman to show his knowledge, energy level or even his non-ordinary nature because of King and Church. This is the very crux of the knowledge about the Other which defines Intuition Function. It is only through quiet self-acknowledgment that the Shaman can come to the point where he follows the direction of the Other. The Other does not force an individual to acknowledge its presence, but it is always there protecting the instrument of Communication.

Points to Consider:

1. Intuition Function governs the energy released through Direct Knowing.
2. The energy governed by Intuition function allows consciousness to be aware of the dictates of the Other or at least of Delta to Beta thinking.
3. Intuition Function is best taught by Shamans being tyrannical with their replacements. In lieu of Shamans being tyrannical, the Other seems to find tyrants in the real world to teach this lesson.
4. Consciousness sometimes seems to need a near life and death situation to relinquish control.
5. Humility is a characteristic of a Shaman who has learned this lesson.
6. It is strange that the Other does not force learning, but without a certain uncomfortable feeling, we seem not to learn to allow the Other full sway in our lives.

Story Chapter XV

Bob has had several "eureka moments" since the last time we talked. With every insight, he has opened avenues for the Other to express. In spite of himself, he is maturing. He is no longer the brash know-it-all he once was. I doubt that he is as aware of the transformation as I am, although he has certainly noticed the change.

He is ready for the next part of the Shaman's belief system which is the Intuition Function. I suppose that "belief system" is not as accurate as the term should be but it's what we have. A problem which all budding Shamans have is how to describe the events they witness. It is difficult to even notice that changes are taking place if you don't have a method for describing them. This is always a problem.

The Be One, Harmony, Do Function set and the associated tools provide a set of information that the new Shaman can use to guide himself. Even so, it is hard to imagine that any but the most adept will have the ability to discipline themselves to the point that they will discover the truths found in those sets all alone. The reason is that no one can see the color of their own eyes, nor can we see what we are looking with. Bob was lucky or the Other wanted him to discover what he was about.

Most searchers fall by the wayside simply because the Other can't express through the existing Programming or they never listen to the benefactors who are placed in their paths. It is hard to fault the searchers. The same can be said of the benefactors who fail. They have also been provided a chance to learn. Hopefully, they learn even in failure.

"What's up, Roberto?"

"Nothing much."

"Why not?"

"I don't know. You know, it's becoming harder and harder to find people to talk to."

"Is it, now?"

"Yes, it is. It has occurred to me that not many people have ever had some of the experiences I have."

"No, I don't suppose they have."

"I don't know that I've met anyone who allows the Other to express itself."

I need to get him to start looking at protecting himself. There are forces in the world that may not cotton to him wandering around talking about the Other, especially with the meager energy levels he has at this point.

"Look, I told you a while back that you weren't very careful. You're still not. To begin with, the path you're on is not for everyone. Actually, the path you're on is only for you. You have to be very, very careful about even letting people, any people, know you are on that path. Not all that many years ago you could have been killed if anyone even suspected that you were entertaining thoughts about Shamanism. Things aren't that dangerous now, but that doesn't mean that you won't threaten people just because you know things."

"Most people I meet are really interested in the things I talk to them about."

"Are they now? Anyone ask you where they can go to get started?"

"No, but they aren't ready to do that yet."

"Is that what they tell you?"

"Yeah."

"Let me say this another way. The path you're on is only for you. No one can walk down that path *but* you. If you try to tell other people about that path, you will threaten them. Think about this for a minute. How much trouble did you have just to accept that the Other might, maybe, once in a while, have a juicy little tidbit just for you?"

"Well, I might have been a little hard-headed about that."

"You were actually easy. The Other had been Stalking you a long time. You were ready. When you came to me, I knew the Other had brought you. You don't know this about the people you're talking to. You don't *see* them."

"Of course I see them, they're standing right in front of me."

"Yeah, yeah. I know you look right at them, but you don't *see* them. You don't observe them from the Other. I've covered this with you."

"Oh yeah, I remember."

"Good for you. You're still young, and because of that you make mistakes that a young person makes. But you can't afford to make *this* mistake. You have to be aware that some people come to you because they are brought to you by the Other, some people come to you because they want your energy, and some people come to you to prove you wrong by using logic against you. You must be more careful. Even people who are brought to you by the Other may not be safe. It is extremely easy to be caught in anyone's web. It is something else again to get out of those webs. You're still trying to be a nice guy. There's nothing wrong with that, but there will be times when you will have to be other than nice to get out of people's webs. Been there, done that."

"You make it sound like I can't talk to anyone because they are some kind of danger to me."

"And?"

"How can some guy off the street, hanging out down at the coffee shop, be that dangerous?"

"Most often, he's not. But every once in a while he's, let's say, an energy ghoul. Do you know which one is which?"

"I've never even thought about an energy ghoul."

"And it shows. Think about it. You'll learn which ones are which. Besides, it will sharpen your Seeing."

"Tell me a little more about Seeing."

"In one way, Seeing and Direct Knowing are connected. Generally, when the Intuition Function is realized, a Shaman has more or less come of age. It is at this point that he is ready to begin to take on the tyrants of the world. Don't make a mistake here. There *are* tyrants about and they absolutely represent a clear and present danger, but without them you won't progress as rapidly as you will when you confront them. Don't think that you can approach someone like that and preach love and peace and everything will be all rosy. You will have to defeat them. Otherwise, they will defeat you."

"You know, you always make things sound like they are a matter of life and death."

"You can pretend they're not if you want. I don't care. You're a grown man and you can play around with things until you've enjoyed all of it you care to."

"I didn't mean it like that."

"Then how did you mean it? That I'm being dramatic? That I'm overreacting? How?"

"Do you really think that there are life and death situations in possessing simple knowledge?"

"Do you really think you possess simple knowledge?"

"Well, it isn't all that difficult to understand."

Right! You've been wrestling with this for how long now? This is not a logical set of thoughts, Bob.

"You've just begun and have yet to apply what you know or to extend it to its logical conclusion."

"I thought you said that the Other isn't concerned with logic."

"That's true, but I didn't say that logic doesn't have a place, nor did I say that you can't apply logic to any of this. I told you that you needed to think from your beliefs out to logic. When you apply this set of beliefs to the world it will have to pass through logic or Beta think, will it not?"

"Oh. I hadn't thought about that."

"I know. That's why I'm telling you that you're careless. You are not considering everything you know as yet. Tsk, tsk, tsk."

"Just when I'm beginning to think I understand something, you come along and tell me how stupid I am."

"I'm not telling you you're stupid. I'm telling you you're careless. You've only considered the Be One, Harmony and Do Function set as a linear concept. What if it can be stacked up in three dimensions?"

"What?"

"You heard me. What if it can be stacked up in three dimensions? Do you think a three dimensional construct would change how you think about all this?"

"I feel a lot like I'm about to find out that what I 'know' so far is going to be torpedoed."

"I suspect you're right."

It's nice to talk to Bob as an adult. He actually walked through this session without running his usual defense programs. I didn't really talk to him about the energies that the Intuition Function controls because I'm going to introduce him to the three dimensional construct of all that he has been learning in the next session we have together. That conversation may be the hardest he has had to date. It will take a while for him to sort through that information.

Points to Consider:

1. Intuition Function is the Other communicating through the body and consciousness.
2. The teacher allowed Bob to demonstrate the Intuition Function for himself. The teacher pushed hard on Bob to be more careful because Bob does not yet have the necessary experience to function as a Shaman.
3. As a Shaman, Bob has an obligation to talk to other people, but he still hasn't realized that the Other brings the Shaman together with the people he is to Communicate with.
4. Bob has come a long way in the 15 lessons reported here. Intuition Function is already operating for him.
5. The teacher has successfully guided Bob through the lessons without leaving his footprints on Bob's Programming.
6. Bob will be able to form his own opinions about what he should do with his knowledge. In other words, he will apply the Intuition Function as he sees best.

Chapter 16: Agreement

As a Shaman becomes proficient with the tools and concepts of his craft, there comes a time when he may long for a greater involvement in the world. Certainly, that involvement is possible, but there is still one concept that he must master before involvement can reflect his Shamanic knowledge. This concept is a culmination of sorts of everything he has learned. In common English we call the concept Agreement.

When Tribal Shaman found himself in a world filled with Kings and the power of Kings, he faced a choice. The choice was simple, really. He could do what the King wanted or he could face the King's displeasure. It would've seemed that Tribal Shaman could have hidden his knowledge and escaped the King's attention, but as society continued to develop, Tribal Shaman's specialized knowledge provided him with a certain notoriety. For some Shamans, the notoriety came as the result of their knowledge of healing. For other Shamans, the notoriety came as the result of their ability to attend social ills. For other Shamans, the notoriety was the result of seemingly magical abilities.

Kings are absolute rulers, or they were at the time of this Shamanic notoriety. Absolute rulers cannot allow other individuals to usurp even a little of their authority or there will be unrest in the populace. As a consequence, the Shamans of notoriety were summoned to the throne to account for their activities. This posed a problem.

Consider the dilemma. A Shaman must Be One. This means that the Shaman would have had to unify his Shamanic commitments to himself and to others with the requirements of the throne. The Shaman must function in Harmony. This means that the Shaman would have had to be in Harmony with the Point of View of the throne and at the same time the Point of View that allows Shamanic activities. The Shaman would have to Do. This means that the Shaman would have had to communicate with the throne about his activities and the throne may not have been terribly sympathetic. The Shaman must practice his Specific Function. This could have meant that he would have to Dream for the throne or Stalk for the throne. The Shaman must utilize Natural Mind Function. This meant that he would have had to Not Do for the throne. The Shaman must employ Empathy Function. This would have meant that he would have to have been Brutally Honest with the throne. The Shaman must gather all his knowledge in Intuition Function. This would have meant that the Shaman would have had to demonstrate Direct Knowing for the throne. But the Shaman would have also known that plying his Craft for the throne would have put him in contact with great energy and power.

To be sure, there were Shamans who availed themselves of the energy and power of the throne and lost. So the remaining Shamans applied their Seeing to the problem. Perhaps it was through Dreaming that the answer finally came forth. The solution they found to the problem was Agreement. This wasn't the nod the head up and down at the right place type of agreement, it was the Shamanic Agreement. The two ideas are notably different.

It was what the Shamans *saw* or Dreamed about Agreement that is the most surprising aspect of all the Shamanic concepts. The first thing they *saw* was that when anyone agrees to something, the way they perceive reality changes. Those Shamans were convinced that every Agreement actually *created* a new piece of reality. In a way, they were absolutely correct. In another way, it would be better to say that every Agreement actually opens a window on a view of a world that has always been there. It doesn't really make any difference which description of the event was used because the description is no more the thing than the word is the thing. The next thing the Shamans *saw* was that no one ever noticed that a new reality had been created. The third thing the Shamans *saw* about Agreement was that every time an Agreement was reached the participants in the Agreement benefited from an increase in their energy levels. Still, how to use this information to avert Kingly ire still eluded the Shamans.

Clarification:

The idea that every Agreement actually creates a new piece of reality may seem to be far-fetched until it is examined carefully. The term "Agreement" as used here signifies an accord between people in which an accomplishment is energized. Excluded in this usage are agreements such as, "I agree with Jack Sprat who is running for Congress because he is a Democrat/Republican," or "I agree with Dr. Whatizit's view of world money markets and if I ever get a Billion dollars I'm going to invest just like he says." The usage here is more in the vein of, "I have $20,000.00 dollars and need a new car." This would be answered with the "Agreement" statement of, "Step right in my office and let's see what we can do for you today."

A new piece of reality would be created which would include a new car for one person and a nice paycheck for another person. Perhaps neither person would realize the perceived reality had changed, but both would experience an increase in their energy levels. They would probably both claim they were simply excited by the advent of the new car and the nice paycheck, but a notable animation would be apparent to an outside observer.

The Shamans then saw a fourth thing about Agreement. Because no one noticed the change in the perceived reality, they never sought out Agreement except for individual, and most often personal, betterment. It was the reason that no one noticed the change that interested the Shamans. When an Agreement is reached, a certain amount of energy is released, or appears to be released, as the Agreement moves from an idea to actualization. That energy burst causes the Point of View, or the Assemblage Point, to move. Such movement carries with it a more or less complete set of instructions for operating the computer from the new position. The old position is "forgotten" because it is not present in the new.

This was the key for the Shamans to interact with the throne. The Shamans considered the King to be the same as any other person, so they thought that he would be no different in his shift of perception. Yet if they asked the King for his Agreement, then he would have the right to control Shamanic activity. What if they deliberately sought out an Agreement that bettered the throne? The King would certainly be disposed to such a proposal, especially if it benefited the King and throne. The question then became: What species of Agreement could be sought that would benefit the King, the throne, and from which the Shamans and the King could benefit from increased energy levels?

It appears that the Agreement the Shamans finally settled on was to begin to hold ceremonies that could become public. As the ceremonies became popular, the throne benefited through increased production, for instance, which would have translated to a larger tax base. In this example, if the ceremony was for rain, the people would have planted more fields expecting the harvest. The King would not have wanted to interfere with the ceremony because of the increase in the royal coffers. The Shamans would have garnered more energy and everyone, it would seem, would have been better off than before. There was a problem with this type of backhanded Agreement, though. It induced a sense of power in the Shamans. To demonstrate that power, they sought to dominate the people. The human sacrifices of the Aztec would seem to be an example of this type of Shamanic domination.

Clarification:

It would not have been necessary for the Shamanic community to actually go to the King and present the benefits to the throne of their proposed ceremonies. Remember here that Communication is a Do Function and can be an action as well as words. If, for instance, the Shamans instituted a Spring Fertility Event and the general populace benefited through having a good time and that good time extended to planting more fields, then the throne would have benefited by an increase of Taxes.

The eventual problem for the Shaman is that this type of Agreement enhances a sense of powerfulness. The Shaman was, in essence, pulling a fast one on the King. This would have certainly been conceived as heady stuff. So there was no one to *disagree* with the Shaman. Because disagreement is as important a part of Agreement as it's more positive counterpart, the Shamans did not have any checks and balances on their activities. In other words, there was no one to *disagree* with them. The King couldn't, because they had not asked for his implicit Agreement and he was benefiting, so it wouldn't make any sense to stop an activity which incremented his power. Even when the ceremonies became macabre, the King could not, or would not, step in because the ceremonies were something which the people themselves supported. As long as the Shamans did nothing to detract from the power of the throne, their ceremonies were not a Kingly concern.

Those who do not learn from History are doomed to repeat it

There exists another type of Agreement which could be called the Shamanic Agreement. This type of Agreement is held and forged in private and does not utilize any secular power. The practice of this type of Agreement employs all eight of the tools and all seven of the Functions. It is focused through Intent and is rarely communicated to the beneficiaries. It generates energy for the Agreement holders and may even facilitate shifts in the position of the Assemblage Point in the society at large.

This type of Agreement is generated by Shamans and often addresses social ills and other issues which may or may not affect the Shaman in any way. Although the structure of this type of Agreement is available to anyone, it usually is realized only by Shamans who employ the eight tools and have acquired an understanding of the energies and practices represented by the seven Functions. The reason for this is that the possibility of the Movement of the Assemblage Point is something that is too easily disbelieved. It is only through the Shamanic practice of *suspending disbelief* that the possibility of Shamanic Agreement can be conceptualized.

Clarification:

It is important to consider that the Shamanic Agreement results in a shift of the Assemblage Point that is not remembered. One reason seems to be that most of the effect of the shift is involved in purely mental activity. Another part of the shift is related to the Other, but that part of the shift has no particular bearing on this consideration.

When the Assemblage Point moves, it is as though the new point has always been in place, just as it seems the old one has always been in place. Neither point has actually always been in place. Still, there is not memory of movements simply because a new Assemblage Point adjusts memory as easily as it adjusts and accommodates programs.

As a result of this phenomenon, believing that nothing has occurred and that memory and Programming is a continuum through time from birth to present is easily accepted. Since there is no Difference, then nothing is seen. Because no Difference is seen, then the reward is not visible to people who have no practice with the tools and Functions which make up Shamanic knowledge.

The Shaman accumulates Points of View and new Assemblage Points as though he were a collector. With enough repetition, the Shaman begins to notice the changes which new Agreements bring. There is another reason Shamans begin to notice the changes. This is that Shamans begin to adopt

Assemblage Points which include other Assemblage Points. There seem to be stages in the understanding of moving the Assemblage Point. At first, it seems that there are nudges around the core Point of View. It is as though the Point of View expands a bit to the left, right, up, or down. As the nudges become understood and the event not as fear-filled, then at times, entirely new positions can be achieved. After more practice, three-dimensional movements can be undertaken. With the advent of three-dimensional movement, several Points of View can be accommodated in a new "higher" Assemblage Point, or one that is "further back." Such a position affords the Shaman a more comprehensive view of the events surrounding the movements of the Assemblage Point brought about through and during Agreements.

Shamanic Agreement addresses both the masculine and feminine aspects of an issue. It addresses the objective and subjective issues. It addresses the Delta to Beta thought processes and Programming and it addresses the Beta to Delta thought processes and Programming. It also focuses Intent on a specific outcome without defining the track for that outcome.

Perhaps the easiest way to illustrate the Shamanic Agreement would be to use the example of a Male and Female Shaman forging a Shamanic Agreement to shift community perceptions concerning a debilitating social perception such as sexual exploitation of children. The Agreement could be forged between two male or two female Shamans as easily but in order to keep the masculine and feminine aspects of the Functions more nearly accessible here it is convenient to use a Male Shaman and a Female Shaman in the example.

The Male Shaman will represent the Objective processes of Specific Function and the Subjective processes of Natural Mind Function. The Female Shaman will represent the Objective processes of Intuition Function and the Subjective processes of Empathy Function. Both Shamans will be assumed to be capable of Shamanic Agreement and the Male Shaman will represent a Stalker and the Female Shaman will represent a Dreamer.

To try to break the process apart into steps is to demean the process to a certain extent, but there are certain parts of Agreement which can be identified as necessary for the Agreement process to take place. The Male Shaman would apply the Be One Function on the field of endeavor known as Specific Function. This would mean that the Male Shaman would Be at One with several aspects of who he is and what his Specific Function is. He would Be at One with his Specific Function as a Stalker, his Specific Function as defined by his energy field or aura, and all the tools of his craft from Programming to Seeing. He would apply the Harmony Function on the field of endeavor known as Natural Mind Function. This would mean that the Male Shaman would be in Harmony with all the Functions, with the community and with the Other.

Meanwhile the Female Shaman would apply the Be One Function to the field of endeavor known as Intuition Function. This would mean that she would Be at One with the Intuitive Function of Dreaming, the Intuitive Function of the Other using the body as an instrument of Communication, and her Intuition Function as defined by all the Functions of her craft from Be One to Intuition. She would apply the Harmony Function on the field of endeavor known as Empathy Function. This would mean that the Female Shaman would be in Harmony with the tools of her craft, the needs of the community, and the effect and healing aspects of the Other when the body is allowed to be an instrument of Communication.

Both Shamans would apply the Do Function of Communication between the objective Beta to Delta thinking and subjective Delta to Beta thinking of the other Shaman. This allows both Shamans to understand exactly what is being communicated and what has been considered before the Communication takes place. If there are points that must be clarified, then either or both can be Brutally Honest while knowing that the other Shaman has nothing to protect. There is another aspect of applying the Do Function of Communication between the objective and subjective thinking for the Shamans. They both will understand that their word is life itself. They will both know that whatever is discussed will be driven by unbending Intent backed by the life force.

Clarification:

> *Unbending* Intent backed by the life force can seem to be a harsh and daunting concept. However, the subject here is Shamans forging Shamanic Agreement. This is a serious endeavor undertaken by serious people. How could they be any less serious than the subject of their Agreement? They are staking the outcome of their Agreement on the lives of children in this instance and must, therefore, be as careful with their words and concepts as though they had physical responsibility for the life of a child. There is no other position available to the serious Shaman.

In the example, the Male Shaman would consider sexual molestation of children as being outside the Specific Function of community protection of children. He would consider the Natural Order or Natural Mind Function in children as being incomplete and therefore children to be unprepared for sex. The Female Shaman would consider the pain and confusion of sexually molested children and be cognizant of their pain as though her own. She would utilize the Intuition Function to understand the reasons for adults thinking that children would be ready for sexual activity and formulate the methods for combating those ideas to protect those who are defenseless.

Perhaps the defense would be in the form of well-considered "rumors" dropped in appropriate ears. Perhaps the defense would be in the form of salty statements about the hypocrisy of those who prey on children delivered in the dulcet tones and rhythms of deep Delta. Perhaps there could even be an outrageous confrontation. Yet the method and execution of the defense would be formulated through the combined Communication, and therefore, Do Function, of the two Shamans. The resulting Shamanic Agreement would have the power and energy of two sets of aligned programs and the consideration of the Functions of human existence. It would be void of moral or religious considerations. Yet it would also release energy to the community to address the social ill.

Because of the Agreement these two Shamans forge, there is an energy release that causes them both to experience a shift in their Assemblage Points. Because the energy release is greater than they can absorb, some of the energy is absorbed by the community. The event can be described in a number of ways. To describe the event as an energy release would be to compare it to a type of creation with an attendant mini big bang. The event could just as well be described as a vibratory event. To say that the vibrations of the new Assemblage Point would set up harmonic vibrations in the community would be as accurate. The event could also be described as something that the Human Collective Other observes and introduces to the community at large. Still, any description would be the domain of the describer more than the accurate observation put to words.

The activity depicted here as Shamanic Agreement must be experienced to be understood. It is not enough to simply state that Shamanic Agreement does not invade another's mind, but allows another to adjust to a new Point of View without being forced. It requires *unbending* Intent on the parts of the Agreement makers and may even require that they go to war to Intend the change.

A famous example from the 20th century is Gandhi. When Gandhi unmasked the Specific Function of the British tax on salt, all of India began to "vibrate" to Gandhi's proposed Agreement. Gandhi himself walked a great distance with a handful of followers to gather salt rather than pay British tax on something that was needed by the human organism as much as oxygen or water. As long as the Indian populace agreed to pay the tax, then the power of the British throne held dominion over them. Yet when the populace refused to pay the tax and decided to collect their own salt, the British throne tried to force the issue. At one point, several hundred Indians were machine-gunned in an enclosed courtyard. Another famous event featured British soldiers standing in the way of salt gatherers with wooden staves. The Indian people walked calmly up to the soldiers, stood quietly while the soldiers beat them over the head, and were carried away to be replaced by the next in line. The force of the British throne was defeated by the strength of Gandhi's peaceful Agreement. Gandhi's Agreement changed the Point of View of the entire world and the modern state of India was formed. This is the power of a well-crafted Agreement.

Points to Consider:

1. There are three "types" of Agreement. Nod your head Agreement, change the reality Agreement and Shamanic Agreement.
2. Agreement which changes the reality or perhaps even creates a piece of reality is not remembered.
3. When an Agreement is made real, a perceived surge of energy occurs which can be and is harvested by the Agreement makers.
4. Disagreement is as much a part of Agreement as creating reality.
5. Disagreement must be counterbalanced with an alternative Agreement.
6. Agreement and disagreement can evoke such strong emotions in holders of a Point of View that the Agreement triggers life-threatening responses. This is especially true when Agreements propose new control mechanisms.
7. A Shaman is cognizant of the force of his proposed Agreements and actually puts his life on the line when he presents his ideas. To do less would make a mockery of his very life and his hard bought experiences.
8. The Shaman avails himself of every Point of View and shift in the Assemblage Point that he encounters. It is through accumulating more and more points of reference that he will eventually be able to note the change in his Programming and memory which coincides with those shifts.
9. Shamanic Agreement is directed by the Other and has far reaching influences. It can even change worldviews.

Story Chapter XVI

The next session with Bob will be the last for a while. This represents a kind of graduation for him. If he continues on the path toward knowledge, the next set he will need involves other people. Up to this point, the information he has is appropriate for a lone Shaman acting on his own behalf. The session has to be presented as though it is regular conversation. It isn't conversational information, it is Communication from the Other presented at 10.5 cycles per second so that it lodges in mid-Alpha. It is information which has effect in both Delta to Beta thinking and Beta to Delta thinking.

The subject matter is about putting everything he has learned into a structure so that it can be applied to real life in real time. It is a concept that may turn his world upside down for a while. Sometimes the integration of the material in this session takes a few years to integrate into the thinking machinery. Sometimes the integration is almost immediate. This can't be helped because the material concerns a wide range of Shamanic activity.

I won't be able to give Bob much in the way of explanation. He will have to supply that through his own experience. In some ways, this material could be thought of as a residency program for a Shaman. Bob has come a long way so I don't have much concern for his maturation at this point.

"Come in, Bob, set yourself down and get comfortable. We have a good deal of information to cover tonight and this will be a conclusion, in a way, of this part of what we have been discussing."

"Okay. Does that mean that after this I'll be a Shaman?"

"Not really. You'll have to spend some degree of time adjusting what you know and putting it into practice, I'm sure. But the basic set of information will be in there."

"When you say, 'basic set of information,' do you mean there's more?"

"That really depends on you. Some people never really get up to this point, some others are satisfied with just this information, and still others go on and add to this information."

"Is there a determining factor for one level or another?"

"I'm sure there is, but I'm not sure that I understand all that's in play for anyone else. I know that some people just don't want to put in the work necessary to progress beyond this point."

"Do you think I'll be back for more information?"

"I don't know. That depends on your 'want to' to a great extent. There is also some reason to think that the actual configuration of the energy body has something to do with what information is required by a given individual."

"So this must be a pretty startling piece of information if you think that it is an 'end' of sorts to what I have been learning."

"It isn't so startling, actually. It is something that you have seen and, no doubt, put to use many, many times. It is the order and relation of this piece of information that carries its importance."

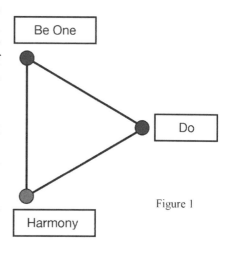

Figure 1

"I didn't get that, I don't think. Why would the order have anything to do with importance?"

"When we started, you had heard of such things as Programming, changing Points of View and so on. When we put them in an order and identified them as tools to learn more complex thoughts which, in our case, were Shamanic Functions, the order then gave each piece of information a unique quality and importance. Did it not?"

"Yes, it did, and I've wondered about that from time to time, but never saw the importance of the order until just now."

"That's as is should be. So what do you say that we begin to look at the last concept in this set?"

"All right."

"The name of this story is Agreement. It is a deceptively simple name and seems easy enough to understand. But the way Shamans deal with the idea is quite a bit different than it is in common usage."

"I agree all the time. There isn't anything earth shaking in that."

"You're absolutely right, but as with many of the concepts we've talked about, things are not always as they appear to be. For the Shaman, Agreement is composed of several parts and concepts. The concepts include all the things we have talked about, but they are arranged in a particular order and structure to give substance to the action of Agreeing. When viewed from the Shaman's Point of View, Agreement becomes more than we normally consider it to be."

"Let's back up here a little bit. You said the concepts we have been talking about are arranged in a particular order and structure, right?"

"Yes, I did."

"I thought that you had already given me the concepts we've talked about in a particular order and structure."

"I did, indeed."

"I didn't hear anything about Agreement in what we have talked about so far, as far as I know."

"You didn't. The reason is that now that you have the tools and Functions as linear concepts. It is time to arrange them into a structure so you can see how they interrelate."

"Oh man, does this mean that I have to learn everything all over again?"

"In a way it does. In another way it simply means that you need to learn how to apply what you have already learned. Ready?"

"I suppose."

"Good. So let's get started. I explained to you the last time we talked that I thought that you were a lot less than careful. Tonight I'm going to explain why. As you know, the first three concepts of the Shamanic belief system are Be One Function, Harmony Function and Do Function. These three Functions form a whole. Take a look at Figure 1 *(left)*.

"This is how these three Functions go together. In a way, there are two Not Doings and one Doing represented here. Be One Function could be considered as a Not Doing, as could Harmony Function. Do Function is, obviously, a Doing. Joined together, they make another concept for the Shaman. I'll get to that in a moment. If you think about this as a symbol, you may remember that if the triangle were pointed down that it would represent the pagan mother symbol.

"Each point on the triangle is named and the order of the names is important because this group of Functions, ordered in this way, represents another concept. In other cultures this symbol would be pointed upward because it actually represents the masculine aspects of the Functions of Be One, Harmony and Do."

"How do you know that this triangle represents male aspects rather than female aspects?"

"The second figure *(right)* here represents the female aspects of the Be One, Harmony and Do Functions. The points are in a different order. Do you see where they are different?"

"It's pointing the other way."

"Yeah, in older or other cultures it would actually point down. But there is something else different as well."

"Well it isn't a mirror image, exactly, but it seems to have simply been rotated."

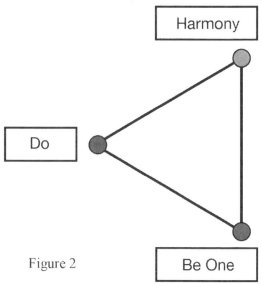

Figure 2

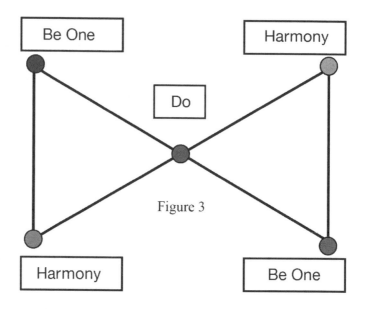

Figure 3

"You are exactly right. But in ages before the computer, these two symbols would have appeared to be non-mirrored images of the same thing. Let's compare them placed together to see the difference. Take a look at Figure 3 *(above)*."

"If the two drawings were mirror images, then Be One would be at the top of both triangles. As you can see, they're not."

"Okay, so I'm guessing that there is a significance in this?"

"Yes, there is. But for now, let's simply observe that when drawn in this way there is a male and there is a female aspect to the three Functions represented in the drawing. The triangle drawing is an ancient symbol. Depending on the direction of the triangle, it can represent male or female aspects of a given concept. At one time it was such a powerful symbol that it was thought to represent the male and female god entities. I'm telling you all this so that you can recognize the component parts of an ancient and powerful symbol. But wait, you ain't seen nothing yet."

"There's more?"

"You betcha."

"In the next figure 4 *(next page)* you probably recognize the four remaining Functions. As I told you, these four Functions are more like fields of endeavor than actions proper. Please notice the arrangement of the quadrants. Specific Function is at the top and on the left side of this diagram. Natural Mind Function is at the bottom of the left side. Empathy Function is at the top of the right side. Intuition Function is at the bottom of the right side. These

Functions are arranged in this order only so that you have a chance to understand what they represent and what they do. Later I'll rearrange them and give you another concept. You may also notice that this drawing is very reminiscent of sand painting and OT/Ancient drawings of the four winds. In some cultures, this symbol was drawn as a circle with a cross in the middle. At times the cross appeared to be an 'X'. However, the square divided by a cross serves our purposes here best.

"You will notice also that the left side is labeled as 'Dod Function' which is an old English concept which carries the approximate meaning of yang as in Yin and Yang. The Yin and Yang duality is a bit over used and I prefer that you consider this with words that are somewhat unknown. The other side is labeled 'Ley Functions' which corresponds to yin. I don't know if you remember or not, but Specific Function is thought to pertain to male objective thinking. By that I mean that, generally speaking, Specific Function has a masculine aspect that is related to Beta to Delta thought processes and is heavily weighted with logical ideas and concepts.

For instance, Specific Function represents the Dod or masculine concepts of 'a place for everything and everything in its place', a calling or a talent, 'a man's gotta do what a man's gotta do', 'you count money', and 'God helps those who help themselves' to give some banal examples.

"You with?"

"I think so."

"Good. Natural Mind Function is thought to pertain to male subjective thinking. By that I mean it has a masculine aspect that is related to Delta to

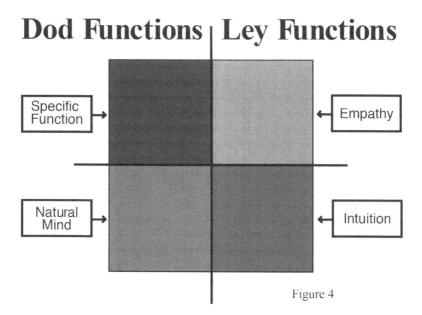

Dod Functions | Ley Functions

Figure 4

Beta thinking. It is weighted with 'non-linear' ideas and thoughts. The Natural Mind Function represents concepts which are specific to the idea, such as: it is possible to observe the movements of animals and then set traps to capture the animal based on those observations; there are no straight lines in nature, music, poetry, and religion, to give some common examples.

"Empathy Function is thought of as pertaining to female subjective thinking. This means that the Function has aspects which are more nearly feminine in nature and represents another aspect of Delta to Beta thinking. Empathy Function represents the Ley or feminine concepts of feeling another's pain or joy directly as though it were your own, understanding another person's thought processes and accepting those processes as valid even though they are foreign to you, giving to a beggar, and 'mothering' those who are less developed physically, mentally, or spiritually than you are.

"Intuition Function is thought to pertain to female objective thinking. This means that the function has aspects which are more nearly feminine and represent Beta to Delta thinking in a way. The Intuition function represents such Ley or feminine concepts as Direct Knowing, healing at a distance, a doctor's ability to diagnose, a mother's awareness of her children, and the rattle of a samurai's sword when danger is near.

"To call any of these Functions masculine or feminine can be misleading. They are not necessarily functions which men perform or functions which women perform, although the concepts are often embodied in men and women. For the Shaman, they are simply concepts which he uses as he needs them.

"You're starting to look a little green around the gills. Need some air?"

"Kind of. Do you expect me to be able to talk about this the way you are?"

"Only if you want to actually understand it."

"Man, this is a bunch of information to absorb all at once."

"Want a little cheese with that whine? We've been over all this before. But when you lay out these four Functions in this way they form another concept altogether. In this regard, these four Functions joined in this drawing are like the first three Functions joined together. Together they have a different meaning than when they are separate and aligned in a linear form."

"I can see that. But I don't see the significance of this drawing *(previous page).*"

"As I mentioned earlier, these four Functions are sometimes drawn in this way to represent the four winds or even the four elements of earth, wind, fire and water. But for now we want to think about this concept from our culture."

"If that will make it any easier to understand, I'm in."

"I don't know if it will make anything any easier or not. But you need to be able to see this from inside your culture and understanding or it becomes even harder to grasp."

"I can see that, I think. I've encountered some of these concepts before, like

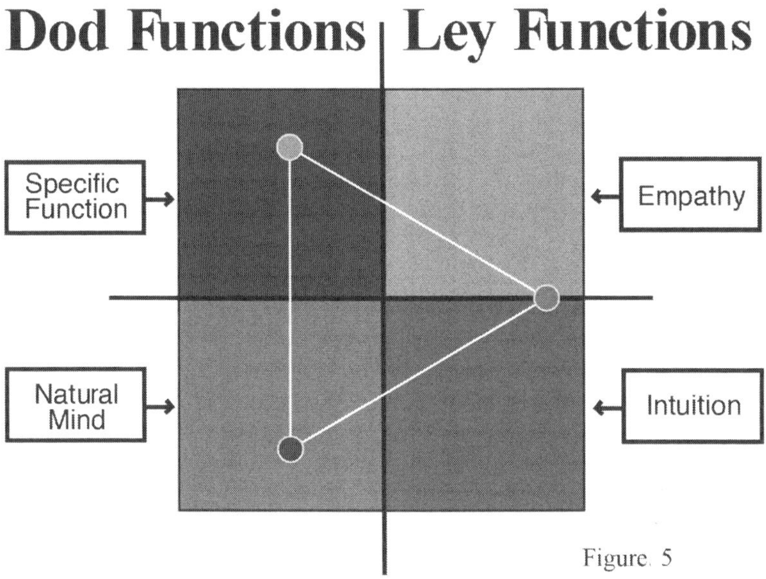

Dod Functions | Ley Functions

Figure 5

the mother symbol you were explaining before, but I never knew that it was made up of parts."

"Exactly! You need to consider these concepts as clearly as possible so you can draw your own conclusions using your culture and your language as a base. Now, let's pile these two drawings on one another to make yet another concept."

"I should have known."

"In Figure 5 *(above)* here you can see the proper alignment of masculine aspects of the Be One, Harmony and Do Functions over the drawing of the four winds or, in this case, the other four Functions. You will notice that the Be One Function is located in the Specific Function quadrant, the Harmony Function is located in the Natural Mind Function, and the Do Function is on the line separating the Empathy and Intuition Functions. Why is that, do you suppose?"

"You got me."

"Think about what you are looking at for a moment. The first thing to consider is that the triangle on this drawing represents the male aspects of Be One, Harmony and Do. Therefore, it is proper that the base of the triangle is located on the side of the four Functions drawing which represents the masculine Functions. But why are the Be One and Harmony Function located where they are? Why not the other way around?"

"Because this is the male representation of the triangle and the order of the structure indicates the male aspects?"

"That's true, but be careful that you don't get the cart before the horse. The

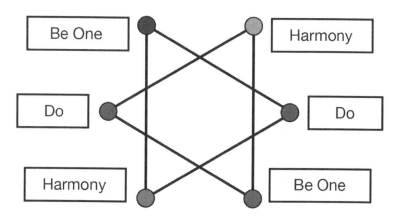

Figure 6

reason for the order of the structure of the triangle is found in the four Functions drawing. Be One Function represents separation to oneness. Specific Function represents that same separation but in terms of separation of Function. Harmony Function represents a joining of two through shared Points of View. Natural Mind Function represents discovery of the contents of other minds through Not Doing which allows for Harmony to be realized."

"You know, I've kind of missed the relationships between the Functions, maybe."

"You may have, but I've presented the Functions to you as stand-alone concepts up to this point so don't be too hard on yourself. There still remains a point in question, though. Why is the dot representing the Do Function located on the feminine side of the four Functions drawing?"

"Because guys like to talk to girls?"

"Actually that is pretty close to correct. When I drew the comparison of the two triangles for you, I showed them as having a shared Do Function. That would have represented the point of Communication, don't you think?"

"Yes, that is what I thought."

"But I am talking to a man who is becoming a Shaman and for that to take place then you will need to place your Do or Communication between the objective and subjective thinking of the feminine constructs whenever they are encountered. We could also say that you will have to address the Beta to Delta thinking at the same time you address the Delta to Beta thinking while addressing the Empathy and Intuition Function of another person. Therefore, you have to actually enter into the thinking of other individuals and this is simply a drawing representing that entrance, in a way."

"I was feeling pretty confident up until that 'in a way' thing slid in there."

"Figure 6 *(above)* represents the way the Shaman communicates. Can you see the two triangles here?"

"Yeah, I can. But I would have thought that the Do Function would have been positioned like it was in the first drawing of the male and female aspects. This one looks kind of familiar though."

"I wouldn't be surprised. This is very similar to the Jewish Star of David. It too is a six-point star. But the symbol is probably older than the Jewish faith and at one time represented various aspects of fertility and other male and female interactions.

But when we place this six pointed star over our four Functions drawing, as in Figure 7 *(below)*, we can see a whole other set of interrelated concepts."

"You want to take a stab at explaining this one?"

"What does 'Reality Created' mean?"

"Originally, when these symbols were presented to tribal people for instance, the Reality Created part of the drawing probably referred to making babies. But not every time that men and women communicated resulted in babies being made. This raised the question about what was being created when they communicated. I imagine it took a while to figure that one out."

"So what does that mean?"

"It means that we have finally come to the point of talking about what Shamans do."

"Shamans create reality!?!"

"In a manner of speaking we could say that, but before we do I want you to look out that window. What do you see?"

"I see the house across the street."

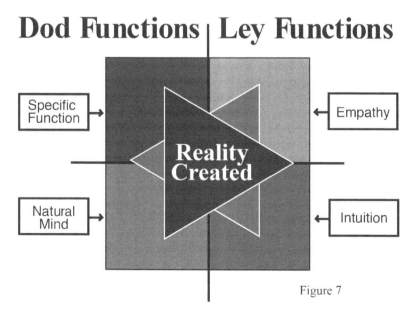

Dod Functions | Ley Functions

Specific Function → Reality Created ← Empathy

Natural Mind → ← Intuition

Figure 7

"What else do you see?"

"I see the street, nine cars, lots of lawns, street lights, the stoplight at the end of the street blinking red, and behind all of that, more of the same."

"Very good. How did all those things get where they are?"

"I don't understand."

"What part didn't you understand? How did they get there?"

"I guess someone built the houses and bought the cars and planted the grass, I don't know."

"You're giving me a simplistic answer. Do you see anything out there that is not man made?"

"Some trees and grass and other plants, I guess."

"You may have to trust me on this, but even those things are man-made."

"I guess so."

"Let me try this from another angle. How much of what you're looking at is real?"

"How much of it is real? It's all real."

"Why yes it is. How did it become real?"

"How did it become real? It's always been real."

"No, it hasn't. I remember when that house right across the street wasn't even there. I'll bet that there are people who live in this neighborhood who remember when that street was not there. They probably remember when the streetlights weren't there. If they remember that, I'll bet that they remember when that stoplight wasn't there. The same could be said of the gardens and cars and so on. So there was a time when the things you are looking at didn't exist or, we could say, they weren't real. How did they become real?"

"Christ, how should I know?"

"See there, you're being sloppy again."

"Well, how am I supposed to know how they *became* 'real'?"

"Sloppy and careless, my, oh, my. Okay, I'll let you up. People agreed to make all those things real. I don't mean they nodded their heads up and down at the right time and made pleasant noises, I mean that they put their money and their life where their mouth was and *agreed*. That kind of Agreement makes things real. What do you Agree to make real?"

"Wait a minute, I'm still trying to sort through making things real by agreeing. You can't *make* the world 'real' by agreeing it's real."

"Why not? You do."

"Oh, come on. I don't make the world real."

"You don't? Then what did you do when you decided that your soul didn't exist because you missed your Grams? Didn't you create a reality that you lived in all by yourself? That may have been a fantasy reality, but for you it was just as real as those trees and houses and cars across the street."

"In a way."

"More than in a way. Think about this before you get all hot and bothered.

Everyone does the same thing. We all run around looking for Agreement for our pet reality projects. Your clients all drive you nuts trying to convince you to agree that they are poor pitiful pumpkins who can't find work or feed their kids. I could give you lots and lots of examples, but you need to figure this out for yourself."

"Okay, you're saying that we all create little mini realities that we live in, right?"

"Yes. I'm also saying that we, as a society, create big old mega realities like cities and towns which we live in, too."

"I guess that's true."

"There's no 'guess' about it. It is true. How we do it is in that little diagram on the table. We may not know the parts of the Agreement, but we all know the dance. In fact, you can look at the reality that someone creates for himself and deduce what is wrong with the Agreements he's made. The Agreements that you or I or anyone makes are programs that we write and what powers the program is the energy lent to us by those with whom we make those Agreements.

"For instance, you agreed with your mom that you could rebel against your dad. When your mom took off for parts unknown, you agreed with your dad that she was an undesirable person. Those Agreements created a reality that you lived in until you recognized it and changed it.

"Not all programs are the result of Agreements. You wrote a program all by yourself about what your mom told you about the soul of your grandmother still being with you. You energized it all by yourself. It took so much energy that you didn't have any left over to do things like find a steady girlfriend. Of course, that Agreement you held with your dad didn't help that situation any."

"Oh man, this is too heavy for me."

"Well, Hotdog, it's too late for you to run now. Now you understand. How can you run from that?"

"I don't understand anything."

"Of course you don't. So when you're down at the coffee shop chatting up your buddies, what Agreements are you Programming yourself to uphold? Do you know?"

"I never thought about that."

"I know. It kind of shows. Like I said, you're careless. You agree to all kinds of, well, to be unkind, foolish things. Then you wonder why you don't have enough energy to blow your nose."

"So this is what Shaman's do? They agree to make things real?"

"In a way. But Shamans do pay attention to the idea that Agreements make things real. Way back in the day when Shamans shook rattles and recited incantations, they probably got the entire clan together and made an Agreement to find a bunch of buffalo. Everybody Agreed and poof, they survived the winter. If there was disagreement in the ranks, then somebody died in the hunt or some other misfortune befell the clan and the Shaman recited more incantations until everyone got tired of listening and found a way to Agree. That was back in the day. These days we live in a world that is a bit more complicated. Incantations and shaking rattles won't do much of anything anymore. We have to rethink the tools of the craft."

"How do we do that?"

"We start over."

"What do you mean, 'we start over'?"

"I mean we have to rebuild the knowledge so that it is relevant to today's world. We have to carefully pick Agreements which fund our energy so that we can communicate from the Other. We have to take care that we maintain ourselves in our Specific Function so that we don't bleed energy off in activities that are contrary to our function. We have to make sure that we follow the natural order of things. That would mean that we use the Natural Mind Function to accent what manner of activity we practice. If we are Dreamers then we use our Dreaming to increase our store of energy. If we are Stalkers, then we Stalk Agreements so that we don't waste our energy on battles that can't be won. That means that we use the Empathy Function to practice kindness with our fellow man so they can offer us their excess energy to help heal them in whatever manner that healing takes place. That means that we use Intuition Function to lift ourselves out of the folly of our own making. That energy is all that separates us from whatever other person. That means that we use the concept of the Be One, Harmony and Do Functions to communicate the Agreements we will choose and live with."

"This all seems pretty relevant to me."

"It is. But then I haven't told you about how to build the Pyramid of the Sacred Flags. And that's another whole story."

Points to Consider:

1. Seeing funds the energy of Agreement for the Shaman.
2. The reality which any person perceives may be nothing more or less than a compilation of the Agreements which he holds. If he perceives a limiting reality, then he holds limiting Agreements. If he perceives reality as full of inviting possibilities, then he holds Agreements which are full of inviting possibilities.
3. The Shaman's "magic" or "healing" abilities are in direct proportion to his ability to adjust the Agreements for those he helps.
4. The Shaman, because of his training, has no right to impose his values on others. He must influence Agreements and even hold Agreements with others, but only the Agreements which others are capable of holding.
5. The actions of the Shaman must be, therefore, covert or wrapped in mystery.
6. The Shaman leaves no tracks, but must influence the world in which he

lives. This is best accomplished through Agreements with other Shamans.

7. Shamanic Agreement can change not only pieces of reality but how entire communities interact. This may even include the Global Village.

What's Next?

When a reader completes *The Office of Shaman,* the question often asked is: "What do I do next?" The confusion seems to be in the idea that the Functions are to be completed as much as they are to be learned. It must be remembered that the Functions already exist. They are constants and are the building blocks of any belief system. They are learned by becoming proficient with the Tools that are found in Part One of *The Office of Shaman.* These Tools and Functions are best learned by Doing. To help the reader become more proficient in this Doing, we have a group of individuals available to speak to about this work, upcoming classes and how to avail oneself of advanced material for the next steps or new perspectives for personal practice. For additional information please visit:

http://mentalartsnetwork.com

Our website has detailed information about classes offered for both individuals and businesses, as well as classes designed specifically for those who are currently working in a float center or who are planning to open one. You may also contact the float centers listed on our site with any questions.

About the Author

John Worthington was born to the Office of Shaman in rural Pennsylvania in 1947 and spent the next four decades discovering and defining exactly what that means. He has studied with consciousness researcher John C. Lilly, been an instructor for the Silva Method, taught and lectured extensively nationwide, owned a consciousness studio featuring sensory deprivation tanks in Boulder, Colorado, and has appeared on numerous radio and television programs, including the Today Show, describing his experiences. His writings have been published internationally in magazines and newspapers on both sides of the border and are currently being used in select college curriculum. He currently lives, writes, holds shamanic intensives and works with students at his home outside of Guadalajara, Mexico. Being unencumbered by personal history and ambiguous abstractions of any kind, he lives a simple, engaged life. John invites you to contact him: **worthington@mentalartsnetwork.com**

25634087R00142

Made in the USA
Middletown, DE
05 November 2015